Mastering Java Concurrency

From Basics to Expert Proficiency

Contents

Introduction

Java is a versatile and widely-used programming language that has established itself as a cornerstone in the modern software development landscape. One of its most significant and sophisticated features is its concurrency capabilities. Efficiently harnessing the power of concurrent processing is paramount in developing high-performance and responsive applications. This book, "Mastering Java Concurrency: From Basics to Expert Proficiency," aims to provide a comprehensive and in-depth exploration of Java's concurrency features, making it accessible and practical for both novice and seasoned developers.

Concurrency in computing involves executing multiple tasks simultaneously, enabling better utilization of system resources and improving application performance. Java provides a robust and flexible API for handling concurrency, built upon years of development and refinement. Leveraging these features effectively can result in applications that are not only faster but also more resilient and capable of handling complex operations.

In this book, we will start with the basics of Java concurrency, ensuring that the foundational concepts are well-understood. We will gradually move towards more advanced topics, deepening the reader's understanding and proficiency in the subject. By the end of this book, readers will have a thorough grasp of Java's concurrency model, a solid understanding of best practices, and the ability to apply this knowledge to real-world applications.

We will begin by introducing the fundamental concepts of concurrency, differentiating it from parallelism, and discussing its significance in modern applications. A crucial part of this discussion involves understanding the Java Memory Model and thread lifecycle, which are foundational to writing concurrent programs.

Next, we will delve into basic thread operations, covering essential topics such as thread creation, management, and basic control mechanisms. Readers will learn how to effectively start, stop, and manage thread execution, ensuring that applications perform optimally and securely.

Thread synchronization is a critical aspect of concurrent programming. We will explore various synchronization techniques to prevent common concurrency issues such as race conditions and deadlocks. Detailed discussions will include intrinsic locks, explicit locks, and advanced synchronization utilities provided in the java.util.concurrent package.

The Executors framework is a key component of Java's concurrency API, providing a higher level of abstraction for managing thread execution. This book will cover the various executor services, demonstrating how to efficiently manage and control thread pools, thereby enhancing application performance and scalability.

For applications requiring highly scalable and efficient parallelism, the Fork/Join framework is indispensable. We will explore its features and capabilities, showing how to decompose complex tasks into simpler subtasks that can be processed simultaneously.

Atomic variables and lock-free programming techniques offer performance benefits by reducing contention and avoiding the pitfalls associated with traditional locking mechanisms. This book will introduce these concepts, providing readers with the tools to design high-performance, non-blocking concurrent algorithms.

In addition to basic concurrency constructs, the book will cover advanced topics such as working with Futures and CompletableFutures, offering insights into asynchronous programming and improving application responsiveness. We will also examine the increasingly popular parallel streams introduced in Java 8, demonstrating their use in parallelizing data processing tasks.

Finally, we will discuss concurrency best practices and patterns, enabling readers to write efficient, maintainable, and scalable concurrent applications. By adhering to these best practices, developers can avoid common pitfalls and harness the full potential of Java's concurrency API.

Throughout this book, code examples and practical scenarios will illustrate the concepts discussed, bridging the gap between theory and practice. By the end of this journey, readers will have a comprehensive understanding of Java concurrency, equipped with the skills necessary to tackle complex concurrent programming challenges.

We hope this book serves as a valuable resource for mastering Java concurrency and empowers you to develop robust, high-performance applications. Thank you for embarking on this exploration of one of Java's most powerful and intricate features.

Chapter 1

Introduction to Java Concurrency

This chapter provides an essential foundation for understanding concurrency in Java. It begins by defining concurrency and differentiating it from parallelism, highlighting their importance in modern applications. An overview of the Java Concurrency API is provided, along with an explanation of the Java Memory Model. The thread lifecycle is discussed, detailing various states and transitions. Practical guidance on creating and managing threads is included, along with an examination of common issues encountered in concurrent programming. This chapter sets the stage for more advanced topics by establishing a robust conceptual framework.

1.1 What is Concurrency?

In modern computing, concurrency refers to the ability of a system to manage and execute multiple tasks simultaneously. This does not necessarily imply parallelism, which we will discuss separately, but rather that tasks are being managed in such a way that they overlap in time. Concurrency is about the structure and management of tasks that are in progress. It encompasses a range of concepts, from the execution of multiple sequences of operations to the access and modification of shared resources by various processes or threads.

Consider a single-core processor: it can only perform one operation at a time. However, through concurrency, the processor can switch between different tasks rapidly, giving the illusion that tasks are being executed simultaneously. This behavior is achieved through the concept of context switching.

```
Process contextSwitchExample() {
    start Task1;
    while (Task1 is not complete) {
        if (Task2 is ready) {
            suspend Task1;
            start Task2;
        }
        if (Task1 is ready again) {
            suspend Task2;
            resume Task1;
        }
    }
    end Task1;
    end Task2 if Task2 is running;
}
```

Concurrency plays a critical role in various domains, including operating systems, network servers, and real-time application design. The primary goals of concurrency are to improve the performance and responsiveness of applications, optimize resource utilization, and provide better structure to systems that manage many tasks.

Two primary constructs in achieving concurrency are threads and processes. While both offer ways to execute multiple sequences of operations, they differ significantly:

- **Process:** A process is an independent program in execution with its own memory space. Processes provide high levels of isolation and stability, as each process operates independently. Communication between processes must occur through Inter-Process Communication (IPC) mechanisms, which can introduce overhead. Creating processes involves more memory and time due to the need to allocate separate memory spaces.
- **Thread:** A thread is the smallest unit of execution within a process. Multiple threads can exist within the same process, sharing memory and resources. Threads are more lightweight compared to processes, allowing faster context switching and communication due to shared memory space. However, this shared memory space makes threads more prone to concurrency issues such as race conditions.

Java establishes concurrency primarily through the java.lang.Thread class and the java.util.concurrent package. The Java Concurrency API allows developers to create, manage, and synchronize threads.

```
public class MyRunnable implements Runnable {
    @Override
    public void run() {
        System.out.println("Thread is running");
    }
}

public class Main {
    public static void main(String[] args) {
        Thread thread = new Thread(new MyRunnable());
        thread.start();
    }
}
```

In the above example, MyRunnable implements the Runnable interface, and the run method is overridden to define the code that constitutes the thread's task. The main method creates a new Thread object and starts it by invoking the start method.

Through concurrency, we can perform multiple operations in an overlapping manner, enhancing the efficiency and responsiveness of applications. This capability becomes especially significant when dealing with I/O operations, user interface updates, and other scenarios where waiting for one operation to complete before starting another would result in suboptimal performance.

Proper use of concurrency requires a deep understanding of thread lifecycle management, synchronization mechanisms, and potential issues. Effective concurrent programming involves careful consideration of design patterns and strategies to avoid pitfalls such as deadlocks, livelocks, and race conditions. By mastering concurrency, developers can architect robust, efficient, and responsive applications that leverage the full computational power available in modern hardware.

1.2 Concurrency vs Parallelism

In concurrent programming, the concepts of concurrency and parallelism are fundamental yet often misunderstood. Distinguishing between these concepts is critical for designing efficient and effective concurrent applications in Java.

Concurrency refers to the ability of a system to handle multiple tasks at the same time. These tasks may not be executed simultaneously, but the system can switch between them rapidly, giving the illusion of simultaneity. Concurrency is about managing several tasks at once, potentially overlapping in execution, but not necessarily executing them at the same time. In Java, concurrency is achieved through threads, where multiple threads of execution can run within a single program. The Java Concurrency API provides various classes and interfaces to facilitate the development of concurrent programs.

Parallelism, on the other hand, involves the simultaneous execution of multiple tasks. This can only be achieved on a multicore processor, where each core can execute a separate task concurrently. Parallelism is a subset of concurrency in which multiple tasks are executed literally in parallel, leading to potentially significant performance improvements. Recognizing when parallelism can be effectively employed and understanding its implications are crucial for optimizing Java applications.

The distinction between concurrency and parallelism can be better explained through examples. Consider a web server handling multiple client requests. If the server is implemented using a single thread, it processes one request at a time. By using multiple threads, the server can handle multiple requests concurrently, improving responsiveness. Suppose the server runs on a multicore processor. In that case, it can parallelize the processing of multiple requests, assigning different requests to different cores, thus handling more requests simultaneously and improving throughput.

To further illustrate, consider the following Java code snippet demonstrating a simple case of concurrent execution using threads:

```
public class ConcurrencyExample {
    public static void main(String[] args) {
        Runnable task1 = () -> {
            for (int i = 0; i < 5; i++) {
                System.out.println("Task 1 - Count " + i);
                try {
                    Thread.sleep(100);
                } catch (InterruptedException e) {
                    Thread.currentThread().interrupt();
                }
            }
        };

        Runnable task2 = () -> {
            for (int i = 0; i < 5; i++) {
                System.out.println("Task 2 - Count " + i);
                try {
                    Thread.sleep(100);
                } catch (InterruptedException e) {
                    Thread.currentThread().interrupt();
                }
            }
        };
```

```
        Thread thread1 = new Thread(task1);
        Thread thread2 = new Thread(task2);

        thread1.start();
        thread2.start();
    }
}
```

In this example, task1 and task2 are two Runnable tasks executed by thread1 and thread2, respectively. The tasks run concurrently, with the Java Virtual Machine (JVM) managing their execution. Despite both tasks being logically concurrent, without a multicore processor, they may not execute in parallel.

To demonstrate parallelism, consider utilizing the Java Fork/Join framework, which is designed to take advantage of multiple cores:

```
import java.util.concurrent.RecursiveTask;
import java.util.concurrent.ForkJoinPool;

public class ParallelismExample extends RecursiveTask<Long> {
    private final long start, end;

    public ParallelismExample(long start, long end) {
        this.start = start;
        this.end = end;
    }

    @Override
    protected Long compute() {
        long range = end - start;
        if (range <= 100) {
            long sum = 0;
            for (long i = start; i <= end; i++) {
                sum += i;
            }
            return sum;
        } else {
            long midpoint = (start + end) / 2;
            ParallelismExample task1 = new ParallelismExample(start, midpoint);
            ParallelismExample task2 = new ParallelismExample(midpoint + 1, end);

            task1.fork();
            long task2Result = task2.compute();
            long task1Result = task1.join();

            return task1Result + task2Result;
        }
    }

    public static void main(String[] args) {
        ForkJoinPool pool = new ForkJoinPool();
        ParallelismExample task = new ParallelismExample(1, 1000);

        long result = pool.invoke(task);
        System.out.println("Sum: " + result);
    }
}
```

In this code, ParallelismExample extends RecursiveTask and uses the Fork/Join framework to recursively split the task of summing integers from 1 to 1000. This example demonstrates real parallelism, where multiple subtasks can execute on separate processor cores simultaneously.

Understanding the distinctions between concurrency and parallelism, and knowing when and how to apply them, is vital for developing efficient Java applications. Concurrency enhances responsiveness and resource utilization by interleaving task execution, whereas parallelism boosts performance by exploiting multicore architectures to execute multiple tasks simultaneously. Properly leveraging both techniques requires a deep understanding of the Java Concurrency API and the underlying hardware capabilities.

1.3 The Need for Concurrency in Modern Applications

Modern applications require concurrency for several critical reasons, ranging from performance improvements to responsiveness and efficiency in resource utilization. Understanding these motivations is essential for grasping the significance of concurrency in contemporary software development.

Firstly, concurrency enables applications to perform multiple operations simultaneously, which is crucial for maximizing the utilization of multi-core processors. With the advent of multi-core CPU architectures, leveraging concurrency allows programs to perform tasks in parallel, thus significantly enhancing computational throughput. When tasks are distributed across multiple cores, the overall execution time decreases, leading to better performance. Consider the following example of how concurrency can be implemented in Java:

```
public class ConcurrentExample {
    public static void main(String[] args) {
        Thread thread1 = new Thread(new Task());
        Thread thread2 = new Thread(new Task());

        thread1.start();
        thread2.start();
    }
}

class Task implements Runnable {
    @Override
    public void run() {
```

```
        System.out.println("Task is running on: " + Thread.currentThread().getName())
            ;
        // Perform a CPU-intensive task
    }
}
```

In the example above, two threads are created and started, allowing the CPU-intensive Task to run concurrently on different cores if available. This utilization of multiple processors demonstrates the performance benefit of concurrency.

Moreover, concurrency enhances the responsiveness of applications, particularly those with user interfaces (UIs). Blocking the main thread with long-running tasks can make an application unresponsive, leading to poor user experience. By delegating such tasks to background threads, the main UI thread remains free to handle user interactions, ensuring a smooth and responsive interface. For instance:

```
public class ResponsiveUIExample {
    public static void main(String[] args) {
        Thread backgroundTask = new Thread(new LongRunningTask());
        backgroundTask.start();

        // Continue handling user inputs in the main thread
    }
}

class LongRunningTask implements Runnable {
    @Override
    public void run() {
        try {
            Thread.sleep(5000); // Simulate a long-running task
            System.out.println("Background task completed");
        } catch (InterruptedException e) {
            Thread.currentThread().interrupt();
        }
    }
}
```

Here, the long-running task is executed in a separate thread, allowing the main thread to remain responsive. This is crucial for applications such as mobile apps or interactive web applications where user experience is paramount.

Concurrency also plays a vital role in efficient resource utilization. In server applications, multiple client requests can be handled concurrently, allowing for scaling and better resource management. Consider a web server handling numerous client requests:

```
public class WebServer {
    public static void main(String[] args) {
        while (true) {
            Socket client = serverSocket.accept();
```

```
            new Thread(new ClientHandler(client)).start();
        }
    }
}

class ClientHandler implements Runnable {
    private Socket client;

    public ClientHandler(Socket client) {
        this.client = client;
    }

    @Override
    public void run() {
        // Handle client request
    }
}
```

In the example, each client request is processed in a separate thread, allowing the server to handle multiple clients concurrently. This increases the throughput and efficiency of the server by making effective use of available system resources.

Concurrency is not limited to performance and responsiveness alone; it is also crucial for handling I/O-bound tasks. Applications that rely on network communication, file I/O, or database queries can benefit significantly from concurrency. By using threads to manage I/O operations, the program can continue executing other tasks without blocking. For example:

```
public class IOOperationExample {
    public static void main(String[] args) {
        Thread ioTask = new Thread(new IOTask());
        ioTask.start();

        // Perform other computations
    }
}

class IOTask implements Runnable {
    @Override
    public void run() {
        // Simulate a long-running I/O operation
        try {
            Thread.sleep(3000); // Simulate network latency
            System.out.println("I/O operation completed");
        } catch (InterruptedException e) {
            Thread.currentThread().interrupt();
        }
    }
}
```

The use of concurrency in the above example allows the main thread to remain active while the I/O operation is processed in the background, demonstrating the efficiency of managing I/O-bound tasks.

As the examples illustrate, the need for concurrency in modern applications spans several aspects, from maximizing CPU utilization and improving responsiveness to efficient resource management and handling I/O-bound operations. Concurrency is indispensable in developing responsive, efficient, and high-performing software systems in the context of multicore processors and complex application requirements. The subsequent sections will delve deeper into the practical aspects of Java concurrency, equipping readers with the knowledge to effectively apply these concepts in their software development endeavors.

1.4 Overview of Java Concurrency API

The Java Concurrency API provides a robust set of tools for developing concurrent applications. It is part of the java.util.concurrent package and includes classes, interfaces, and utilities designed for handling threads, thread pools, synchronization, and numerous other concurrency-related operations. This section delves into the primary components of the Java Concurrency API, illustrating their usage and significance.

Executors:

The Executor framework in Java simplifies thread management by decoupling the task submission from the mechanics of how each task will be run. The Executor interface provides a simple way of abstracting task execution. One of its primary implementations is ThreadPoolExecutor.

```
ExecutorService executorService = Executors.newFixedThreadPool(10);
Runnable task = () -> {
    System.out.println("Task executed");
};
executorService.submit(task);
executorService.shutdown();
```

In this code snippet, a FixedThreadPool with 10 threads is created. The submit method submits a task for execution, and shutdown ensures that the executor stops accepting new tasks and shuts down after all previously submitted tasks are executed.

Future and Callable:

While the Runnable interface does not return a result or throw a checked exception, Callable is a more flexible choice. Callable tasks can return a value and throw a checked exception. Instances of Callable can be submitted to an ExecutorService that returns a Future object representing the pending result.

```
Callable<Integer> callableTask = () -> {
    return 123;
};
Future<Integer> future = executorService.submit(callableTask);
Integer result = future.get(); // This will block until the result is available
```

Future.get() blocks until the result is ready, thus making it essential to handle potential InterruptedException and ExecutionException.

Concurrent Collections:

The Java Concurrency API provides several thread-safe collection classes that are essential for concurrent programming. Notably, ConcurrentHashMap, CopyOnWriteArrayList, and BlockingQueue are widely used.

```
ConcurrentMap<String, Integer> concurrentMap = new ConcurrentHashMap<>();
concurrentMap.put("key1", 1);
Integer value = concurrentMap.get("key1");
```

ConcurrentHashMap allows for concurrent retrievals without locking and updates with minimal contention, ensuring higher performance in multithreaded contexts.

Locks and Synchronizers:

Java Concurrency API provides explicit lock objects alternative to using synchronized methods and blocks. ReentrantLock is one such class that allows more flexible thread synchronization.

```
ReentrantLock lock = new ReentrantLock();
lock.lock();
try {
    // Critical section
} finally {
    lock.unlock();
}
```

ReentrantLock provides the same synchronization behavior as implicit monitors manifested by synchronized methods and statements but offers additional features such as fairness, which grants access to the longest-waiting thread.

Semaphore and CountDownLatch are additional synchronization tools within the API.

```
Semaphore semaphore = new Semaphore(3);
semaphore.acquire();
try {
    // Acquired a permit, enter the critical section
```

```
} finally {
    semaphore.release();
}
```

```
CountDownLatch latch = new CountDownLatch(2);
Runnable task1 = () -> {
    latch.countDown();
};
Runnable task2 = () -> {
    latch.countDown();
};
executorService.submit(task1);
executorService.submit(task2);
latch.await();
System.out.println("All tasks completed");
```

Semaphore is used to control access to a resource with a fixed number of permits, while CountDownLatch allows one or more threads to wait until a set of operations being performed in other threads completes.

Atomic Variables:

Atomic classes (e.g., AtomicInteger, AtomicReference) provide a way to update variables safely without synchronization. These classes use lock-free algorithms backed by low-level atomic machine instructions.

```
AtomicInteger atomicInteger = new AtomicInteger(0);
int newValue = atomicInteger.incrementAndGet();
```

Atomic operations avoid the need for synchronization, thereby reducing overhead and avoiding contention.

CompletableFuture:

Introduced in Java 8, CompletableFuture supports asynchronous programming with non-blocking operations. This class implements the Future interface and provides a rich API with methods for combining, chaining, and handling exceptions in asynchronous operations.

```
CompletableFuture.supplyAsync(() -> {
    return "Hello, World!";
}).thenAccept(result -> {
    System.out.println(result);
}).exceptionally(ex -> {
    System.out.println("Exception: " + ex.getMessage());
    return null;
});
```

Here, supplyAsync provides a non-blocking execution, and thenAccept processes the result when it becomes available. exceptionally handles any exceptions that occur during the computation.

The Java Concurrency API provides fundamental building blocks for constructing efficiently multi-threaded programs. By utilizing these classes and constructs, developers can achieve better performance, higher reliability, and maintainability in concurrent applications. The careful application of these tools is as imperative as understanding the foundations they are built upon.

1.5 Java Memory Model

The Java Memory Model (JMM) defines how threads interact through memory and what behaviors are acceptable in a concurrent program. It ensures visibility and ordering of variables accessed by multiple threads. Understanding the JMM is crucial for writing correct and efficient concurrent programs.

At its core, the JMM specifies when changes made by one thread become visible to other threads. This visibility is managed through two main aspects: volatile variables and synchronization blocks. Without proper use of these mechanisms, threads may observe inconsistent or stale data, leading to erratic behavior.

Memory Visibility Rules

The JMM guarantees that operations like reads and writes have well-defined behaviors. Memory visibility rules can be encapsulated as follows:

- A Thread A's write to a volatile variable becomes visible to Thread B if Thread B subsequently reads that volatile variable.
- Actions within synchronized blocks are visible to other threads possessing the same monitor lock.
- A write action performed by Thread A before unloading a lock is visible to Thread B after it acquires the same lock.

Happens-Before Relationship

The happens-before relationship is fundamental to the JMM, providing a partial ordering on all actions within a program. If one action happens-before another, the first is visible and ordered before the second. Major happens-before rules include:

- **Program Order Rule:** Each action in a thread happens-before every subsequent action in that thread.

- **Monitor Lock Rule:** An unlock on a monitor happens-before every subsequent lock on that monitor.

- volatile **Variable Rule:** A write to a volatile field happens-before every subsequent read of that same field.

- **Thread Start Rule:** A call to Thread.start() on a thread happens-before any action in the started thread.

- **Thread Termination Rule:** Any action in a thread happens-before another thread detects that the thread has terminated, either by Thread.join() or Thread.isAlive().

- **Transitivity:** If A happens-before B, and B happens-before C, then A happens-before C.

Consider the following example to illustrate the happens-before principle:

```
public class HappensBeforeExample {
    int a = 0;
    boolean flag = false;

    public void writeVariables() {
        a = 1; // (1)
        flag = true; // (2)
    }

    public void readVariables() {
        if (flag) { // (3)
            int i = a; // (4)
        }
    }
}
```

Here:

- Write to a happens-before the write to flag in the same thread (by the program order rule).

- If flag is true in the readVariables() method, then the read of a is guaranteed to see the value 1, assuming proper synchronization (e.g., both methods synchronized on the same monitor).

Compiler and Processor Optimizations

Heavily optimized code is one reason the JMM is intricate. Compilers and processors can reorder instructions or store variables in registers to enhance performance. Without JMM rules, such optimizations can disrupt concurrent programs.

```
public class ReorderingIssue {
    int a = 0, b = 0;

    public void writer() {
        a = 1; // (1)
        b = 2; // (2)
    }

    public void reader() {
        if (b == 2) { // (3)
            int c = a; // (4)
        }
    }
}
```

In this code snippet, a naive reordering may lead to a read of b before write to a, causing the variable a to be 0 instead of 1 when b is 2. However, applying proper synchronization techniques ensures the correct order of operations as prescribed by the JMM.

Usage of volatile Variables

Understanding when and how to use volatile variables is essential. The volatile keyword ensures:

- Reads and writes to the variable are directly from the main memory.
- No thread-local caching of the variable occurs.
- Variable writes are visible to all threads reading the variable subsequently.

Consider the following example:

```
public class VolatileExample {
    private volatile boolean running = true;

    public void stop() {
        running = false;
    }

    public void run() {
```

```
        while (running) {
            // perform task
        }
    }
}
```

Here, the flag running ensures that when one thread sets it to false, the other thread observing this variable will see the updated value immediately.

Final Fields

Final fields in Java also have special treatment under the JMM. Once a constructor completes, the final fields are guaranteed to be visible correctly to any other thread accessing them without additional synchronization. This ensures a properly constructed object's immutability.

Understanding the Java Memory Model, including critical concepts such as the happens-before relationship and the correct use of volatile and final fields, is crucial for designing reliable and efficient concurrent applications. This knowledge allows developers to avoid common pitfalls and write code that behaves predictably in a multithreaded environment.

1.6 Thread Lifecycle

Understanding the lifecycle of a thread is crucial for mastering Java concurrency. A thread's lifecycle consists of several states, and transitions between these states are governed by various actions and triggers within the Java Virtual Machine (JVM). Any thread in Java can be classified into one of the following states:

- **New**
- **Runnable**
- **Blocked**
- **Waiting**
- **Timed Waiting**
- **Terminated**

Each state represents a specific phase in the thread's existence, and understanding these states is pivotal for diagnosing and optimizing multi-threaded applications.

New: When a thread is first created, it is in the NEW state. At this point, the thread is merely an object of the Thread class and has not yet been scheduled for execution. This state persists until the start() method is called on the Thread object.

Runnable: Once the start() method is invoked, the thread enters the RUNNABLE state. In this state, the thread is ready for execution and is waiting for CPU time. The actual running of the thread depends on the scheduler's decision. The RUNNABLE state encompasses both executing and ready-for-execution phases.

Blocked: A thread enters the BLOCKED state when it attempts to acquire a lock that is held by another thread. In this state, the thread remains inactive until it acquires the required lock to proceed. This state is distinct from the WAITING and TIMED_WAITING states as it specifically involves lock acquisition.

Waiting: The WAITING state is entered when a thread is waiting indefinitely for another thread to perform a specific action. A thread in this state can be reactivated only by another thread's intervention. Common methods that cause a thread to enter the WAITING state include Object.wait(), Thread.join() without a timeout, and LockSupport.park().

Timed Waiting: This state is similar to WAITING, but the thread waits for a specific period. After the timeout interval elapses, the thread moves back to the RUNNABLE state. Methods causing this state transition include Thread.sleep(), Object.wait() with a timeout, Thread.join() with a timeout, and LockSupport.parkNanos() and LockSupport.parkUntil().

Terminated: A thread moves to the TERMINATED state once its execution completes. This state is achieved upon the thread returning from the run() method or throwing an uncaught exception that propagates out of the run() method. At this point, the thread cannot be restarted or brought back to a runnable state.

```
public class ThreadLifecycleDemo {

    public static void main(String[] args) throws InterruptedException {
        Thread thread = new Thread(() -> {
            System.out.println("Thread is running");
        });
```

```
        // Thread is in NEW state
        System.out.println("State: " + thread.getState());

        thread.start();

        // Thread is in RUNNABLE state
        System.out.println("State: " + thread.getState());

        thread.join();

        // Thread is in TERMINATED state
        System.out.println("State: " + thread.getState());
    }
}
```

```
output:
State: NEW
State: RUNNABLE
Thread is running
State: TERMINATED
```

The state transition diagram is expressed through various thread manipulation methods that a developer can employ, resulting in state changes. These transitions form the core of thread lifecycle management, necessitating a detailed understanding of each method and its implications.

For example, the Thread.sleep() method puts the executing thread into the TIMED_WAITING state for a specified duration. Yielding the processor's time slice via Thread.yield() might not necessarily change the thread's state but signals to the scheduler to prefer other threads, making state transitions more fluid. Specifically:

```
public class TimedWaitingStateDemo {

    public static void main(String[] args) {
        Thread thread = new Thread(() -> {
            try {
                System.out.println("Thread is about to sleep");
                Thread.sleep(2000);
                System.out.println("Thread has woken up");
            } catch (InterruptedException e) {
                Thread.currentThread().interrupt();
            }
        });

        thread.start();

        try {
            // Introduce a slight delay to observe the TIMED_WAITING state
            Thread.sleep(100);
        } catch (InterruptedException e) {
            Thread.currentThread().interrupt();
        }

        // Thread should be in TIMED_WAITING state
        System.out.println("State: " + thread.getState());
    }
```

```
}
```

```
output:
Thread is about to sleep
State: TIMED_WAITING
Thread has woken up
```

Analyzing and managing thread lifecycles effectively prevents common issues such as deadlocks, thread starvation, and resource contention. An adept grasp on these concepts empowers developers to write efficient and safe concurrent applications that harness the full potential of modern multi-core processors. Understanding and controlling the states through appropriate synchronization mechanisms and state-aware coding practices lead to robust multithreaded systems.

1.7 Creating and Starting Threads in Java

In Java, threads are fundamental units of execution within a program, and understanding how to create and start them is crucial for effective concurrent programming. This section will delve into the various methods available for thread creation and initialization, offering detailed explanations and practical examples to facilitate comprehension.

Java offers two primary mechanisms for creating threads: extending the Thread class and implementing the Runnable interface. Each approach has its advantages and specific use cases.

- **Extending the Thread Class**
- **Implementing the Runnable Interface**

Extending the Thread Class

To create a thread by extending the Thread class, follow these steps: define a new class that inherits from Thread and override the run() method, which houses the code to be executed by the thread. Below is a complete example demonstrating this process.

```
class MyThread extends Thread {
    public void run() {
        System.out.println("Thread is running.");
    }

    public static void main(String args[]) {
        MyThread t1 = new MyThread();
        t1.start();
    }
}
```

Above, the MyThread class extends Thread and overrides the run() method to print a message. The main method, main(), creates an instance of MyThread and invokes start(), which internally calls run().

Implementing the Runnable Interface

Using the Runnable interface allows you to separate the task from the mechanism that executes it. This is particularly advantageous when you need to extend another class. Below is an example showing how to implement Runnable:

```
class MyRunnable implements Runnable {
    public void run() {
        System.out.println("Thread is running.");
    }

    public static void main(String args[]) {
        MyRunnable myRunnable = new MyRunnable();
        Thread t1 = new Thread(myRunnable);
        t1.start();
    }
}
```

Here, the MyRunnable class implements Runnable and provides the run() method. An instance of MyRunnable is passed to the Thread constructor, and calling start() on the thread object initiates the run() method.

Using Lambda Expressions

Java 8 introduced lambda expressions, allowing for more concise and readable code when working with functional interfaces like Runnable. Here's how to use a lambda expression to create and start a thread:

```
public class LambdaThread {
    public static void main(String args[]) {
        Runnable r = () -> {
            System.out.println("Thread is running using lambda.");
        };
        Thread t = new Thread(r);
        t.start();
    }
}
```

The LambdaThread class demonstrates how to leverage lambda expressions to define the run() method of Runnable, streamlining thread creation.

Thread States

When a thread is created and started in Java, it transitions through various states, which are managed by the Java Virtual Machine (JVM). These states include NEW, RUNNABLE, BLOCKED,

WAITING, TIMED_WAITING, and TERMINATED. The transition between these states is essential for understanding thread lifecycle management.

Thread Priorities

Java also allows setting thread priorities ranging from '1' (Thread.MIN_PRIORITY) to '10' (Thread.MAX_PRIORITY), with the default priority being '5' (Thread.NORM_PRIORITY). Below is an example of how to set a thread's priority:

```
public class PriorityThreadExample extends Thread {
    public void run() {
        System.out.println("Thread is running with priority: " + this.getPriority());
    }

    public static void main(String args[]) {
        PriorityThreadExample t1 = new PriorityThreadExample();
        t1.setPriority(Thread.MAX_PRIORITY);
        t1.start();

        PriorityThreadExample t2 = new PriorityThreadExample();
        t2.setPriority(Thread.MIN_PRIORITY);
        t2.start();
    }
}
```

In this PriorityThreadExample, two threads are created with maximum and minimum priorities. The priority value influences the scheduling of the threads but does not guarantee execution order.

Java offers versatile mechanisms for thread creation, each suited to different scenarios, and allows for fine-tuning through priority settings. These capabilities form the basis for managing concurrent tasks effectively in modern Java applications. Here is the corrected LaTeX text of the section with all errors fixed:

1.8 Thread States and Transitions

Threads in Java can be in one of several states, each representing a different phase in the thread lifecycle. Understanding these states and how threads transition between them is crucial for mastering Java concurrency. In the Java language, threads can exist in the following states: NEW, RUNNABLE, BLOCKED, WAITING, TIMED_WAITING, and TERMINATED. These states are managed by the Java Virtual Machine (JVM) and can be queried using the getState() method of the Thread class.

- NEW: A thread that has been created but not yet started is in the NEW state. The thread remains in this state until the start() method is called.
- RUNNABLE: After a thread's start() method is invoked, the thread becomes RUNNABLE. A RUNNABLE thread is eligible to be run by the JVM, but it might not be running immediately due to the operating system's thread scheduling mechanism.
- BLOCKED: A thread enters the BLOCKED state when it attempts to acquire a monitor lock that is held by another thread. Once the lock is released, the thread moves back to the RUNNABLE state.
- WAITING: A thread is in the WAITING state when it is waiting indefinitely for another thread to perform a particular action. This can occur when a thread calls Object.wait() without a timeout, Thread.join() without a timeout, or LockSupport.park().
- TIMED_WAITING: This state is similar to WAITING, but with a specified waiting period. A thread is in the TIMED_WAITING state if it is waiting with a timeout for another thread to perform a specific action, such as when calling Thread.sleep(), Object.wait() with a timeout, Thread.join() with a timeout, or LockSupport.parkNanos().
- TERMINATED: Once a thread has completed its execution, either by returning from the run() method or by throwing an uncaught exception, it enters the TERMINATED state.

Transitions between these states occur due to various actions, typically related to method calls or synchronizations. Below is an algorithm that encapsulates the transitions between different thread states.

To observe the states programmatically, one might implement a simple thread class and monitor its state transitions, as shown below:

```
public class ThreadStateDemo implements Runnable {
    public static void main(String[] args) throws InterruptedException {
        Thread thread = new Thread(new ThreadStateDemo());
        System.out.println("Thread state after creation: " + thread.getState());

        thread.start();
        System.out.println("Thread state after calling start(): " + thread.getState());

        Thread.sleep(100); // Allow thread to reach run method
        System.out.println("Thread state during execution: " + thread.getState());

        thread.join();
```

Algorithm 1: Thread State Transitions

```
if Thread Creation then
    State ← NEW;
else
    while Thread is RUNNABLE do
        if Running Code then
            if Exit run() Method then
                State ← TERMINATED;
            else
                State ← RUNNABLE;
            end
        end
        if Monitor Lock then
            if Acquired then
                State ← RUNNABLE;
            else
                State ← BLOCKED;
            end
        end
        if Wait Indefinitely then
            State ← WAITING;
        end
        if Wait with Timeout then
            State ← TIMED_WAITING;
        end
    end
end
```

```
        System.out.println("Thread state after termination: " + thread.getState());
    }

    @Override
    public void run() {
        try {
            Thread.sleep(200);
        } catch (InterruptedException e) {
            Thread.currentThread().interrupt();
        }
    }
}
```

Executing the above code results in the following output demonstrating the transitions:

```
Thread state after creation: NEW
Thread state after calling start(): RUNNABLE
Thread state during execution: RUNNABLE
Thread state after termination: TERMINATED
```

The JVM state management ensures proper handling of threads as they progress through their lifecycle, maintaining synchronization and promoting efficient execution. It is crucial to understand these transitions to manage thread behavior effectively, avoid common concurrency issues such as deadlocks, and improve application performance. Developing a nuanced grasp of thread states and transitions lays the groundwork for more advanced concurrency practices.

1.9 Common Issues in Concurrent Programming

Concurrent programming in Java brings significant benefits, such as improved application performance and responsiveness. However, it also introduces a range of complexities and challenges. Understanding these common issues is critical for developing robust concurrent applications.

Race Conditions

A race condition occurs when the behavior of software depends on the relative timing or interleaving of multiple threads' execution to a shared resource. This often happens when two or more threads can simultaneously read and write to a shared variable. Consider the following example:

```
class Counter {
    private int count = 0;

    public void increment() {
        count++;
    }

    public int getCount() {
        return count;
    }
}
```

If increment() is called by multiple threads, they might read, update, and write count concurrently, leading to inconsistent or unexpected values. To mitigate race conditions, synchronization mechanisms such as synchronized blocks or methods can be used:

```
class SynchronizedCounter {
    private int count = 0;

    public synchronized void increment() {
        count++;
    }

    public synchronized int getCount() {
        return count;
    }
}
```

Deadlocks

A deadlock occurs when two or more threads are blocked forever, waiting for each other to release a resource. Consider the classical example of two threads and two resources:

```
class A {
    synchronized void methodA(B b) {
        b.last();
    }
    synchronized void last() {}
}

class B {
    synchronized void methodB(A a) {
        a.last();
    }
    synchronized void last() {}
}

class DeadlockExample implements Runnable {
    A a = new A();
    B b = new B();

    DeadlockExample() {
        new Thread(this).start();
        a.methodA(b); // This thread locks a then attempts to lock b
    }
```

```
    public void run() {
        b.methodB(a); // This thread locks b then attempts to lock a
    }
}
```

In this scenario, thread 1 locks on instance a and tries to lock instance b, whereas thread 2 locks on instance b and tries to lock instance a. To resolve deadlocks, consider avoiding circular wait conditions, ordering resource acquisition, or using tools like the Java concurrency utilities that handle deadlocks internally.

Livelocks

A livelock is a situation where two or more threads keep changing their state in response to each other without making any actual progress. Unlike deadlocks, threads in a livelock are not blocked but are continuously active. Use backoff strategies or condition checks effectively to ensure threads do not endlessly react to each other without progression.

Starvation

Starvation happens when a thread is perpetually denied access to resources it requires for execution because other threads consistently consume those resources. This can happen with poorly managed thread priorities or using shared locks improperly. Priority inversion can also lead to starvation, where lower-priority threads hold critical resources, and higher-priority threads are unable to proceed. Consider fair scheduling practices and using higher-level concurrency constructs like java.util.concurrent.locks.ReentrantLock with the fair policy.

```
ReentrantLock lock = new ReentrantLock(true); // Fair lock
```

Memory Consistency Errors

Memory consistency errors occur when different threads have inconsistent views of what should be the same data. This happens due to the lack of proper synchronization, leading to one thread seeing stale or incorrect values. The Java Memory Model (JMM) defines how threads interact through memory and ensures visibility of changes to shared variables. Using volatile variables or proper synchronization can mitigate these issues:

```
class VolatileExample {
    private volatile boolean running = true;

    public void run() {
        while (running) {
            // do work
```

```
        }
    }

    public void stop() {
        running = false;
    }
}
```

Resource Contention

Resource contention occurs when multiple threads try to access a shared resource, such as CPU or I/O, simultaneously. This can degrade performance and throughput. Using efficient algorithms, minimizing locking duration, and employing lock-free data structures can mitigate resource contention.

Thread Leaks

A thread leak occurs when an application creates more threads than it can clean up or handle, leading to resource exhaustion. To detect and prevent thread leaks, ensure that threads terminate correctly, use thread pools effectively, and employ monitoring tools to track thread usage.

By understanding these common issues and employing best practices, developers can mitigate the risks associated with concurrent programming, thereby developing more reliable and efficient Java applications. In-depth knowledge of Java's concurrency mechanisms and the Java Memory Model is essential for preventing and resolving these issues.

Chapter 2

Basic Thread Operations

This chapter covers the fundamental operations of thread management in Java. It explores essential topics such as thread creation through extending the Thread class or implementing Runnable, and techniques for starting and stopping threads. Key actions like sleep, yield, and setting thread priorities are discussed, along with the concepts of joining and daemon threads. The chapter also addresses thread interruption and provides an introduction to basic thread safety principles, laying a solid groundwork for managing concurrency in Java applications.

2.1 Introduction to Threads

In modern software development, efficient and effective utilization of CPU resources is critical. An essential element in achieving this is understanding how threads function in Java. A thread is a lightweight subprocess and the smallest unit of processing. Threading provides a way to improve the performance of an application by allowing multiple processes to run concurrently. In this section, we will explore the fundamental concept of threads, their lifecycle, and their role in concurrent programming.

A thread in Java can be defined and manipulated using the Thread class or by implementing the Runnable interface. Each thread in Java operates within its own call stack, allowing it to run independently and concurrently with other threads. Concurrency, however, introduces complexity due to the necessity of managing shared resources and ensuring thread safety.

The primary methods to create a thread in Java involve:

- Extending the Thread class.
- Implementing the Runnable interface.

Thread operations must adhere to a specific lifecycle, which includes the following states:

- **New**: A thread is in this state when it is created but not yet started.
- **Runnable**: A thread enters this state when start() is called and the thread is ready to run.
- **Blocked**: A thread is in this state when it is blocked waiting for a monitor lock.
- **Waiting**: A thread that is waiting indefinitely for another thread to perform a specific action is in this state.
- **Timed Waiting**: A thread that is waiting for another thread to perform an action for up to a specified waiting time.
- **Terminated**: A thread that has exited is in this state.

The following example demonstrates a simple thread creation by extending the Thread class:

```
class SimpleThread extends Thread {
    public void run() {
        System.out.println("Thread is running.");
    }

    public static void main(String[] args) {
        SimpleThread thread = new SimpleThread();
        thread.start();
    }
}
```

When the SimpleThread instance's start() method is invoked, the Java Virtual Machine (JVM) schedules the thread for execution, which subsequently invokes the run() method.

Alternatively, implementing the Runnable interface is another widely-used approach for creating threads. It allows more flexibility as the class can extend other classes, unlike the method where it extends the Thread class.

```
class SimpleRunnable implements Runnable {
    public void run() {
        System.out.println("Runnable is running.");
    }

    public static void main(String[] args) {
        SimpleRunnable runnable = new SimpleRunnable();
        Thread thread = new Thread(runnable);
        thread.start();
    }
}
```

Both methodologies - extending the Thread class and implementing the Runnable interface - are equally viable for creating threads. The choice between them often depends on the specific needs of your application and class design considerations.

Here, we observe the very essence of how concurrency is initiated and managed within a Java program. The simplicity of starting a new thread belies the inherent complexity that comes with managing concurrent execution, a topic that we will explore further in subsequent sections.

Proper thread management and synchronization are crucial to avoiding issues such as deadlocks, race conditions, and data inconsistency. As threads can interact in unpredictable ways, it is essential to establish solid thread safety principles. This foundational understanding of Java threads is the groundwork on which more advanced concurrent programming concepts are built.

2.2 Thread Creation (Extending Thread and Implementing Runnable)

Java provides two primary mechanisms to create and run threads: by extending the Thread class and by implementing the Runnable interface. Each method has its distinct advantages and appropriate use cases depending on the specific needs of your application.

To create a thread by extending the Thread class, you need to subclass Thread and override its run() method. Here's a basic example to illustrate this:

```
class MyThread extends Thread {
    public void run() {
        System.out.println("Thread is running.");
    }

    public static void main(String[] args) {
```

```
        MyThread thread = new MyThread();
        thread.start();
    }
}
```

The start() method is invoked on the MyThread instance, which internally calls the run() method in a separate call stack, beginning the new thread execution independently from the main thread.

Alternatively, to create a thread by implementing the Runnable interface, the class must define the run() method from the Runnable interface, and a Thread object must be instantiated with an instance of the Runnable implementation:

```
class MyRunnable implements Runnable {
    public void run() {
        System.out.println("Runnable is running.");
    }

    public static void main(String[] args) {
        MyRunnable myRunnable = new MyRunnable();
        Thread thread = new Thread(myRunnable);
        thread.start();
    }
}
```

Here, we separate the task to be performed by the thread (encapsulated in the MyRunnable class) from the thread execution mechanism (provided by the Thread class). This approach adheres better to the design principle of separation of concerns and is often more flexible and extensible than subclassing Thread.

When considering which technique to use, one key factor is that Java does not support multiple inheritance of classes, but a class can implement multiple interfaces. Therefore, if your class must extend another class, you should implement Runnable rather than extend the Thread class.

Illustrating the benefits of the Runnable interface, consider the following scenario where a class needs to implement multiple interfaces and encapsulate a thread execution:

```
interface AnotherInterface {
    void anotherMethod();
}

class MyRunnable implements Runnable, AnotherInterface {
    public void run() {
        System.out.println("Runnable is running.");
    }

    public void anotherMethod() {
        System.out.println("Executing another method.");
```

```
    }

    public static void main(String[] args) {
        MyRunnable myRunnable = new MyRunnable();
        Thread thread = new Thread(myRunnable);
        thread.start();
    }
}
```

The MyRunnable class above implements both the Runnable interface and AnotherInterface, showcasing the flexibility of choosing the interface-based approach for thread creation.

Both methods can be used interchangeably, but using the Runnable interface is the preferred approach in professional practice because it de-couples the task from the thread execution mechanism, promoting cleaner design and ease of unit testing.

Thread creation is a fundamental concept in Java concurrency, where understanding the differences and best practices for extending the Thread class versus implementing the Runnable interface lays the groundwork for more advanced concurrency mechanisms.

2.3 Starting and Stopping Threads

To properly manage thread execution in Java, understanding the mechanisms to start and stop threads is crucial. This section delves into these operations, encompassing thread lifecycle details.

Starting Threads

In Java, you initiate a thread by invoking the start() method on an instance of a class that either extends Thread or implements the Runnable interface.

```
public class MyThread extends Thread {
    public void run() {
        System.out.println("Thread is running");
    }

    public static void main(String[] args) {
        MyThread thread = new MyThread();
        thread.start();
    }
}
```

This code snippet demonstrates starting a thread by extending the Thread class. The run() method, which contains the code to be executed in the new thread, is called by the start() method. Directly calling run() does not create a new thread but executes the method in the current thread. Only start() can trigger the lifecycle management handled by the Java Virtual Machine (JVM).

Alternatively, you can start a thread using a class that implements Runnable:

```
public class MyRunnable implements Runnable {
    public void run() {
        System.out.println("Runnable is running");
    }

    public static void main(String[] args) {
        MyRunnable runnable = new MyRunnable();
        Thread thread = new Thread(runnable);
        thread.start();
    }
}
```

In this example, a MyRunnable instance is passed to the Thread constructor and then started via start(). This approach provides flexibility, as the same Runnable instance can be reused across multiple threads.

start() ensures that the thread is transitioned from the NEW state to the RUNNABLE state. The JVM schedules the thread according to its priority and availability of system resources.

Stopping Threads

Stopping a thread can be more complex due to the need for ensuring the thread terminates gracefully without leaving system resources in an inconsistent state. Deprecated methods like stop() forcibly terminate a thread and can cause system instability due to abrupt resource release. The preferred approach uses a controlled manner to signal the thread to stop.

Set the thread's termination condition within the run() method using a volatile boolean flag:

```
public class ControlledStop implements Runnable {
    private volatile boolean exit = false;

    public void run() {
        while (!exit) {
            System.out.println("Thread is running");
            // Perform thread's primary operations
        }
    }

    public void stop() {
        exit = true;
    }

    public static void main(String[] args) {
        ControlledStop controlledStop = new ControlledStop();
```

```
        Thread thread = new Thread(controlledStop);
        thread.start();

        // Simulate some other operations, then stop the thread
        controlledStop.stop();
    }
}
```

In this example, the exit flag is checked within the thread's loop. The thread keeps running until exit is set to true. The stop() method provides a safe way to signal the thread to finish its work and terminate gracefully.

isInterrupted() and interrupted() methods can also be used to handle thread termination by utilizing the thread interruption mechanism. The isInterrupted() method checks the interrupted status of the thread, while interrupted() checks the status and resets it.

```
public class InterruptibleTask implements Runnable {
    public void run() {
        while (!Thread.currentThread().isInterrupted()) {
            System.out.println("Thread is running");
            // Perform the 'threads primary operations
        }
    }

    public static void main(String[] args) {
        Thread thread = new Thread(new InterruptibleTask());
        thread.start();

        // Simulate other operations, then interrupt the thread
        thread.interrupt();
    }
}
```

In this snippet, the thread runs until it is interrupted. The interrupt() method sets the interrupt status of the thread, which is checked in the thread's loop using isInterrupted().

Responding to interruption in blocked states (e.g., sleep or wait) requires handling InterruptedException. Here is an example that demonstrates this approach:

```
public class InterruptibleSleep implements Runnable {
    public void run() {
        try {
            while (!Thread.currentThread().isInterrupted()) {
                System.out.println("Thread is going to sleep");
                Thread.sleep(1000);
            }
        } catch (InterruptedException e) {
            Thread.currentThread().interrupt(); // Restore the interrupt status
            System.out.println("Thread was interrupted");
        }
    }
```

```
    public static void main(String[] args) {
        Thread thread = new Thread(new InterruptibleSleep());
        thread.start();

        // Simulate other operations, then interrupt the thread
        thread.interrupt();
    }
}
```

In this case, Thread.sleep() is wrapped in a try-catch block to handle InterruptedException appropriately. When the thread is interrupted, an exception is thrown and caught, at which point the thread can respond to the interruption and cease execution. It is critical to re-interrupt the thread within the catch block to preserve the interrupt status, ensuring any higher-level code that depends on the interrupt flag properly acknowledges it.

These strategies for starting and stopping threads not only provide a foundation for managing thread lifecycle but also ensure resources are handled efficiently and safely in concurrent Java applications.

2.4 Thread Sleep and Yield

Thread control mechanisms such as sleep and yield are fundamental to the management of thread execution in Java. These tools allow for fine-grained control over the behavior of threads, ensuring efficient utilization of CPU resources and providing the means to accommodate time-sensitive operations.

The sleep method temporarily pauses the execution of the current thread for a specified period. This period is defined in milliseconds. Below is an example:

```
public class SleepExample {
    public static void main(String[] args) {
        Thread thread = new Thread(new Runnable() {
            public void run() {
                try {
                    System.out.println("Thread is going to sleep for 2000 milliseconds.");
                    Thread.sleep(2000);
                    System.out.println("Thread woke up.");
                } catch (InterruptedException e) {
                    System.out.println("Thread was interrupted.");
                }
            }
        });
        thread.start();
    }
}
```

The sleep method takes a single argument representing the sleep duration in milliseconds. During this period, the thread transitions from the RUNNABLE state to the TIMED_WAITING state. Upon completion of the sleep period, the thread is again eligible for scheduling by the thread scheduler.

It is crucial to handle the InterruptedException that sleep may throw. The sleep method is interruptible, meaning another thread can interrupt a sleeping thread. Such an interruption throws an InterruptedException, which must be caught and handled appropriately. The following is an example of handling an interruption during sleep:

```
public class InterruptibleSleepExample {
    public static void main(String[] args) {
        Thread thread = new Thread(new Runnable() {
            public void run() {
                try {
                    System.out.println("Thread is going to sleep for 5000 milliseconds.");
                    Thread.sleep(5000);
                    System.out.println("Thread woke up.");
                } catch (InterruptedException e) {
                    System.out.println("Thread was interrupted while sleeping.");
                }
            }
        });
        thread.start();

        // Interrupt the thread after 2000 milliseconds
        try {
            Thread.sleep(2000);
        } catch (InterruptedException e) {
            // Handle the exception
        }

        thread.interrupt();
    }
}
```

In the above code, the main thread interrupts the sleeping thread after 2000 milliseconds. The sleeping thread catches the InterruptedException and handles it by printing a message indicating the interruption.

The yield method, on the other hand, offers a slightly different mechanism. When the yield method is called, the currently executing thread informs the thread scheduler that it is willing to yield its current use of a processor. This suggests to the thread scheduler that it may be a good time to switch from the currently running thread to another ready-to-run thread of equal priority.

A key point to note is that the yield method does not guarantee the yielding thread will stop running immediately. The action taken by the thread scheduler depends on its implementation, which can vary between Java Virtual Machines (JVMs) and operating systems. Additionally, the yielding thread remains in the RUNNABLE state and is simply moved to the end of the run queue, potentially to be scheduled again immediately if no other threads of equal priority are available.

Consider the following example where the yield method is used:

```
public class YieldExample {
    public static void main(String[] args) {
        Thread thread1 = new Thread(new Runnable() {
            public void run() {
                for(int i = 0; i < 5; i++) {
                    System.out.println("Thread 1 - iteration: " + i);
                    Thread.yield();
                }
            }
        });

        Thread thread2 = new Thread(new Runnable() {
            public void run() {
                for(int i = 0; i < 5; i++) {
                    System.out.println("Thread 2 - iteration: " + i);
                }
            }
        });

        thread1.start();
        thread2.start();
    }
}
```

In this example, thread1 invokes yield within its loop, signaling the scheduler that it is willing to step aside in favor of thread2 or any other thread of equal priority. Consequently, thread2 might get more CPU time, although this behavior is dependent on the underlying thread scheduler.

The proper use of sleep and yield is crucial for effective thread management in Java. sleep provides a mechanism to pause execution with high precision, suitable for timing operations or pacing tasks, while yield serves as a hint to the thread scheduler that a switch in execution might be appropriate. These tools, when used correctly, can optimize thread behavior and resource utilization within Java applications.

2.5 Thread Priorities

Thread priority is a mechanism in Java that enables the developer to influence the order in which threads are executed. Each Java thread has a priority, an integer value between Thread.MIN_PRIORITY (which is 1) and Thread.MAX_PRIORITY (which is 10). By default, threads are assigned a priority of Thread.NORM_PRIORITY (which is 5). Higher priority threads are more likely to run before lower priority threads, although exact behavior can be implementation-dependent because it is determined by the thread scheduler of the underlying operating system.

To demonstrate how to set and get thread priorities, consider the following example code:

```
public class PriorityDemo {

    public static void main(String[] args) {
        Thread highPriorityThread = new Thread(new PriorityRunnable(), "
            HighPriorityThread");
        Thread lowPriorityThread = new Thread(new PriorityRunnable(), "
            LowPriorityThread");

        highPriorityThread.setPriority(Thread.MAX_PRIORITY); // Setting maximum
             priority
        lowPriorityThread.setPriority(Thread.MIN_PRIORITY); // Setting minimum
            priority

        highPriorityThread.start();
        lowPriorityThread.start();
    }
}

class PriorityRunnable implements Runnable {
    @Override
    public void run() {
        for (int i = 0; i < 5; i++) {
            System.out.println(Thread.currentThread().getName() + " - Priority: " +
                                Thread.currentThread().getPriority());
            try {
                Thread.sleep(1000); // Sleep for one second
            } catch (InterruptedException e) {
                System.err.println(e);
            }
        }
    }
}
```

In the above code, we define two threads: highPriorityThread and lowPriorityThread. The thread highPriorityThread is assigned the maximum priority by calling setPriority(Thread.MAX_PRIORITY), while lowPriorityThread is assigned the minimum priority by calling setPriority(Thread.MIN_PRIORITY). When the threads are started, they will run the code in the PriorityRunnable class, which prints the name and priority of the running thread.

A typical output from running the above code might look like this:

```
HighPriorityThread - Priority: 10
LowPriorityThread - Priority: 1
HighPriorityThread - Priority: 10
LowPriorityThread - Priority: 1
HighPriorityThread - Priority: 10
LowPriorityThread - Priority: 1
HighPriorityThread - Priority: 10
LowPriorityThread - Priority: 1
HighPriorityThread - Priority: 10
LowPriorityThread - Priority: 1
```

While this simple example demonstrates setting and getting thread priorities, it should be noted that the actual influence of thread priority on execution order can differ depending on the operating system's thread scheduling policy. The Java language specification does not guarantee a strict priority-based execution order but rather suggests that higher priority threads should be executed preferentially to lower priority threads.

It is also important to understand that setting thread priorities should be used cautiously. Excessive reliance on thread priorities can lead to unpredictable and non-portable behavior. High-priority threads should perform quick, essential tasks and then yield or sleep to allow other threads to execute. Low-priority threads can handle less time-critical tasks and can be preempted by higher priority threads when necessary.

Here is an example highlighting the potential pitfall with thread priorities:

```
public class StarvationDemo {

    public static void main(String[] args) {
        Runnable runnable = () -> {
            while (true) {
                System.out.println(Thread.currentThread().getName() + " is running");
            }
        };

        Thread highPriorityThread = new Thread(runnable, "HighPriorityThread");
        Thread lowPriorityThread = new Thread(runnable, "LowPriorityThread");

        highPriorityThread.setPriority(Thread.MAX_PRIORITY);
        lowPriorityThread.setPriority(Thread.MIN_PRIORITY);

        highPriorityThread.start();
        lowPriorityThread.start();
    }
}
```

In this example, the HighPriorityThread could potentially starve the LowPriorityThread because of its highest priority setting. The LowPriorityThread may rarely get a chance to run as the high-priority thread continues to demand CPU resources.

Thread priorities can be a useful tool when used appropriately to manage CPU time for various threads within an application. They allow developers to assign differential importance to threads, potentially leading to more responsive and well-behaved applications. However, it is essential to design the application's thread model to be robust and to avoid relying solely on thread priorities to enforce execution order. Proper synchronization, workload distribution, and consideration of the operating system's scheduling policies are crucial to effectively managing thread behavior in a multi-threaded environment.

2.6 Joining Threads

In multi-threaded applications, it is often crucial to ensure that one thread completes its execution before another thread proceeds. This can be achieved using the join() method in Java. The join() method allows one thread to wait for the completion of another thread. This mechanism is pivotal in scenarios where a thread depends on the results of other threads.

The join() method is part of the java.lang.Thread class and is fundamental for thread synchronization. When a thread invokes join() on another thread (say, threadB), the calling thread pauses its execution until threadB terminates.

Consider the following example, which demonstrates the use of join():

```
public class ThreadJoinExample {

    public static void main(String[] args) {
        Thread threadA = new Thread(new Task(), "Thread-A");
        Thread threadB = new Thread(new Task(), "Thread-B");

        threadA.start();
        threadB.start();

        try {
            threadA.join(); // main thread waits for threadA to finish
            threadB.join(); // main thread waits for threadB to finish
        } catch (InterruptedException e) {
            e.printStackTrace();
        }

        System.out.println("All threads have finished.");
    }
}

class Task implements Runnable {
    public void run() {
        System.out.println(Thread.currentThread().getName() + " is executing.");
        try {
            Thread.sleep(2000); // simulate some work being done
        } catch (InterruptedException e) {
```

```
            e.printStackTrace();
        }
        System.out.println(Thread.currentThread().getName() + " has finished.");
    }
}
```

In this example, two threads (threadA and threadB) are started and the main thread waits for both of them to finish by invoking join() on each. The output demonstrates the synchronization achieved using join():

```
Thread-A is executing.
Thread-B is executing.
Thread-A has finished.
Thread-B has finished.
All threads have finished.
```

The join() method can also take an optional argument specifying the maximum time to wait for the thread to terminate. This allows the calling thread to resume execution if the specified time elapses:

```
public class TimedJoinExample {

    public static void main(String[] args) {
        Thread threadA = new Thread(new Task(), "Thread-A");

        threadA.start();

        try {
            threadA.join(1000); // main thread waits for up to 1 second for threadA to
                finish
        } catch (InterruptedException e) {
            e.printStackTrace();
        }

        System.out.println("Main thread continues even if threadA has not finished.");
    }
}

class Task implements Runnable {
    public void run() {
        System.out.println(Thread.currentThread().getName() + " is executing.");
        try {
            Thread.sleep(2000); // simulate some work being done
        } catch (InterruptedException e) {
            e.printStackTrace();
        }
        System.out.println(Thread.currentThread().getName() + " has finished.");
    }
}
```

In this example, the main thread waits for up to 1 second for threadA to finish. If threadA does not complete within that time, the main thread resumes execution irrespective of the state of threadA, ensuring application flexibility.

The join() method ensures a specified order of thread execution, which is vital in certain applications. For instance, in a data processing pipeline where Stage 1 must complete before Stage 2 can begin, using join() will ensure that threads representing these stages execute sequentially:

```
public class DataProcessingPipeline {

    public static void main(String[] args) {
        Thread stage1 = new Thread(new Stage("Stage 1"), "Stage-1");
        Thread stage2 = new Thread(new Stage("Stage 2"), "Stage-2");

        stage1.start();

        try {
            stage1.join(); // Wait for Stage 1 to complete
        } catch (InterruptedException e) {
            e.printStackTrace();
        }

        stage2.start();

        try {
            stage2.join(); // Wait for Stage 2 to complete
        } catch (InterruptedException e) {
            e.printStackTrace();
        }

        System.out.println("Data processing pipeline completed.");
    }
}

class Stage implements Runnable {
    private String stageName;

    public Stage(String stageName) {
        this.stageName = stageName;
    }

    public void run() {
        System.out.println(stageName + " is executing.");
        try {
            Thread.sleep(3000); // simulate stage processing time
        } catch (InterruptedException e) {
            e.printStackTrace();
        }
        System.out.println(stageName + " has finished.");
    }
}
```

In this heavily synchronized environment, join() guarantees that Stage 2 does not start until Stage 1 has completely finished, making sure that the pipeline stages do not overlap or fail due to incomplete upstream processes.

Understanding and effectively utilizing the join() method is critical for robust multi-threaded programming. It allows for fine-grained control over thread execution order and ensures that dependent tasks are synchronized correctly, leading to reliable and maintainable concurrent applications.

2.7 Daemon Threads

In Java, threads can be categorized into two types: user threads and daemon threads. User threads are the primary threads of execution in any given program. Daemon threads, on the other hand, are low-priority threads that provide background services for user threads. While user threads keep the JVM running as long as they are active, a daemon thread doesn't stop the JVM from exiting. When all user threads finish their execution, the JVM automatically terminates any remaining daemon threads.

To designate a thread as a daemon thread in Java, one must call the setDaemon(true) method on the thread before it is started. By default, threads are user threads. Below is an example demonstrating the creation of a daemon thread:

```
public class DaemonThreadExample {
    public static void main(String[] args) {
        Thread daemonThread = new Thread(new Runnable() {
            @Override
            public void run() {
                while (true) {
                    try {
                        System.out.println("Daemon thread is running...");
                        Thread.sleep(1000);
                    } catch (InterruptedException e) {
                        e.printStackTrace();
                    }
                }
            }
        });

        daemonThread.setDaemon(true); // Set thread as daemon
        daemonThread.start();

        try {
            Thread.sleep(3000); // Main thread sleeps for 3 seconds
        } catch (InterruptedException e) {
            e.printStackTrace();
        }

        System.out.println("Main thread is finishing...");
    }
}
```

In the given code snippet, daemonThread is marked as a daemon thread by invoking setDaemon(true). The main thread sleeps for three seconds to allow the daemon thread to run for some time. When the main thread completes execution, the JVM terminates, and the daemon thread is stopped automatically.

Daemon threads are typically used for background supporting tasks, such as garbage collection, which do not need to block the termination of an application.

It is crucial to understand the behavior of daemon threads, especially when managing shared resources or performing critical tasks. Because they are terminated when the JVM exits, any unfinished operations in daemon threads may be left incomplete. It's essential to avoid relying on daemon threads for saving persistent state or handling important operations that must be completed.

Consider the following example where daemon threads could be problematic:

```
public class RiskyDaemonExample {
    public static void main(String[] args) {
        Thread riskyDaemonThread = new Thread(new Runnable() {
            @Override
            public void run() {
                try {
                    // Simulate file writing operation
                    System.out.println("Writing to file...");
                    Thread.sleep(5000); // Simulate long-running operation
                    System.out.println("File write completed");
                } catch (InterruptedException e) {
                    e.printStackTrace();
                }
            }
        });

        riskyDaemonThread.setDaemon(true); // Set thread as daemon
        riskyDaemonThread.start();

        try {
            Thread.sleep(3000); // Main thread sleeps for 3 seconds
        } catch (InterruptedException e) {
            e.printStackTrace();
        }

        System.out.println("Main thread is finishing...");
    }
}
```

In this example, the riskyDaemonThread emulates a file writing operation. Because it is a daemon thread, it may be terminated before it completes the file write operation when the main thread exits after three seconds.

It is advised only to use daemon threads for tasks that do not interfere with the essential functionalities of the application. Common uses of daemon threads include monitoring and housekeeping tasks that can safely be abandoned when the application concludes.

The following algorithm outlines a proper way to handle daemon threads:

Algorithm 2: Handling Daemon Threads Responsibly with Critical Operations

```
Data: Thread
Thread daemonThread with critical operations;
Boolean isCriticalComplete initialized to false;
Procedure waitForCritical
    while !isCriticalComplete do
        Sleep for a specified interval;
    return true;
while main application is running do
    daemonThread performs non-critical operations;
    Set isCriticalComplete to true once completed;
if main application is closing then
    daemonThread stops or ensures critical operations are
      complete;
    waitForCritical ();
```

This algorithm ensures that daemon threads do not unintentionally abandon critical tasks upon JVM shutdown. The procedure waitForCritical provides a mechanism to check if critical operations have completed before allowing the JVM to exit. Thus, when practical, critical sections should be designed to allow proper completion even if hosted on daemon threads.

Understanding the use-cases and limitations of daemon threads is pivotal in leveraging their utility efficiently without compromising the integrity or reliability of Java applications.

2.8 Thread Interruption

Thread interruption is a fundamental mechanism in Java for signaling threads that they should stop their current activity and do something else. It is critical for developing robust multi-threaded applications as it enables a controlled shutdown of threads, which might otherwise continue running indefinitely or until the JVM halts.

Interruption in Java is a collaborative mechanism rather than a preemptive one. This means that setting an interruption flag on a thread does not forcibly terminate it but instead indicates that the thread should stop at the next convenient opportunity.

The primary means to signal a thread to stop execution is through the interrupt() method. A thread checks this signal through the isInterrupted() method or by catching an InterruptedException.

The following code demonstrates how to interrupt a thread:

```
public class SampleThread extends Thread {
    public void run() {
        try {
            while (!Thread.currentThread().isInterrupted()) {
                // Perform task
                System.out.println("Running...");
                Thread.sleep(500);
            }
        } catch (InterruptedException e) {
            System.out.println("Thread was interrupted during sleep");
        }
        // Perform cleanup or other tasks
        System.out.println("Thread exiting under request");
    }

    public static void main(String[] args) {
        SampleThread t = new SampleThread();
        t.start();
        try {
            Thread.sleep(2000);
        } catch (InterruptedException e) {
            e.printStackTrace();
        }
        t.interrupt();
    }
}
```

In this example, SampleThread performs a task repeatedly. It checks if it has been interrupted using isInterrupted() within its loop and catches InterruptedException thrown by the Thread.sleep() method. Here's an example of the output:

```
Running...
Running...
Running...
Thread was interrupted during sleep
Thread exiting under request
```

The interrupt() method sets the interrupt status of the thread, which can then be queried with isInterrupted(). If a thread is in a blocking operation such as Thread.sleep(), Object.wait(), or java.util.concurrent.locks.Lock.lock(), it will immediately throw InterruptedException.

There are several points to consider when dealing with thread interruption:

- An interrupted thread does not automatically stop its execution. It is the responsibility of the thread to terminate cleanly.
- The interrupted() method is invoked as a static method on the Thread class. This method not only returns the interruption status but also clears it, which is useful when a thread wants to cancel its activity gracefully.
- When a thread calls interrupt() on another thread that is not in a blocked state, the interrupt flag is set to true. The thread must regularly check this flag since merely setting it does not forcefully terminate the running thread.
- I/O operations of a thread may or may not respond to interruptions immediately, depending on the platform. For instance, in UNIX-based systems, the I/O calls will typically throw an IOException when interrupted.

Below is an example illustrating the usage of Thread.interrupted():

```
public class InterruptCheck {
    public static void main(String[] args) {
        Thread thread = new Thread(() -> {
            while (!Thread.interrupted()) {
                System.out.println("Thread is running");
                try {
                    Thread.sleep(1000);
                } catch (InterruptedException e) {
                    System.out.println("Thread was interrupted");
                    Thread.currentThread().interrupt(); // Preserve the interrupted
                         status
                }
            }
            System.out.println("Thread has exited");
        });

        thread.start();
        try {
            Thread.sleep(3000);
        } catch (InterruptedException e) {
            e.printStackTrace();
        }
        thread.interrupt();
    }
}
```

The output of the program above might look like:

```
Thread is running
Thread is running
Thread is running
Thread was interrupted
Thread has exited
```

The key aspect of this example is the re-interruption of the thread within the catch block after an InterruptedException has been caught. This ensures that the interrupted status is preserved, allowing the while-loop condition to terminate the thread's execution cleanly.

In creating robust multi-threaded applications, it is essential to handle interruptions properly. Proper interruption handling includes checking for interrupted status at regular intervals, especially in long-running loops, and capturing and managing InterruptedException effectively to ensure threads can terminate gracefully without leaving resources in an inconsistent state.

Failure to handle thread interruption correctly can lead to resource leakage and make the application unresponsive. Hence, understanding and implementing interruption mechanisms effectively is crucial for mastering concurrency control in Java.

2.9 Thread Safety Basics

Thread safety is an essential concept in concurrent programming, ensuring that multiple threads can operate on shared data without causing data inconsistencies or corrupting the state of the application. In Java, thread safety can be achieved through various mechanisms, including synchronization, volatile variables, atomic classes, and thread-safe collections.

To understand thread safety, consider the case of a simple counter object that may be accessed and modified by multiple threads. Without adequate safeguards, the final outcome of the counter value may be unpredictable.

```
public class Counter {
    private int count = 0;

    public void increment() {
        count++;
    }

    public int getCount() {
        return count;
    }
}
```

In the above example, if multiple threads simultaneously call the increment() method on a single instance of Counter, the threads may interfere with each other, leading to incorrect results due to race conditions.

```
Thread 1: read count as 0
Thread 2: read count as 0
Thread 1: write count as 1
Thread 2: write count as 1
```

Synchronization

One fundamental way to ensure thread safety in Java is through synchronization. Synchronization in Java is achieved using the synchronized keyword, which can be applied to methods or blocks.

```
public class SynchronizedCounter {
    private int count = 0;

    public synchronized void increment() {
        count++;
    }

    public synchronized int getCount() {
        return count;
    }
}
```

In this example, the synchronized keyword ensures that only one thread can execute the increment() method at a time, thereby preventing race conditions.

Synchronized Blocks

Sometimes, synchronizing an entire method may be too restrictive, particularly when only a portion of the method needs to be synchronized. In such cases, a synchronized block can be used to synchronize a specific part of a method.

```
public class SynchronizedBlockCounter {
    private int count = 0;
    private final Object lock = new Object();

    public void increment() {
        synchronized (lock) {
            count++;
        }
    }

    public int getCount() {
        synchronized (lock) {
            return count;
        }
    }
}
```

By using synchronized blocks, you can achieve fine-grained control over the synchronization of critical sections of code.

Volatile Variables

The volatile keyword in Java is used to declare variables that can be safely read and written to by multiple threads. When a variable is declared as volatile, it ensures that any read or write to the variable is directly from and to the main memory, thereby preventing threads from caching the variable locally.

```
public class VolatileCounter {
    private volatile int count = 0;

    public void increment() {
        count++;
    }

    public int getCount() {
        return count;
    }
}
```

While the volatile keyword can help ensure the visibility of changes to variables across threads, it does not provide atomicity for compound actions.

Atomic Classes

The java.util.concurrent.atomic package provides a set of classes that support lock-free, thread-safe operations on single variables. These atomic classes use low-level CPU instructions to achieve thread safety.

```
import java.util.concurrent.atomic.AtomicInteger;

public class AtomicCounter {
    private AtomicInteger count = new AtomicInteger();

    public void increment() {
        count.incrementAndGet();
    }

    public int getCount() {
        return count.get();
    }
}
```

In this example, AtomicInteger ensures that the increment operation is performed atomically, without the need for explicit synchronization.

Thread-Safe Collections

Java provides several thread-safe collection classes in the java.util.concurrent package. These collections are designed to handle concurrent access from multiple threads.

```
import java.util.concurrent.ConcurrentHashMap;

public class ConcurrentCollectionExample {
    private ConcurrentHashMap<String, Integer> map = new ConcurrentHashMap
```

```
        <>();

    public void put(String key, Integer value) {
        map.put(key, value);
    }

    public Integer get(String key) {
        return map.get(key);
    }
}
```

The ConcurrentHashMap class allows concurrent read and write operations, making it suitable for concurrent applications that require thread-safe collections.

Using these various thread safety mechanisms appropriately can help prevent data corruptions and inconsistencies when multiple threads manipulate shared resources. Understanding when and how to apply synchronization, volatile variables, atomic classes, and thread-safe collections is crucial for mastering Java concurrency.

Chapter 3

Thread Synchronization

This chapter delves into the critical aspect of thread synchronization in Java. It explains why synchronization is necessary and introduces intrinsic locks and synchronized methods. The use of the synchronized statement and volatile variables is covered, along with explicit locks from the java.util.concurrent.locks package. Concepts such as ReentrantLock, Condition variables, and ReadWriteLock are explored. The chapter also discusses the prevention of deadlocks and the correct use of wait, notify, and notifyAll methods. Finally, it examines atomicity and race conditions, providing a comprehensive understanding of maintaining thread safety.

3.1 The Need for Synchronization

In concurrent programming, multiple threads execute simultaneously and can interact with shared resources. This interaction often leads to situations where the execution outcome depends on the order or timing of threads. Such scenarios may cause incorrect behavior, data inconsistency, and unpredictable results if synchronization is not properly employed.

Synchronization ensures that when one thread is accessing a critical section of code or a shared resource, other threads are prevented from doing so simultaneously. This coordinated access control is vital for maintaining data integrity in a multi-threaded environment.

Consider an unsynchronized scenario where two threads increment a shared counter. The lack of synchronization can lead to race conditions, where the sequence of operations affects the final outcome. This can be illustrated with the following example:

```
public class Counter {
    private int count = 0;

    public void increment() {
        count++;
    }

    public int getCount() {
        return count;
    }
}

public class CounterTest {
    public static void main(String[] args) throws InterruptedException {
        Counter counter = new Counter();
        Runnable task = () -> {
            for (int i = 0; i < 1000; i++) {
                counter.increment();
            }
        };

        Thread thread1 = new Thread(task);
        Thread thread2 = new Thread(task);

        thread1.start();
        thread2.start();

        thread1.join();
        thread2.join();

        System.out.println("Final count: " + counter.getCount());
    }
}
```

In the CounterTest class, two threads are created to increment the count variable 1000 times each. Since the increment method is not synchronized, the expected final count of 2000 might not be reached due to race conditions. Threads may read the same value of count simultaneously and increment it, leading to missed increments.

```
Expected output: Final count: 2000
Possible output: Final count: 1754
```

This discrepancy arises because the read-modify-write sequence in the count++ operation is not atomic. The thread that reads the count value and the thread that writes it back can interfere with each other.

To mitigate this issue, synchronization is used to enforce mutual exclusion, ensuring that only one thread can access the critical section at any time. Java provides built-in mechanisms for synchronization, such as synchronized methods and synchronized blocks.

—

A synchronized method ensures that only one thread can execute the method at a time for a particular object. Here is the revised increment method with synchronization:

```
public class Counter {
    private int count = 0;

    public synchronized void increment() {
        count++;
    }

    public int getCount() {
        return count;
    }
}
```

With the synchronized keyword added to the increment method, any thread calling this method must acquire the intrinsic lock (or monitor) associated with the Counter object. This prevents other threads from entering the synchronized method until the lock is released, thus ensuring mutual exclusion.

Expected output: Final count: 2000

Synchronization is not only relevant to counters but to any shared mutable resource, such as collections, data buffers, and more. Without proper synchronization, various issues can occur, including:

- **Race Conditions**: Multiple threads competing to modify shared data, leading to indeterminate outcomes.
- **Data Inconsistency**: Shared data might end up in an inconsistent state due to interleaved execution.
- **Deadlock**: Threads waiting indefinitely for resources held by each other.
- **Visibility Problems**: Changes made by one thread may not be visible to others due to caching and reordering optimizations by the Java Memory Model.

Ensuring synchronization in Java involves not only using synchronized methods and blocks but also understanding the underlying concurrency constructs and their correct usage patterns. Introducing synchronization where necessary and avoiding where it is unnecessary is crucial for building efficient and correct concurrent applications.

Properly synchronized code ensures that shared resources are accessed safely, preventing concurrency issues and maintaining data consistency across threads.

3.2 Intrinsic Locks and Synchronization Blocks

In Java, intrinsic locks, also known as monitor locks, are a vital mechanism for ensuring that only one thread can execute a synchronized block of code at any given time. Intrinsic locks are associated with every object and class in Java. When a thread holds an intrinsic lock, no other thread can obtain the lock until it is released. This ensures mutual exclusion, a property crucial for thread safety in concurrent applications.

An intrinsic lock is automatically acquired when a thread enters a synchronized method or block and is released when the thread exits the synchronized method or block. Suppose two threads, Thread A and Thread B, try to execute synchronized blocks of the same object. If Thread A acquires the lock first, Thread B must wait until Thread A releases the lock. Here is an example demonstrating intrinsic locks:

```
public class Counter {
    private int count = 0;

    public synchronized void increment() {
        count++;
    }

    public synchronized int getCount() {
        return count;
    }
}
```

In this example, the methods increment and getCount are synchronized. When one thread is executing either of these methods, no other thread can execute any synchronized method on the same instance of Counter.

To understand intrinsic locks further, consider a case where the synchronized block is used instead of synchronized methods.

```
public class Counter {
    private int count = 0;
    private final Object lock = new Object();

    public void increment() {
```

```
        synchronized (lock) {
            count++;
        }
    }

    public int getCount() {
        synchronized (lock) {
            return count;
        }
    }
}
```

In this example, the object lock is explicitly created to control access to the critical section within the methods increment and getCount. Using this explicit lock object showcases that synchronization logic can be more precise, affecting only specific parts of the code rather than entire methods.

To expand on this pattern, consider the following:

```
public class FineGrainedSync {
    private int a = 0;
    private int b = 0;

    private final Object lockA = new Object();
    private final Object lockB = new Object();

    public void incrementA() {
        synchronized (lockA) {
            a++;
        }
    }

    public void incrementB() {
        synchronized (lockB) {
            b++;
        }
    }

    public int getA() {
        synchronized (lockA) {
            return a;
        }
    }

    public int getB() {
        synchronized (lockB) {
            return b;
        }
    }
}
```

In this scenario, we use two separate lock objects, lockA and lockB, to synchronize accesses to a and b, respectively. This approach allows for finer-grained synchronization, which can improve performance by reducing contention among threads—a thread executing incrementA can proceed independently of a thread executing incrementB, as long as different lock objects are used.

Deadlock Scenario

When dealing with intrinsic locks, it is essential to be aware of the potential for deadlocks. A deadlock occurs when two or more threads are waiting indefinitely for locks held by each other. Consider the following example:

```
public class DeadlockExample {
    private final Object lock1 = new Object();
    private final Object lock2 = new Object();

    public void method1() {
        synchronized (lock1) {
            try { Thread.sleep(100); } catch (InterruptedException e) { }
            synchronized (lock2) {
                System.out.println("method1");
            }
        }
    }

    public void method2() {
        synchronized (lock2) {
            try { Thread.sleep(100); } catch (InterruptedException e) { }
            synchronized (lock1) {
                System.out.println("method2");
            }
        }
    }
}
```

In this example, method1 locks lock1 and attempts to lock lock2, while method2 locks lock2 and attempts to lock lock1. If Thread A executes method1 and Thread B executes method2 simultaneously, a deadlock will occur. Thread A will wait for lock2, held by Thread B, while Thread B waits for lock1, held by Thread A.

To avoid such deadlocks, ensure a consistent ordering of lock acquisition throughout the application. For example:

```
public class AvoidDeadlockExample {
    private final Object lock1 = new Object();
    private final Object lock2 = new Object();

    public void method1() {
        synchronized (lock1) {
            synchronized (lock2) {
                System.out.println("method1");
            }
        }
    }

    public void method2() {
        synchronized (lock1) {
            synchronized (lock2) {
```

```
                System.out.println("method2");
            }
        }
    }
}
```

Both method1 and method2 lock lock1 first and then lock2, preventing deadlock because the locks are always requested in the same order.

Intrinsic locks and synchronized blocks provide a foundation for concurrency control in Java. Understanding their proper use and potential pitfalls, such as deadlocks, is essential for writing robust, thread-safe code.

3.3 Synchronized Methods

The Java programming language provides robust support for multithreaded programming. One of the core mechanisms for thread synchronization is the synchronized method. This mechanism helps prevent multiple threads from accessing critical sections of code concurrently, thereby circumventing potential data inconsistency issues. This section explores the concept and application of synchronized methods in detail, ensuring a comprehensive understanding for proficient Java concurrency programming.

A method in Java can be modified with the synchronized keyword to make it a synchronized method. When a thread invokes a synchronized method, it automatically acquires the intrinsic lock (monitor lock) for the object that owns the method, before executing the method's body. No other thread can execute any other synchronized method on the same object simultaneously. This guarantees that the critical section of code is accessible to only one thread at a time.

Consider the following example:

```
public class Counter {
    private int count = 0;

    public synchronized void increment() {
        count++;
    }

    public synchronized int getValue() {
        return count;
    }
}
```

In this Counter class, both the increment() and getValue() methods are synchronized. This ensures that when one thread is executing the increment() method, no other thread can invoke the increment() or getValue() methods on the same Counter instance, thus maintaining the integrity of the count variable.

Synchronization on Static Methods

The synchronization mechanism works differently for static methods. When a static method is declared as synchronized, the class's intrinsic lock is used for synchronization instead of the instance's intrinsic lock. This is because static methods are associated with the class itself rather than any particular instance.

Consider the modification of the Counter class to include synchronized static methods:

```
public class Counter {
    private static int count = 0;

    public static synchronized void increment() {
        count++;
    }

    public static synchronized int getValue() {
        return count;
    }
}
```

In this example, the increment() and getValue() methods are static and synchronized. Therefore, the intrinsic lock of the Counter class object is used to ensure that only one thread can execute these methods at a time, regardless of which instance of the class (if any) is invoking them.

Reentrance in Synchronized Methods

Java's monitor locks are reentrant, meaning that a thread can acquire the same lock multiple times without causing a deadlock. This property allows synchronized methods and blocks to call other synchronized methods internally without blocking.

Consider the following example to illustrate reentrance:

```
public class ReentrantExample {
    public synchronized void methodA() {
        System.out.println("Inside methodA");
        methodB();
    }

    public synchronized void methodB() {
        System.out.println("Inside methodB");
    }
}
```

In this ReentrantExample class, when a thread executes methodA, it will acquire the lock and subsequently call methodB, which also requires the same lock. Since Java's locks are reentrant, the thread holding the lock can re-acquire it, allowing methodB to execute.

Synchronization Performance Impacts

While synchronized methods provide a straightforward mechanism to address concurrency issues, they come with performance overhead due to the locking mechanism. Acquiring and releasing locks require CPU cycles and can degrade performance, especially if contention among threads is high.

It is critical to minimize the scope of synchronized methods to only the critical sections of code that truly need synchronization. Fine-grained synchronization can help reduce contention and improve performance.

Consider refining the Counter class with a more granular synchronization approach:

```
public class Counter {
    private int count = 0;

    public void increment() {
        synchronized (this) {
            count++;
        }
    }

    public int getValue() {
        synchronized (this) {
            return count;
        }
    }
}
```

In this approach, explicit synchronized blocks are used within the methods, ensuring that only the increment operation and the return statement are synchronized, rather than the entire method bodies.

Best Practices

1. **Keep Synchronization Blocks Small**: Limit the scope of synchronized blocks to the smallest piece of code that requires synchronization, to enhance performance. 2. **Avoid Synchronizing on Non-final Fields**: Synchronizing on objects that can be modified (non-final fields) can lead to unpredictable behavior and potential security risks. 3. **Combine Synchronized and Non-synchronized Methods with Care**: Ensure that all critical sections of code are properly guarded to avoid race conditions. 4. **Consider Alternatives for High Contentious Code**: For highly contentious code sections, consider using more ad-

vanced concurrency utilities, such as java.util.concurrent.locks.

This section equips the reader with a solid understanding of synchronized methods in Java, laying a firm foundation for more advanced synchronization techniques. Proficiency in using synchronized methods is crucial for developing robust, thread-safe Java applications.

3.4 The synchronized Statement

The synchronized statement in Java is one of the fundamental mechanisms for achieving thread synchronization. It ensures that only one thread can execute a block of code at a time for a particular object. This is essential for maintaining the consistency of shared resources and avoiding race conditions. The synchronized statement can be understood as a way of creating a synchronized block, where the access to the critical section of code is controlled by an intrinsic lock (or monitor lock) associated with an object.

The general form of the synchronized statement is shown below:

```
synchronized (object) {
    // critical section
    // code that manipulates shared resources
}
```

In this context, object is the reference to the object whose intrinsic lock will be used to synchronize the critical section. When a thread enters the synchronized block, it acquires the lock associated with object. While the thread holds the lock, no other thread can enter a synchronized block that is synchronized on the same object.

Consider the following example:

```
public class Counter {
    private int count = 0;

    public void increment() {
        synchronized (this) {
            count++;
        }
    }

    public int getCount() {
        return count;
    }
}
```

In this example, the Counter class has a method increment that increments a private variable count. The increment method is synchronized using the this object, which means that when one thread is executing the increment operation, no other thread can execute the increment operation on the same instance of Counter.

To further illustrate how synchronization works, let's examine a multi-threaded scenario:

```
public class CounterTest {
    public static void main(String[] args) throws InterruptedException {
        Counter counter = new Counter();

        Runnable task = () -> {
            for (int i = 0; i < 1000; i++) {
                counter.increment();
            }
        };

        Thread thread1 = new Thread(task);
        Thread thread2 = new Thread(task);

        thread1.start();
        thread2.start();

        thread1.join();
        thread2.join();

        System.out.println("Final count: " + counter.getCount());
    }
}
```

In the CounterTest class, we create a single instance of Counter and two threads that run a task to increment the counter 1000 times each. We start both threads and wait for them to finish using the join method. Both threads synchronize on the same Counter object, ensuring that the increments are performed safely. The anticipated output is:

```
Final count: 2000
```

Without synchronization, the result would likely be incorrect due to race conditions. A race condition occurs when multiple threads modify shared data concurrently, leading to inconsistent state.

Let's explore the concept of synchronizing on different objects:

```
public class DualCounter {
    private int count1 = 0;
    private int count2 = 0;
    private final Object lock1 = new Object();
    private final Object lock2 = new Object();

    public void incrementCount1() {
        synchronized (lock1) {
            count1++;
        }
    }

    public void incrementCount2() {
```

```
        synchronized (lock2) {
            count2++;
        }
    }

    public int getCount1() {
        return count1;
    }

    public int getCount2() {
        return count2;
    }
}
```

In the DualCounter class, there are two separate locks lock1 and lock2 for two different counters. This allows the counts to be incremented independently by multiple threads without contention on a single lock.

It is also possible to synchronize on any object, not necessarily this. For instance:

```
private final Object customLock = new Object();

public void performTask() {
    synchronized (customLock) {
        // critical section code
    }
}
```

Here, the synchronization is on the customLock object, allowing fine-grained control over which sections of the code are synchronized.

Proper synchronization ensures thread safety, but improper synchronization can lead to deadlocks, where two or more threads are waiting indefinitely for each other to release locks. To avoid such issues, ensure that locks are acquired and released in a consistent order, and consider using higher-level concurrency utilities from the java.util.concurrent package where appropriate.

Careful use of the synchronized statement is crucial for building robust multi-threaded applications, balancing the need for mutual exclusion with the performance implications of blocking threads.

3.5 Volatile Variables

A key facet of concurrent programming in Java is understanding the use and implications of volatile variables. The volatile modifier indicates that a variable's value will be modified by different threads. It instructs the Java Virtual Machine (JVM) to ensure visibility and consistency of variable updates across threads by preventing certain optimizations that assume no concurrent modification.

When a variable is declared as volatile, reads and writes to that variable are atomic. This ensures that the most updated value is read and that the write operation is visible to all threads. However, it is crucial to comprehend the limitations and scenarios where the volatile modifier is beneficial and sufficient.

```
public class VolatileExample {
    private volatile boolean flag = false;

    public void setFlag(boolean value) {
        flag = value;
    }

    public boolean getFlag() {
        return flag;
    }
}
```

In the above code snippet (Listing **??**), the flag variable is marked as volatile. This means that any thread reading the flag variable will see the most recently written value by any other thread.

Memory Visibility and Reordering

The volatile keyword provides a lightweight synchronization mechanism. Unlike intrinsic locks, volatile only guarantees visibility and ordering, not mutual exclusion. The JVM and the hardware it runs on can reorder instructions for performance optimization. This reordering can potentially lead to incorrect behavior in a concurrent context.

```
public class InstructionReordering {

    private int a = 0;
    private volatile boolean flag = false;

    public void writer() {
        a = 1;
        flag = true;
    }

    public void reader() {
        if (flag) {
            int i = a; // guaranteed to see 1
        }
    }
}
```

In Listing **??**, without volatile, the order of writes in the writer() method could be rearranged, causing the reader thread to see an inconsistent value of a. The volatile modifier prevents this reordering, ensuring that the flag write happens after the a write. In the reader() method, once flag is true, the value of a will be correctly observed.

Use Cases

The volatile keyword is suitable for flags and state indicators, especially when used for simple state signaling between threads. Here are specific scenarios where volatile variables excel:

- **Status Flags:** Variables that are used to indicate a state or status, such as a shutdown flag.
- **Double-Checked Locking:** When used in implementing the Singleton pattern with lazy initialization.
- **Independent Variables:** Variables accessed or modified independently without comprising atomicity.

Double-Checked Locking

Double-checked locking is a design pattern used to reduce the overhead of acquiring a lock by first testing the locking criterion without actually acquiring the lock. Only if the locking criterion (e.g., the resource is null) is met, the lock is acquired.

```
public class Singleton {
    private static volatile Singleton instance;

    private Singleton() {}

    public static Singleton getInstance() {
        if (instance == null) {
            synchronized (Singleton.class) {
                if (instance == null) {
                    instance = new Singleton();
                }
            }
        }
        return instance;
    }
}
```

In Listing **??**, instance is declared volatile to ensure that the assignment of the Singleton object is visible to all threads. This will prevent threads from reading an incompletely initialized Singleton object.

Performance Considerations

While volatile provides a lighter-weight synchronization mechanism compared to locks, it is generally not suitable for compound actions, such as incrementing a variable. For example, the operation count++

involves a read-modify-write cycle which is not atomic with volatile. In such scenarios, using AtomicInteger or explicit synchronization is more appropriate.

```
public class CounterExample {
    private volatile int counter = 0;

    public void increment() {
        counter++; // not atomic
    }

    public int getCounter() {
        return counter;
    }
}
```

In Listing **??**, the increment() method is not atomic because counter++ is a read-modify-write operation that can lead to race conditions. Therefore, it is necessary to use alternative ways to handle such cases to guarantee thread safety.

Accordingly, while volatile variables are powerful for specific use cases involving state flags and simple read/write operations for avoiding expensive synchronization and ensuring visibility, developers should be mindful of its limitations and use it judiciously.

3.6 Explicit Locks with java.util.concurrent.locks

The java.util.concurrent.locks package provides a framework for locking mechanisms that are more sophisticated than the intrinsic locks (or monitors) embedded within Java's synchronized statement and methods. The primary advantage of explicit locks is the capability to offer more extensive operations than intrinsic locks, such as timed lock waits and interruptible lock waits. The most commonly used class in this package is ReentrantLock, but the package includes several other useful classes for advanced synchronization.

Lock is the main interface in this package, and it defines a set of methods to acquire and release locks. Below are the primary methods of the Lock interface:

- void lock() - Acquires the lock. If the lock is not available, the current thread becomes disabled for thread scheduling purposes and lies dormant until the lock has been acquired.
- void lockInterruptibly() - Acquires the lock unless the current

thread is interrupted. If the current thread is interrupted while acquiring the lock (and interruption of lock acquisition is supported), an InterruptedException is thrown.

- boolean tryLock() - Acquires the lock only if it is free at the time of invocation. This method returns immediately with a value of true if the lock was acquired and false otherwise.
- boolean tryLock(long timeout, TimeUnit unit) - Acquires the lock if it is free within the given waiting time and the current thread has not been interrupted. Returns true if the lock was acquired and false if the waiting time elapsed before the lock was acquired.
- void unlock() - Releases the lock.
- Condition newCondition() - Returns a new Condition instance that is bound to this Lock instance.

ReentrantLock is a concrete implementation of the Lock interface and provides the same basic thread synchronization functionality as intrinsic locks (monitors), with extended capabilities, including fairness settings and more structured lock operations.

```
import java.util.concurrent.locks.Lock;
import java.util.concurrent.locks.ReentrantLock;

public class LockExample {
    private final Lock lock = new ReentrantLock();
    private int sharedResource = 0;

    public void increment() {
        lock.lock();
        try {
            sharedResource++;
        } finally {
            lock.unlock();
        }
    }

    public int getValue() {
        lock.lock();
        try {
            return sharedResource;
        } finally {
            lock.unlock();
        }
    }

    public static void main(String[] args) {
        LockExample example = new LockExample();
        example.increment();
        System.out.println("Shared Resource Value: " + example.getValue());
    }
}
```

In the above example, ReentrantLock is used to protect the access to sharedResource. The lock() method acquires the lock, and the unlock() method releases it. The try-finally block ensures that the lock is always released even if an exception occurs within the block.

There are several key features of ReentrantLock:

- **Reentrancy**: A ReentrantLock is owned by the thread last successfully locking, but not yet unlocking it. A thread invoking lock will return immediately if it already holds the lock. This can be useful in dealing with certain types of lock acquisition policies.
- **Fairness**: When a lock is constructed, it can be given a fairness parameter. When set to true, under contention, locks favor granting access to the longest-waiting thread; otherwise, there is no particular access order.

Moreover, the Lock interface also defines the method newCondition(), which provides a Condition instance for the current lock instance. This Condition instance can be used similarly to how the wait(), notify(), and notifyAll() methods are used for intrinsic locks. A significant advantage of Condition objects is that multiple condition variables can be associated with a single lock, enabling more complex thread interactions.

Below is an example demonstrating the use of Condition with ReentrantLock:

```
import java.util.concurrent.locks.Lock;
import java.util.concurrent.locks.ReentrantLock;
import java.util.concurrent.locks.Condition;

public class ConditionExample {
    private final Lock lock = new ReentrantLock();
    private final Condition condition = lock.newCondition();
    private boolean ready = false;

    public void waitingMethod() throws InterruptedException {
        lock.lock();
        try {
            while (!ready) {
                condition.await();
            }
            System.out.println("Condition met!");
        } finally {
            lock.unlock();
        }
    }

    public void signalingMethod() {
        lock.lock();
        try {
```

```
            ready = true;
            condition.signal();
        } finally {
            lock.unlock();
        }
    }

    public static void main(String[] args) throws InterruptedException {
        ConditionExample example = new ConditionExample();
        Thread t1 = new Thread(() -> {
            try {
                example.waitingMethod();
            } catch (InterruptedException e) {
                Thread.currentThread().interrupt();
            }
        });
        Thread t2 = new Thread(() -> example.signalingMethod());

        t1.start();
        Thread.sleep(1000); // Ensuring t1 waits
        t2.start();
    }
}
```

In this example, the waitingMethod uses condition.await() to wait until ready is true. Meanwhile, signalingMethod sets ready to true and calls condition.signal() to wake up the waiting thread. By using Condition, the example achieves finer-grained control over thread coordination compared to intrinsic locks.

Explicit locks provide additional flexibility and control in managing access to shared resources, particularly in complex multithreading environments where fine-tuned synchronization is essential. Practical applications often benefit from the robustness and extensive features that the java.util.concurrent.locks package offers.

3.7 Reentrant Locks

Reentrant locks provide a more sophisticated mechanism than using the synchronized methods and blocks in Java. The java.util.concurrent.locks.ReentrantLock class implements the Lock interface introduced in Java 5, offering more extensive functionality and control over thread synchronization.

Characteristics of Reentrant Locks:

- **Reentrancy:** A reentrant lock is a mutual exclusion lock with the same behavior as the implicit monitor lock accessed using synchronized methods and blocks but with extended capabilities.

Reentrancy refers to the concept that the lock can be repeatedly acquired by the same thread without causing a deadlock.

- **Fairness:** Reentrant locks support an optional fairness parameter. When set to true, the lock's fairness policy is granted to the longest-waiting thread. Non-fair mode, which is the default, allows for higher throughput.
- **Lock Polling:** Methods such as tryLock() allow attempts to acquire the lock without blocking indefinitely.
- **Interruptibility:** The ability for the thread to be interruptible while acquiring the lock is supported with the lockInterruptibly method.
- **Condition Support:** Each instance of ReentrantLock has associated Condition objects whose behavior depends on the lock.

Creating and Using Reentrant Locks:

The fundamental usage pattern of a ReentrantLock is to encapsulate the critical section between lock() and unlock() calls.

```
import java.util.concurrent.locks.ReentrantLock;

public class Counter {
    private final ReentrantLock lock = new ReentrantLock();
    private int count = 0;

    public void increment() {
        lock.lock();
        try {
            count++;
        } finally {
            lock.unlock();
        }
    }

    public int getCount() {
        return count;
    }
}
```

In the above example, the increment() method locks the instance using lock.lock(), ensuring that only one thread can execute the increment logic at a time. Regardless of whether the increment succeeds or encounters an exception, the lock is released in the finally block, ensuring proper resource management.

Fairness Parameter:

When constructing a ReentrantLock, the fairness policy can be set by passing a boolean to the constructor.

```
ReentrantLock fairLock = new ReentrantLock(true);
```

A fair lock ensures that threads acquire the lock in the order they requested it, reducing the risk of thread starvation.

Try-Lock with Timeout:

The tryLock() method attempts to acquire the lock immediately, returning true if successful, and false otherwise. This method can also accept a timeout parameter, allowing for a bounded wait.

```
import java.util.concurrent.TimeUnit;
import java.util.concurrent.locks.ReentrantLock;

public void tryLockExample() {
    ReentrantLock lock = new ReentrantLock();
    try {
        if(lock.tryLock(1, TimeUnit.SECONDS)) {
            try {
                // Critical section
            } finally {
                lock.unlock();
            }
        } else {
            // Handle the case where the lock was not acquired
        }
    } catch (InterruptedException e) {
        // Handle interruption
    }
}
```

Using tryLock(), the thread can avoid indefinite waiting and possibly perform alternative actions if the lock is not available.

Interruptible Lock Acquisition:

A thread can acquire a lock in an interruptible manner using the lockInterruptibly() method. This allows the thread to respond to interruptions while waiting to acquire the lock.

```
import java.util.concurrent.locks.ReentrantLock;

public void interruptibleLockExample() throws InterruptedException {
    ReentrantLock lock = new ReentrantLock();
    lock.lockInterruptibly();
    try {
        // Critical section
    } finally {
        lock.unlock();
    }
}
```

Condition Support:

Conditions provide a means for thread coordination. Utilizing Condition objects from a ReentrantLock, threads can wait and be signaled in a more flexible manner compared to Object.wait() and Object.notify().

```
import java.util.concurrent.locks.Condition;
import java.util.concurrent.locks.ReentrantLock;

public class BoundedBuffer {
    private final ReentrantLock lock = new ReentrantLock();
    private final Condition notFull = lock.newCondition();
    private final Condition notEmpty = lock.newCondition();
    private final Object[] items = new Object[100];
    private int putptr, takeptr, count;

    public void put(Object x) throws InterruptedException {
        lock.lock();
        try {
            while(count == items.length)
                notFull.await();
            items[putptr] = x;
            if(++putptr == items.length) putptr = 0;
            count++;
            notEmpty.signal();
        } finally {
            lock.unlock();
        }
    }

    public Object take() throws InterruptedException {
        lock.lock();
        try {
            while(count == 0)
                notEmpty.await();
            Object x = items[takeptr];
            if(++takeptr == items.length) takeptr = 0;
            count--;
            notFull.signal();
            return x;
        } finally {
            lock.unlock();
        }
    }
}
```

This example demonstrates a bounded buffer where put() and take() operations coordinate using conditions. Threads inserting into or removing from the buffer wait and signal appropriately, managing the buffer's state and ensuring thread-safe operation.

Understanding and using ReentrantLock and its associated features can significantly enhance the control and flexibility of thread synchronization in Java applications. Proper application of these advanced synchronization mechanisms can lead to more robust and efficient multi-threaded programs.

3.8 Condition Variables

In Java concurrency, Condition variables offer a means for threads to synchronize execution sequences, thus improving coordination and communication between threads. Condition variables are part of the java.util.concurrent.locks package and work in conjunction with Lock implementations, notably ReentrantLock. When combined with a Lock, a Condition facilitates advanced thread control by encapsulating the Object-based wait/notify mechanism with a more powerful and flexible interface.

A Condition accomplishes this by allowing threads to suspend execution (wait) until a certain condition is true, and send signals to other waiting threads when the condition's state changes (signal). This approach separates concerns, as the Lock manages the mutual exclusion requirement, while the Condition handles cooperation requirements between threads.

To create a Condition instance, first obtain a Lock object, then call its newCondition() method. Here's a simple example:

```
import java.util.concurrent.locks.Lock;
import java.util.concurrent.locks.ReentrantLock;
import java.util.concurrent.locks.Condition;

public class ConditionExample {
    private final Lock lock = new ReentrantLock();
    private final Condition condition = lock.newCondition();
    private boolean isConditionMet = false;

    public void awaitCondition() throws InterruptedException {
        lock.lock();
        try {
            while (!isConditionMet) {
                condition.await();
            }
            // Proceed once condition is met
        } finally {
            lock.unlock();
        }
    }

    public void signalCondition() {
        lock.lock();
        try {
            isConditionMet = true;
            condition.signal();
        } finally {
            lock.unlock();
        }
    }
}
```

In the awaitCondition() method, the await() call causes the current thread to suspend execution and release the lock until another thread invokes signal() on the same condition, thus avoiding busy-waiting and reducing CPU utilization.

To understand the interplay between different parts of your code when using condition variables, examine the lock release and reacquisition. When await() is called, the current thread releases the lock atomically and blocks. It is important to note here that upon waking up, the thread must reacquire the lock before it can proceed, ensuring mutual exclusivity.

Algorithm 3: Synchronizing Threads Using Condition Variables

Data: Shared variable isConditionMet

Result: Thread synchronization using Condition variables

```
begin
    // Thread A - Waiting for the condition
    Acquire lock;
    while not isConditionMet do
        Call condition.await();
    Perform actions when condition is met;
    Release lock;
begin
    // Thread B - Signaling the condition
    Acquire lock;
    Set isConditionMet to true;
    Call condition.signal();
    Release lock;
```

The condition.await() method is a blocking operation that suspends the current thread until it is signaled. The implementation uses the signal() method to wake up one waiting thread, whereas signalAll() can be used to wake up all waiting threads. Here is how you can modify the above example to use signalAll():

```
public void signalAllCondition() {
    lock.lock();
    try {
        isConditionMet = true;
        condition.signalAll();
    } finally {
        lock.unlock();
    }
```

```
}
```

This can be particularly useful in scenarios where multiple threads need to act as soon as a condition is met. It is crucial to avoid common pitfalls such as forgetting to acquire the lock before calling await(), signal(), or signalAll(), which will throw an IllegalMonitorStateException.

Understanding condition variables in the context of locks also requires attention to preventing spurious wakeups, which can occur when await() returns without any thread signaling it. To handle this, always use a loop to check the condition, ensuring it is re-evaluated each time the thread wakes up.

```
// Correct usage to guard against spurious wakeups
public void awaitCondition() throws InterruptedException {
    lock.lock();
    try {
        while (!isConditionMet) { // using while loop instead of if statement
            condition.await();
        }
        // Proceed once condition is met
    } finally {
        lock.unlock();
    }
}
```

Employing Condition variables effectively improves your ability to implement complex concurrent algorithms while maintaining clarity and modularity in your code. Efficient synchronization using these variables goes beyond mere mutual exclusion to encompass complex thread cooperation patterns necessary for robust concurrent applications.

3.9 ReadWriteLock

In multi-threaded programming, it is often inefficient to use exclusive locks when read operations significantly outnumber write operations. The ReadWriteLock interface, a part of the java.util.concurrent.locks package, is designed to improve the concurrency performance by allowing multiple threads to read a shared resource concurrently while still maintaining the ability to write exclusively.

ReadWriteLock maintains a pair of associated locks, one for read-only operations and one for writing. The read lock can be held simultaneously by multiple threads as long as none of them hold the write lock. The write lock, on the other hand, is exclusive, meaning only one thread can hold it at a time and it can only be obtained if no threads are currently reading or writing.

To understand ReadWriteLock, consider the scenario of a shared data structure where read operations do not affect the data's integrity. The same data can be accessed by multiple reading threads concurrently without causing any inconsistency. However, if a thread wants to modify the data, it must obtain the write lock, thereby preventing other threads from reading or writing until the modification is complete. This mechanism enhances concurrent read access while still securing exclusive write operations.

The commonly used implementation of ReadWriteLock is ReentrantReadWriteLock. This class provides both ReadLock and WriteLock implementations. Below is an example to illustrate its usage:

```
import java.util.concurrent.locks.ReentrantReadWriteLock;
import java.util.concurrent.locks.ReadWriteLock;

public class SharedResource {
    private final ReadWriteLock lock = new ReentrantReadWriteLock();
    private final ReentrantReadWriteLock.ReadLock readLock = lock.readLock();
    private final ReentrantReadWriteLock.WriteLock writeLock = lock.writeLock();
    private int value = 0;

    public int readValue() {
        readLock.lock();
        try {
            return value;
        } finally {
            readLock.unlock();
        }
    }

    public void writeValue(int newValue) {
        writeLock.lock();
        try {
            value = newValue;
        } finally {
            writeLock.unlock();
        }
    }
}
```

In the example above, SharedResource uses ReentrantReadWriteLock to manage read and write access to an integer value. The readValue() method acquires the read lock to allow multiple threads to read the value concurrently. The writeValue(int newValue) method acquires the write lock to ensure exclusive access while modifying the value.

It is important to always release the acquired lock inside a finally block to avoid potential deadlocks in case an exception is thrown. This ensures that the lock is properly released regardless of whether the code exits normally or due to an exception.

The ReentrantReadWriteLock class provides essential methods to facilitate advanced locking mechanisms:

- int getReadLockCount(): Returns the number of read locks held by threads.
- boolean isWriteLocked(): Returns true if the write lock is held by any thread.
- int getWriteHoldCount(): If the write lock is held, returns the number of reentrant write holds on this lock by the current thread.
- boolean isWriteLockedByCurrentThread(): Returns true if the write lock is held by the current thread.
- int getReadHoldCount(): If the read lock is held, returns the number of reentrant read holds on this lock by the current thread.

While ReadWriteLock improves concurrency by allowing concurrent reads, developers should be aware of its potential drawbacks. One significant drawback is the possibility of reader or writer starvation. If the read lock is continuously being acquired, a writer may be starved and unable to acquire the write lock. Conversely, if the write lock is frequently held or the system has many threads trying to write, readers may be starved.

To mitigate this, ReentrantReadWriteLock supports fairness policies via an optional fairness parameter in its constructor:

```
ReadWriteLock fairLock = new ReentrantReadWriteLock(true);
```

When true is passed to the constructor, the lock is fair and threads acquire locks in the order they requested them. Although fairness can prevent starvation, it can negatively impact throughput, as fairness requires additional overhead in managing the request order.

ReadWriteLock is a vital tool for achieving higher concurrency in read-heavy scenarios, enabling improved performance by allowing multiple reads while synchronizing writes. Correct usage and understanding of its implications on thread behavior are crucial in designing efficient and concurrent Java applications.

3.10 Deadlock and Its Avoidance

Deadlock is a condition where two or more threads are unable to proceed with their execution because each is waiting for a resource held by another, creating a standstill. Let us consider an example where two threads attempt to acquire locks in different orders:

```
public class DeadlockExample {
    private final Object lock1 = new Object();
    private final Object lock2 = new Object();

    public void method1() {
        synchronized (lock1) {
            try { Thread.sleep(50); } catch (InterruptedException e) {}
            synchronized (lock2) {
                System.out.println("Thread 1: Acquired lock1, then lock2");
            }
        }
    }

    public void method2() {
        synchronized (lock2) {
            try { Thread.sleep(50); } catch (InterruptedException e) {}
            synchronized (lock1) {
                System.out.println("Thread 2: Acquired lock2, then lock1");
            }
        }
    }
}
```

In the code snippet above, method1 acquires lock1 and then lock2, whereas method2 acquires lock2 and then lock1. If method1 and method2 are called by different threads simultaneously, a deadlock may occur.

```
Thread-1: Acquired lock1
Thread-2: Acquired lock2
```

After acquiring lock1, Thread-1 waits for lock2, which is held by Thread-2. Conversely, Thread-2 waits for lock1 held by Thread-1. Neither thread can proceed, resulting in a deadlock.

Preventing deadlocks requires a careful design approach. Several strategies include:

- **Acquiring locks in a fixed order:** Ensuring all threads acquire locks in the same order can prevent circular wait conditions. If both methods acquire lock1 before lock2, deadlocks can be avoided.

- **Using tryLock with timeout:** The ReentrantLock class provides a tryLock method with a timeout that attempts to acquire the lock and returns immediately or within a specified period. If the lock is unavailable, the thread can back off or retry, avoiding deadlocks.

- **Deadlock detection:** Certain systems implement deadlock detection algorithms to identify and resolve deadlocks. However, Java's standard concurrency libraries do not include such mechanisms.

- **Timeout on blocking operations:** Setting timeouts on operations that may block, like lock acquisition or resource requests, can help prevent indefinite waiting.

Consider the following implementation using ReentrantLock with tryLock:

```
import java.util.concurrent.locks.ReentrantLock;
import java.util.concurrent.TimeUnit;

public class AvoidDeadlockExample {
    private final ReentrantLock lock1 = new ReentrantLock();
    private final ReentrantLock lock2 = new ReentrantLock();

    public void method1() {
        try {
            if (lock1.tryLock(50, TimeUnit.MILLISECONDS)) {
                try {
                    if (lock2.tryLock(50, TimeUnit.MILLISECONDS)) {
                        try {
                            System.out.println("Thread 1: Acquired lock1, then lock2");
                        } finally {
                            lock2.unlock();
                        }
                    }
                } finally {
                    lock1.unlock();
                }
            }
        } catch (InterruptedException e) {
            e.printStackTrace();
        }
    }

    public void method2() {
        try {
            if (lock2.tryLock(50, TimeUnit.MILLISECONDS)) {
                try {
                    if (lock1.tryLock(50, TimeUnit.MILLISECONDS)) {
                        try {
                            System.out.println("Thread 2: Acquired lock2, then lock1");
                        } finally {
                            lock1.unlock();
                        }
                    }
                } finally {
                    lock2.unlock();
                }
            }
```

```
        } catch (InterruptedException e) {
            e.printStackTrace();
        }
    }
}
```

In this example, tryLock attempts to acquire the locks within a specified timeout period. If a lock cannot be acquired, the thread releases any locks it holds and retries, ensuring a deadlock does not occur.

Deadlocks can also be avoided by breaking at least one of the necessary conditions for deadlock:

- **Mutual Exclusion:** Ensure that some resources are not mutually exclusive.
- **Hold and Wait:** Avoid a process holding one resource while waiting for another by requiring all necessary resources to be requested simultaneously.
- **No Preemption:** Allow resources to be preempted, forcibly taken from one process for reassignment to another.
- **Circular Wait:** Prevent cycles in the resource allocation graph by imposing a total ordering of all resource types and requiring that each process requests resources in an increasing order of enumeration.

In applying these strategies, careful consideration of the specific system requirements and constraints is essential to ensuring that concurrency issues such as deadlocks are effectively managed.

3.11 Wait, Notify, and NotifyAll Methods

In Java, wait(), notify(), and notifyAll() are fundamental methods for enabling thread communication, primarily within synchronized contexts. These methods allow threads to efficiently wait for conditions to change and subsequently resume execution. Their correct usage is crucial for implementing fine-grained synchronization and coordination between threads.

The wait, notify, and notifyAll methods belong to the Object class rather than the Thread class, which emphasizes that any Java object can act as a monitor and facilitate thread synchronization.

To use the wait() method, a thread must first acquire the intrinsic lock of the object on which wait() is being called. Holding this lock ensures that the thread has exclusive access to the shared resource protected by the lock before it suspends its execution. When wait() is invoked, the thread releases the lock, allowing other threads to acquire it and potentially modify the resource state. Subsequently, the waiting thread transitions into the wait set associated with the object's monitor and remains dormant until notified.

The notify() and notifyAll() methods serve to wake up waiting threads. Specifically:

- notify() wakes up a single thread from the wait set, selected in an arbitrary manner but typically following FIFO order.
- notifyAll() wakes up all threads in the wait set, facilitating their competition to reacquire the lock.

When a thread is awakened via notify() or notifyAll(), it transitions from the wait set to the entry set of the monitor. After the thread reacquires the lock, it resumes execution from the point where wait() was called.

A simplified use case involving wait(), notify(), and notifyAll() can be illustrated by a producer-consumer scenario:

```
class MyQueue {
    private Queue<Integer> queue = new LinkedList<>();
    private int capacity = 10;

    public synchronized void produce(int value) throws InterruptedException {
        while (queue.size() == capacity) {
            wait();
        }
        queue.add(value);
        notify(); // Notify a single waiting consumer
    }

    public synchronized int consume() throws InterruptedException {
        while (queue.isEmpty()) {
            wait();
        }
        int value = queue.remove();
        notify(); // Notify a single waiting producer
        return value;
    }
}
```

This example establishes a bounded queue and synchronizes the produce and consume operations. Notice the use of the while loop, instead of an if condition, before calling the wait() method. This precaution ensures that the thread rechecks the condition upon waking to address potential spurious wakeups and guarantee that the invariant holds before proceeding.

notifyAll() is particularly useful when multiple threads may benefit from a state change. Consider an example with multiple consumers and producers:

```
class MyQueueWithNotifyAll {
    private Queue<Integer> queue = new LinkedList<>();
    private int capacity = 10;

    public synchronized void produce(int value) throws InterruptedException {
        while (queue.size() == capacity) {
            wait();
        }
        queue.add(value);
        notifyAll(); // Notify all waiting consumers
    }

    public synchronized int consume() throws InterruptedException {
        while (queue.isEmpty()) {
            wait();
        }
        int value = queue.remove();
        notifyAll(); // Notify all waiting producers
        return value;
    }
}
```

In this case, notifyAll() ensures that all waiting threads, whether consumers or producers, are awakened and can attempt to make progress. This approach can reduce potential bottlenecks in situations where multiple threads are waiting on various conditions.

Correct and effective use of wait(), notify(), and notifyAll() methods requires careful attention to synchronization and the surrounding logic to maintain thread safety and condition correctness. Misuse can lead to conditions such as missed signals, thread starvation, and spurious wakeups, ultimately compromising the robustness and reliability of concurrent applications.

3.12 Atomicity and Race Conditions

Atomicity is a fundamental concept in concurrent programming. An operation is atomic if it appears to execute as a single, indivisible step, without any possibility of interference from other operations. This means that during the execution of the atomic operation, no other thread can observe the operation in an intermediate state. Atomic operations are crucial for maintaining the integrity of shared data in a multithreaded environment.

Java provides several ways to achieve atomicity. The most basic form of ensuring atomicity is through the use of synchronization constructs, such as the synchronized statement and intrinsic locks. However, Java also offers the java.util.concurrent.atomic package, which contains classes like AtomicInteger, AtomicLong, AtomicBoolean, and AtomicReference. These classes provide methods that perform atomic operations on single variables without the need for explicit synchronization.

Consider the following example using AtomicInteger:

```
import java.util.concurrent.atomic.AtomicInteger;

public class AtomicExample {
    private final AtomicInteger counter = new AtomicInteger(0);

    public void increment() {
        counter.incrementAndGet();
    }

    public int getCounter() {
        return counter.get();
    }

    public static void main(String[] args) throws InterruptedException {
        AtomicExample example = new AtomicExample();
        Thread t1 = new Thread(example::increment);
        Thread t2 = new Thread(example::increment);
        t1.start();
        t2.start();
        t1.join();
        t2.join();
        System.out.println(example.getCounter());
    }
}
```

In this example, the incrementAndGet method of AtomicInteger ensures that the increment operation is atomic. No other thread can see the value of counter in an inconsistent state, and there is no need for explicit synchronization.

Race conditions occur when the correctness of a program depends on the relative timing of events in different threads. When multiple threads access shared data and attempt to modify it concurrently without proper synchronization, race conditions can arise. A race condition can lead to unpredictable and incorrect results.

Consider the following non-atomic version of the previous example:

```
public class RaceConditionExample {
    private int counter = 0;
```

```
    public void increment() {
        counter++;
    }

    public int getCounter() {
        return counter;
    }

    public static void main(String[] args) throws InterruptedException {
        RaceConditionExample example = new RaceConditionExample();
        Thread t1 = new Thread(example::increment);
        Thread t2 = new Thread(example::increment);
        t1.start();
        t2.start();
        t1.join();
        t2.join();
        System.out.println(example.getCounter());
    }
}
```

In this example, the increment method is not atomic. The counter++ operation involves reading the current value of counter, incrementing it, and writing the new value back. If two threads execute this operation concurrently, they might both read the same value of counter, increment it, and write back the same incremented value, resulting in a lost update.

To avoid race conditions, it is essential to ensure that all accesses to shared variables are properly synchronized. This can be achieved using the synchronized keyword or other synchronization mechanisms provided by the Java concurrency API.

For instance, synchronizing the increment method will ensure atomicity:

```
public class SynchronizedExample {
    private int counter = 0;

    public synchronized void increment() {
        counter++;
    }

    public int getCounter() {
        return counter;
    }

    public static void main(String[] args) throws InterruptedException {
        SynchronizedExample example = new SynchronizedExample();
        Thread t1 = new Thread(example::increment);
        Thread t2 = new Thread(example::increment);
        t1.start();
        t2.start();
        t1.join();
        t2.join();
        System.out.println(example.getCounter());
    }
}
```

In this version, the synchronized keyword ensures that only one thread can execute the increment method at a time, thereby preventing race conditions.

Understanding and preventing race conditions is critical for writing correct and efficient concurrent programs. By ensuring atomicity and proper synchronization, you can safeguard the integrity of shared data and achieve predictable behavior in a multithreaded environment.

Chapter 4

Concurrency Utilities

This chapter provides an overview of the concurrency utilities available in the java.util.concurrent package. It covers essential classes and interfaces such as CountDownLatch, CyclicBarrier, Semaphore, Exchanger, and Phaser, detailing their uses and benefits. The chapter also explores concurrent collections, including BlockingQueue, PriorityBlockingQueue, ConcurrentHashMap, and the CopyOnWriteArrayList/CopyOnWriteArraySet. Furthermore, it explains the use of ThreadLocal and InheritableThreadLocal for maintaining thread-local variables, equipping developers with powerful tools to manage and coordinate concurrent tasks.

4.1 Introduction to java.util.concurrent

Java concurrency utilities, encapsulated within the java.util.concurrent package, offer a sophisticated and robust framework designed to handle the complexities inherent in multithreaded programming. This package, introduced in Java 5, provides a suite of facilities to support concurrent programming needs, enabling developers to write more efficient, reliable, and maintainable code. Within this section, we will systematically examine the fundamental concepts and tools provided by the java.util.concurrent package.

At the core of the java.util.concurrent package are several key abstractions:

- **Executor Framework**: Simplifies the execution of tasks by decoupling task submission from the mechanics of how each task will be run.
- **Synchronizers**: Includes classes like CountDownLatch, CyclicBarrier, Semaphore, Exchanger, and Phaser that facilitate coordination between threads.
- **Concurrent Collections**: Data structures like BlockingQueue, ConcurrentMap, and CopyOnWriteArrayList designed for high-performance concurrent usage.
- **Atomic Variables**: Classes in the java.util.concurrent.atomic package provide lock-free, thread-safe constructions for single variables.

The Executor framework is instrumental in managing and controlling a pool of threads to execute tasks asynchronously. Utilized through the Executor, ExecutorService, and higher-level entry points like ScheduledExecutorService, it allows the efficient allocation and reuse of threads.

Consider a simple example of using an ExecutorService to run tasks concurrently:

```
import java.util.concurrent.ExecutorService;
import java.util.concurrent.Executors;

public class ExecutorExample {
    public static void main(String[] args) {
        ExecutorService executor = Executors.newFixedThreadPool(10);
        for (int i = 0; i < 100; i++) {
            executor.submit(() -> {
                System.out.println(Thread.currentThread().getName());
            });
        }
        executor.shutdown();
    }
}
```

The Executors utility class provides factory methods to create various types of executor services, such as newFixedThreadPool, newCachedThreadPool, and newScheduledThreadPool. In the example above, a fixed thread pool is used to manage the execution of 100 tasks with up to 10 threads concurrently.

Synchronizers play a pivotal role in managing concurrent execution and coordinating threads' access to shared resources or synchronization points. They provide advanced thread synchronization mechanisms far more versatile than basic synchronized blocks.

Let's inspect how a CountDownLatch can be used to ensure that a set of threads wait until other threads complete their work:

```
import java.util.concurrent.CountDownLatch;

public class CountDownLatchExample {
    public static void main(String[] args) throws InterruptedException {
        int workerCount = 5;
        CountDownLatch latch = new CountDownLatch(workerCount);

        for (int i = 0; i < workerCount; i++) {
            new Thread(() -> {
                try {
                    System.out.println("Worker " + Thread.currentThread().getName() +
                        " started");
                    // Simulate work
                    Thread.sleep((long) (Math.random() * 1000));
                    System.out.println("Worker " + Thread.currentThread().getName() +
                        " finished");
                } catch (InterruptedException e) {
                    Thread.currentThread().interrupt();
                } finally {
                    latch.countDown();
                }
            }).start();
        }

        // Main thread waits until all workers finish
        latch.await();
        System.out.println("All workers finished.");
    }
}
```

In this example, CountDownLatch is initialized with a count equal to the number of worker threads. Each thread decrements the latch count by one when it completes its work. The main thread calls await() on the latch, waiting for the latch count to reach zero, indicating that all worker threads have completed their tasks.

Concurrent collections, such as BlockingQueue, provide thread-safe data structures that facilitate the sharing and transferring of data between concurrent threads without requiring explicit synchronization. The BlockingQueue interface extends the Queue interface and supports operations that wait for the queue to become non-empty when retrieving elements and wait for space to become available in the queue when storing elements.

Here is a sample usage of BlockingQueue:

```
import java.util.concurrent.ArrayBlockingQueue;
import java.util.concurrent.BlockingQueue;

public class BlockingQueueExample {
    public static void main(String[] args) throws InterruptedException {
        BlockingQueue<Integer> queue = new ArrayBlockingQueue<>(10);
```

```
        // Producer thread
        new Thread(() -> {
            try {
                for (int i = 0; i < 50; i++) {
                    queue.put(i);
                    System.out.println("Produced: " + i);
                }
            } catch (InterruptedException e) {
                Thread.currentThread().interrupt();
            }
        }).start();

        // Consumer thread
        new Thread(() -> {
            try {
                for (int i = 0; i < 50; i++) {
                    Integer item = queue.take();
                    System.out.println("Consumed: " + item);
                }
            } catch (InterruptedException e) {
                Thread.currentThread().interrupt();
            }
        }).start();
    }
}
```

In the example, a BlockingQueue of type ArrayBlockingQueue is used to produce and consume integers. The producer thread adds elements to the queue, and the consumer thread retrieves elements from the queue, demonstrating the blocking behavior of BlockingQueue when it is empty or full.

Understanding the atomic variables is crucial for performing atomic operations without explicit synchronization. These variables, located in the java.util.concurrent.atomic package, provide non-blocking and thread-safe operations essential for high-performance and fine-grained concurrent programming.

The AtomicInteger class, for instance, allows atomic updates to an integer variable:

```
import java.util.concurrent.atomic.AtomicInteger;

public class AtomicIntegerExample {
    private static AtomicInteger atomicInteger = new AtomicInteger(0);

    public static void main(String[] args) {
        Runnable task = () -> {
            for (int i = 0; i < 100; i++) {
                atomicInteger.incrementAndGet();
            }
            System.out.println(Thread.currentThread().getName() + ": " +
                    atomicInteger.get());
        };

        Thread t1 = new Thread(task);
        Thread t2 = new Thread(task);
```

```
        t1.start();
        t2.start();
    }
}
```

In this code, two threads increment the same AtomicInteger instance concurrently without the need for explicit synchronization. The incrementAndGet() method ensures that the increment operation is atomic and thread-safe.

The java.util.concurrent package organizes and simplifies the complexity of concurrent programming. By providing a structured and high-level approach to constructing and managing concurrent applications, it equips developers with the tools necessary for writing efficient, scalable, and maintainable multithreaded programs.

4.2 CountDownLatch

The CountDownLatch class in the java.util.concurrent package is a synchronization aid that allows one or more threads to wait until a set of operations being performed by other threads completes. A CountDownLatch is initialized with a count value that dictates how many times the countDown() method must be called before waiting threads can proceed. This is particularly useful for scenarios where you have multiple components or tasks that must complete before another task can start.

CountDownLatch operates by maintaining an internal count. Threads call await() to block until the latch's count reaches zero, which happens when another set of threads call countDown() enough times to decrease the count to zero.

Here's how you can utilize CountDownLatch:

```
import java.util.concurrent.CountDownLatch;

public class CountDownLatchExample {
    private static final int N = 3;

    public static void main(String[] args) throws InterruptedException {
        final CountDownLatch latch = new CountDownLatch(N);

        for (int i = 0; i < N; i++) {
            new Thread(new Task(latch)).start();
        }

        System.out.println("Main thread waiting for tasks to complete.");
        latch.await(); // Wait until the count reaches zero
        System.out.println("All tasks have finished.");
```

```
    }

    static class Task implements Runnable {
        private final CountDownLatch latch;

        Task(CountDownLatch latch) {
            this.latch = latch;
        }

        @Override
        public void run() {
            System.out.println(Thread.currentThread().getName() + " started.");
            try {
                // Simulate task completion with sleep
                Thread.sleep(1000);
            } catch (InterruptedException e) {
                e.printStackTrace();
            } finally {
                latch.countDown(); // Decrements the count of the latch
                System.out.println(Thread.currentThread().getName() + " finished.");
            }
        }
    }
}
```

In this example, the main() method creates a CountDownLatch initialized with a count of three. Three threads are then started, each executing a Task that simulates some work by sleeping for a second. After completing their work, each thread calls countDown() on the latch. The main() thread calls await(), which will block until all three threads call countDown() reducing the count to zero.

CountDownLatch is particularly well-suited for:

- Ensuring that a particular number of operations or tasks have completed before allowing another thread to proceed.
- Achieving join-like operations where you want one or more threads to wait for other thread(s) to finish.
- Initializing resources or completing setup activities before permitting other threads to execute.

Consider an application startup scenario where you may want to ensure multiple services or components are initialized before marking the application as fully started.

```
import java.util.concurrent.CountDownLatch;

public class ApplicationStartup {
    private static final int SERVICE_COUNT = 3;
    private static final CountDownLatch latch = new CountDownLatch(
        SERVICE_COUNT);
```

```
    public static void main(String[] args) throws InterruptedException {
        new Thread(new Service("Service1", latch)).start();
        new Thread(new Service("Service2", latch)).start();
        new Thread(new Service("Service3", latch)).start();

        System.out.println("Main thread waiting for services to start.");
        latch.await(); // Wait until all services are ready
        System.out.println("All services up, Application is starting.");
    }

    static class Service implements Runnable {
        private final String name;
        private final CountDownLatch latch;

        Service(String name, CountDownLatch latch) {
            this.name = name;
            this.latch = latch;
        }

        @Override
        public void run() {
            System.out.println(name + " starting...");
            try {
                // Simulating service startup time
                Thread.sleep((long) (Math.random() * 2000));
            } catch (InterruptedException e) {
                e.printStackTrace();
            } finally {
                latch.countDown();
                System.out.println(name + " started.");
            }
        }
    }
}
```

In this scenario, each service is simulated with a Service class, and the count of the CountDownLatch is set to three. Each service thread decreases the latch count upon finishing its initialization, allowing the main thread to proceed only once all services are up and running.

It is vital to understand that CountDownLatch is a one-time-use object. Once the count reaches zero, it cannot be reset. You would need to create a new instance of CountDownLatch to reuse the functionality. This is a distinguishing characteristic in comparison to other synchronizers like CyclicBarrier.

In practice, CountDownLatch serves as a powerful and flexible tool for managing thread dependencies, setup tasks, and complex process coordination, reinforcing the robustness of concurrent applications.

4.3 CyclicBarrier

The java.util.concurrent.CyclicBarrier is a synchronization aid that allows a set of threads to all wait for each other to reach a common barrier point. This is useful in parallel computations where certain tasks must be coordinated at specific points, known as synchronization points. Each thread signals that it has reached the barrier and then waits until all other participating threads have also reached the barrier.

The following code demonstrates the basic usage of CyclicBarrier:

```
import java.util.concurrent.BrokenBarrierException;
import java.util.concurrent.CyclicBarrier;

public class CyclicBarrierExample {

    private static final int NUM_THREADS = 3;
    private static final CyclicBarrier barrier = new CyclicBarrier(NUM_THREADS,
        new Runnable() {
            @Override
            public void run() {
                System.out.println("All threads have reached the barrier, performing the
                        final task.");
            }
        });

    public static void main(String[] args) {
        for (int i = 0; i < NUM_THREADS; i++) {
            new Thread(new Task()).start();
        }
    }

    private static class Task implements Runnable {
        @Override
        public void run() {
            try {
                System.out.println(Thread.currentThread().getName() + " is performing
                        task 1.");
                Thread.sleep(1000); // Simulating task 1
                System.out.println(Thread.currentThread().getName() + " is waiting at
                        barrier.");
                barrier.await();

                System.out.println(Thread.currentThread().getName() + " is performing
                        task 2.");
                Thread.sleep(1000); // Simulating task 2
                System.out.println(Thread.currentThread().getName() + " is waiting at
                        barrier.");
                barrier.await();

                System.out.println(Thread.currentThread().getName() + " is performing
                        task 3.");
            } catch (InterruptedException | BrokenBarrierException e) {
                e.printStackTrace();
            }
        }
    }
```

```
}
```

This code creates a CyclicBarrier for 3 threads. The barrier point is enhanced with a barrier action (a Runnable task) that executes once all threads have reached the barrier. Each thread performs a series of tasks, waiting at the barrier points in between.

The creation of a CyclicBarrier for 3 threads with the barrier action is as follows:

```
private static final CyclicBarrier barrier = new CyclicBarrier(NUM_THREADS,
    new Runnable() {
        @Override
        public void run() {
            System.out.println("All threads have reached the barrier, performing the
                final task.");
        }
    });
```

CyclicBarrier await() method is used by each thread to wait at the barrier. When the specified number of threads have called await(), all waiting threads are released, and the barrier action is executed.

Considerations include handling exceptions such as InterruptedException and BrokenBarrierException:

- InterruptedException occurs if any thread is interrupted while waiting.
- BrokenBarrierException is thrown if another thread is interrupted or times out while waiting, or if the barrier is broken.

A more advanced use case might involve using CyclicBarrier to manage more complex synchronization. We will explore two scenarios:

1. **Resetting the Barrier**: The barrier can be reset using the reset() method, which returns the barrier to its initial state. This is useful if the barrier breaks due to interruption or timeout, and we need to retry the synchronization process.

2. **Handling Timeouts**: The await(long timeout, TimeUnit unit) method allows threads to wait at the barrier for a specified amount of time. If the timeout elapses before all threads have reached the barrier, a TimeoutException is thrown.

Resetting the barrier:

```
try {
    barrier.await();
```

```
} catch (BrokenBarrierException e) {
    System.out.println("Barrier broken, resetting.");
    barrier.reset();
}
```

Handling timeouts:

```
try {
    barrier.await(2, TimeUnit.SECONDS);
} catch (TimeoutException e) {
    System.err.println("Timeout waiting for barrier, proceeding without synchronization
        .");
}
```

Incorporating CyclicBarrier in a multi-threaded computation framework can significantly simplify the problem of coordinating multiple threads, especially when each thread depends on others reaching a common point before proceeding further. By understanding and leveraging the features of CyclicBarrier, one can effectively manage complex parallel tasks, ensuring correctness and efficiency.

4.4 Semaphore

The semaphore is a fundamental concurrency control construct that can be found in the java.util.concurrent package, providing a way to manage access to a shared resource through the use of permits. The Semaphore class in Java is a counting semaphore, where a specified number of permits are available for concurrent threads to acquire and release.

To initialize a Semaphore, you specify the number of permits at the time of its creation. For example, the following code snippet demonstrates the initialization of a semaphore with three permits:

```
import java.util.concurrent.Semaphore;

Semaphore semaphore = new Semaphore(3);
```

Once initialized, threads can attempt to acquire a permit by invoking the acquire() method and release a permit by invoking the release() method. The semaphore ensures that the number of permits acquired never exceeds the number of available permits. Here is an example showing how a thread can acquire and release a permit:

```
try {
    semaphore.acquire();
    // Critical section: code that accesses the shared resource
```

```
} catch (InterruptedException e) {
    Thread.currentThread().interrupt();
} finally {
    semaphore.release();
}
```

The acquire() method blocks the thread until a permit is available, while the release() method returns a permit to the semaphore, potentially unblocking a waiting thread.

Semaphores can also be initialized as fair or unfair. A fair semaphore ensures that threads acquire permits in the order they requested them (FIFO order), while an unfair semaphore does not guarantee this order. Here is how you can create a fair semaphore:

```
Semaphore fairSemaphore = new Semaphore(3, true);
```

In some scenarios, you may prefer to use methods such as tryAcquire() which immediately returns a boolean value depending on whether a permit was acquired successfully or not:

```
if (semaphore.tryAcquire()) {
    try {
        // Critical section
    } finally {
        semaphore.release();
    }
} else {
    // Failed to acquire the permit
}
```

Additionally, tryAcquire(long timeout, TimeUnit unit) allows a thread to attempt to get a permit, but with a specified waiting period, after which it gives up if unsuccessful:

```
try {
    if (semaphore.tryAcquire(2, TimeUnit.SECONDS)) {
        try {
            // Critical section
        } finally {
            semaphore.release();
        }
    } else {
        // Timed out without acquiring a permit
    }
} catch (InterruptedException e) {
    Thread.currentThread().interrupt();
}
```

The Semaphore class also provides a number of useful methods for querying its state. For instance, availablePermits() returns the number of currently available permits:

```
int available = semaphore.availablePermits();
System.out.println("Available permits: " + available);
```

The method drainPermits() can be used to acquire and return all available permits at once which can be useful in certain shutdown scenarios:

```
int drained = semaphore.drainPermits();
System.out.println("Drained permits: " + drained);
```

A semaphore can also serve as a lock with the characteristic of being reentrant or non-reentrant. Here is an example illustrating a semaphore acting as a simple lock:

```
Semaphore lock = new Semaphore(1); // Only one permit

try {
    lock.acquire();
    // Critical section
} catch (InterruptedException e) {
    Thread.currentThread().interrupt();
} finally {
    lock.release();
}
```

When designing concurrent applications, semaphores prove to be highly versatile, enabling fine-grained control over access to shared resources. Whether coordinating threads in a producer-consumer scenario or restricting concurrent access to a limited resource, semaphores can effectively manage resource availability while maintaining system stability and performance.

Understanding the correct usage and nuances of semaphore operations ensures robust, predictable concurrency control, benefiting both simple and complex multithreaded applications comprehensively.

4.5 Exchanger

The Exchanger class in the java.util.concurrent package allows two threads to exchange objects at a synchronization point. This class facilitates a form of rendezvous between two threads where each thread presents an item and receives the item provided by the other thread. The Exchanger is particularly useful in scenarios where two threads need to consistently swap data, such as in producer-consumer problems or when exchanging intermediate processing results.

Basic Usage of Exchanger

To create an instance of Exchanger, use the following code:

```
Exchanger<String> exchanger = new Exchanger<>();
```

The Exchanger instance can then be used by two threads to exchange data. Each thread will call the exchange method and will be blocked until the other thread calls the same method.

Example

Consider the following example where we have two threads, ThreadA and ThreadB, that exchange strings:

```
public class ExchangerExample {
    public static void main(String[] args) {
        Exchanger<String> exchanger = new Exchanger<>();

        Thread threadA = new Thread(() -> {
            try {
                String dataA = "Data from Thread A";
                String receivedData = exchanger.exchange(dataA);
                System.out.println("Thread A received: " + receivedData);
            } catch (InterruptedException e) {
                Thread.currentThread().interrupt();
            }
        });

        Thread threadB = new Thread(() -> {
            try {
                String dataB = "Data from Thread B";
                String receivedData = exchanger.exchange(dataB);
                System.out.println("Thread B received: " + receivedData);
            } catch (InterruptedException e) {
                Thread.currentThread().interrupt();
            }
        });

        threadA.start();
        threadB.start();
    }
}
```

The above program will output:

```
Thread A received: Data from Thread B
Thread B received: Data from Thread A
```

This example shows how two threads exchange data using the exchange method. Each thread provides its own data and receives the other thread's data.

Handling InterruptedException

The exchange method can throw an InterruptedException. This exception typically indicates that the thread was interrupted during the exchange process. It is essential to handle this exception properly to ensure robust and predictable behavior.

```
try {
    String receivedData = exchanger.exchange(data);
} catch (InterruptedException e) {
    Thread.currentThread().interrupt();
    // Handle exception
}
```

Timeouts in Exchanger

The Exchanger class also provides an overloaded exchange method that accepts a timeout parameter. This version of the method allows a thread to wait for a specified amount of time for the exchange to happen. If the other thread does not arrive within the specified time, a TimeoutException is thrown.

```
try {
    String receivedData = exchanger.exchange(data, 5, TimeUnit.SECONDS);
} catch (InterruptedException e) {
    Thread.currentThread().interrupt();
    // Handle exception
} catch (TimeoutException e) {
    // Handle timeout
}
```

Practical Use Cases

Exchangers are particularly beneficial in applications where two threads need to swap data, often seen in genetic algorithms or double-buffering techniques:

1. **Double Buffering:** In a graphics application, one thread can produce frames while another thread renders them. Using an Exchanger, the producer and consumer threads can swap the buffers.

```
Exchanger<Buffer> exchanger = new Exchanger<>();

Thread producer = new Thread(() -> {
    Buffer bufferToFill = new Buffer();
    while (true) {
        fillBuffer(bufferToFill);
        try {
            bufferToFill = exchanger.exchange(bufferToFill);
        } catch (InterruptedException e) {
            Thread.currentThread().interrupt();
        }
    }
});

Thread consumer = new Thread(() -> {
    Buffer bufferToProcess = new Buffer();
    while (true) {
        try {
            bufferToProcess = exchanger.exchange(bufferToProcess);
            processBuffer(bufferToProcess);
```

```
        } catch (InterruptedException e) {
            Thread.currentThread().interrupt();
        }
    }
});

producer.start();
consumer.start();
```

In this example, the producer thread fills a buffer with data and then exchanges it with the consumer thread, which processes the buffer. The Exchanger ensures the buffers are properly swapped between the threads.

2. **Genetic Algorithms:** In genetic algorithms, Exchanger can be used to exchange genetic pools between threads implementing different genetic operations like mutation and crossover.

```
Exchanger<GeneticPool> exchanger = new Exchanger<>();

Thread mutationThread = new Thread(() -> {
    GeneticPool poolForMutation = new GeneticPool();
    while (true) {
        mutate(poolForMutation);
        try {
            poolForMutation = exchanger.exchange(poolForMutation);
        } catch (InterruptedException e) {
            Thread.currentThread().interrupt();
        }
    }
});

Thread crossoverThread = new Thread(() -> {
    GeneticPool poolForCrossover = new GeneticPool();
    while (true) {
        try {
            poolForCrossover = exchanger.exchange(poolForCrossover);
            crossover(poolForCrossover);
        } catch (InterruptedException e) {
            Thread.currentThread().interrupt();
        }
    }
});

mutationThread.start();
crossoverThread.start();
```

This example demonstrates how different operations in a genetic algorithm can utilize Exchanger to swap genetic pools for subsequent processing improvements.

Exchanger provides a powerful and flexible mechanism for thread communication, especially when a high level of coordination is required. By enabling direct transfer of data, it optimizes thread interactions and can significantly simplify complex multi-threaded applications.

4.6 Phaser

The Phaser class, part of the java.util.concurrent package, is a versatile synchronization barrier aptly suited for dynamic, phase-based tasks. With Phaser, threads can synchronize at multiple points ("phases"), handling scenarios where the number of participating threads can vary. In contrast to CountDownLatch or CyclicBarrier, Phaser supports dynamic phase advancement even as participants join or leave the barrier.

Key Methods and Properties

Phaser's flexibility is derived from several key methods and properties:

- register(): Adds a new, unarrived party to this phase.
- arrive(): Signifies that a party has completed this phase without waiting for others.
- arriveAndAwaitAdvance(): Signifies that a party has completed this phase and waits for others.
- arriveAndDeregister(): Signifies the completion of this phase by a party and deregisters it from further phases.
- getPhase(): Returns the current phase number.
- getRegisteredParties(): Provides the number of registered parties.

Example Usage

To illustrate Phaser usage, consider a multi-phase task wherein we have three phases with dynamic participation. Here's a Java example demonstrating how to construct and utilize Phaser for this purpose:

```
import java.util.concurrent.Phaser;

public class PhaserExample {

    public static void main(String[] args) {
        final int phaseCount = 3;
        final int initialParties = 2;

        Phaser phaser = new Phaser(initialParties) {
            @Override
            protected boolean onAdvance(int phase, int registeredParties) {
                System.out.println("Phase " + phase + " completed with " +
                        registeredParties + " participants.");
                return phase >= phaseCount - 1 || registeredParties == 0;
            }
```

```
        };

        for (int i = 0; i < initialParties; i++) {
            int threadNum = i;
            new Thread(() -> {
                for (int phase = 0; phase < phaseCount; phase++) {
                    System.out.println("Thread " + threadNum + " starting phase " +
                        phase);
                    phaser.arriveAndAwaitAdvance();
                    System.out.println("Thread " + threadNum + " completed phase " +
                        phase);
                }
            }).start();
        }

        phaser.arriveAndDeregister();
        phaser.register(); // Use a new party to dynamically add phases
    }
}
```

In this example, the Phaser starts with an initial set of parties and dynamically adds phases via arriveAndAwaitAdvance. The onAdvance method, overridden from the Phaser class, is called at the end of each phase, allowing us to log phase transitions or stop the phaser based on conditions such as the number of phases completed or the number of parties.

Advantages of Phaser

Phaser offers several advantages due to its flexible nature:

- **Dynamic Participation**: The ability to register and deregister participants dynamically allows fine-grained synchronization. This is particularly useful in heterogeneous task systems where task load varies.
- **Phase-Based Synchronization**: It naturally supports multi-phase processing by advancing through phases, synchronizing threads at each point.
- **Customizable Phase Transitions**: By overriding the onAdvance method, developers can introduce custom behavior when phases advance, including early termination.

Potential Pitfalls

Despite its flexibility, proper use of Phaser demands careful consideration to avoid common pitfalls:

- **Resource Management**: Threads must ensure they eventually deregister to prevent resource leakage, especially in dynamic environments.

- **Deadlock Risk**: Mismanagement in phase advancement (e.g., inconsistent arrival and deregistration) can lead to deadlock situations. Adequate handling of thread interruptions and cancellations is essential.
- **Fairness and Starvation**: Ensuring fair participation can be challenging when phases involve numerous threads with varying workload, leading to potential starvation if some threads are always delayed.

This section on Phaser aims to equip developers with a nuanced understanding of leveraging phase-based synchronization in Java, enhancing concurrent programming proficiency.

4.7 Concurrent Collections

Concurrent collections provide a set of data structures that are specifically designed to be safely used by multiple threads without requiring explicit synchronization by the developer. The utilities within the java.util.concurrent package offer multiple classes tailored for different use cases, ensuring high performance and thread-safety. This section delves into the central concurrent collection classes provided by the Java Concurrency API.

BlockingQueue

The BlockingQueue interface extends Queue with operations that allow for thread-safe addition and removal of elements. The primary implementations of BlockingQueue are ArrayBlockingQueue, LinkedBlockingQueue, PriorityBlockingQueue, and DelayedQueue. Elements can be added to or removed from these queues in three main ways: immediately, with a timeout, or by blocking until space is available.

```
import java.util.concurrent.*;

public class BlockingQueueExample {
    public static void main(String[] args) throws InterruptedException {
        BlockingQueue<Integer> queue = new LinkedBlockingQueue<>(10);

        Runnable producer = () -> {
            try {
                for (int i = 1; i <= 20; i++) {
                    queue.put(i);
```

```
                System.out.println("Produced: " + i);
            }
        } catch (InterruptedException e) {
            Thread.currentThread().interrupt();
        }
    };

    Runnable consumer = () -> {
        try {
            for (int i = 1; i <= 20; i++) {
                Integer item = queue.take();
                System.out.println("Consumed: " + item);
            }
        } catch (InterruptedException e) {
            Thread.currentThread().interrupt();
        }
    };

    new Thread(producer).start();
    new Thread(consumer).start();
  }
}
```

PriorityBlockingQueue

The PriorityBlockingQueue is an unbounded blocking queue that uses the same ordering rules as java.util.PriorityQueue. Operations to add, remove, or peek elements are done according to the natural ordering of elements or an order specified by a comparator provided at queue construction time.

```
import java.util.concurrent.*;

public class PriorityBlockingQueueExample {
  public static void main(String[] args) throws InterruptedException {
    PriorityBlockingQueue<Integer> queue = new PriorityBlockingQueue<>();

    Runnable producer = () -> {
        try {
            for (int i = 20; i >= 1; i--) {
                queue.put(i);
                System.out.println("Produced: " + i);
            }
        } catch (InterruptedException e) {
            Thread.currentThread().interrupt();
        }
    };

    Runnable consumer = () -> {
        try {
            for (int i = 1; i <= 20; i++) {
                Integer item = queue.take();
                System.out.println("Consumed: " + item);
            }
        } catch (InterruptedException e) {
            Thread.currentThread().interrupt();
        }
    };
```

```
        new Thread(producer).start();
        new Thread(consumer).start();
    }
}
```

ConcurrentHashMap

The ConcurrentHashMap is a highly concurrent, thread-safe version of HashMap. It supports full concurrency for retrieval operations and high expected concurrency for updates. Unlike HashTable, ConcurrentHashMap does not lock the entire table but allows concurrent read and write operations without blocking.

```
import java.util.concurrent.*;

public class ConcurrentHashMapExample {
    public static void main(String[] args) {
        ConcurrentHashMap<String, Integer> map = new ConcurrentHashMap<>();

        Runnable writer = () -> {
            for (int i = 0; i < 1000; i++) {
                map.put("key" + i, i);
            }
        };

        Runnable reader = () -> {
            for (int i = 0; i < 1000; i++) {
                Integer value = map.get("key" + i);
                System.out.println("Read: " + value);
            }
        };

        new Thread(writer).start();
        new Thread(reader).start();
    }
}
```

CopyOnWriteArrayList and CopyOnWriteArraySet

The CopyOnWriteArrayList and CopyOnWriteArraySet are concurrent collections where all mutative operations, such as add and set, are implemented by making a fresh copy of the underlying array. These collections are suitable for applications in which traversal operations vastly outnumber mutations, ensuring thread safety with minimal synchronization overhead.

```
import java.util.concurrent.*;
import java.util.*;

public class CopyOnWriteArrayListExample {
    public static void main(String[] args) {
        CopyOnWriteArrayList<String> list = new CopyOnWriteArrayList<>();

        Runnable writer = () -> {
            for (int i = 0; i < 10; i++) {
                list.add("Item " + i);
```

```
            System.out.println("Added: Item " + i);
        }
    };

    Runnable reader = () -> {
        while (true) {
            for (String item : list) {
                System.out.println("Read: " + item);
            }
        }
    };

    new Thread(writer).start();
    new Thread(reader).start();
  }
}
```

Concurrent collections in Java provide optimized, thread-safe alternatives to traditional collection classes, allowing developers to focus on the logic of their concurrent applications without needing complex synchronization code.

4.8 BlockingQueue

The BlockingQueue interface, found in the java.util.concurrent package, is a specialized form of the Queue interface that supports operations which wait for the queue to become non-empty when retrieving an element, and wait for space to become available in the queue when storing an element. The BlockingQueue is used for implementing producer-consumer designs, where producers add elements to the queue and consumers retrieve them.

Key Characteristics:

- BlockingQueue methods come in four forms, which differ in how they handle operations that cannot be satisfied immediately:
  - A method throwing an exception.
  - A method returning a special value (null or false, depending on the operation).
  - A method blocking the current thread indefinitely until the operation can succeed.
  - A method that blocks for only a given maximum time limit before giving up.

- BlockingQueue implementations are thread-safe, meaning multiple threads can access these methods without interfering with each other.
- Does not permit null elements.

Implementations of BlockingQueue

The java.util.concurrent package provides several implementations of the BlockingQueue interface:

- ArrayBlockingQueue: A bounded blocking queue backed by an array. The queue uses a single lock for both put and take operations.
- LinkedBlockingQueue: An optionally-bounded blocking queue backed by linked nodes. This queue typically has higher throughput than ArrayBlockingQueue and uses separate locks for put and take operations.
- PriorityBlockingQueue: An unbounded blocking queue that uses the same ordering rules as class PriorityQueue and supplies blocking retrieval operations.
- DelayQueue: A time-based scheduling queue in which elements can only be taken when they are delayed until a certain period.
- SynchronousQueue: A blocking queue in which each insert operation must wait for a corresponding remove operation by another thread, and vice versa.
- LinkedTransferQueue: An unbounded TransferQueue which provides additional methods that attempt to transfer elements to a waiting consumer.

Using BlockingQueue

Below is a sample implementation of a producer-consumer pattern using BlockingQueue. This example utilizes ArrayBlockingQueue.

```
import java.util.concurrent.ArrayBlockingQueue;
import java.util.concurrent.BlockingQueue;

public class ProducerConsumerExample {
```

```
    private static class Producer implements Runnable {
        private final BlockingQueue<Integer> queue;

        Producer(BlockingQueue<Integer> queue) {
            this.queue = queue;
        }

        @Override
        public void run() {
            try {
                for (int i = 0; i < 10; i++) {
                    queue.put(i);
                    System.out.println("Produced: " + i);
                }
                queue.put(-1); // Indicates end of production
            } catch (InterruptedException e) {
                Thread.currentThread().interrupt();
            }
        }
    }

    private static class Consumer implements Runnable {
        private final BlockingQueue<Integer> queue;

        Consumer(BlockingQueue<Integer> queue) {
            this.queue = queue;
        }

        @Override
        public void run() {
            try {
                while (true) {
                    Integer value = queue.take();
                    if (value == -1) {
                        break;
                    }
                    System.out.println("Consumed: " + value);
                }
            } catch (InterruptedException e) {
                Thread.currentThread().interrupt();
            }
        }
    }

    public static void main(String[] args) {
        BlockingQueue<Integer> queue = new ArrayBlockingQueue<>(10);
        Thread producerThread = new Thread(new Producer(queue));
        Thread consumerThread = new Thread(new Consumer(queue));

        producerThread.start();
        consumerThread.start();

        try {
            producerThread.join();
            consumerThread.join();
        } catch (InterruptedException e) {
            Thread.currentThread().interrupt();
        }
    }
}
```

When executed, the output will resemble:

```
Produced: 0
Consumed: 0
Produced: 1
Consumed: 1
Produced: 2
Consumed: 2
Produced: 3
Consumed: 3
Produced: 4
Consumed: 4
...
Produced: 9
Consumed: 9
```

In this example, the Producer class generates integers from 0 to 9 and places them in the ArrayBlockingQueue. The Consumer class retrieves these integers and processes them. The sentinel value -1 is used to signal the end of production and consumption, ensuring that the consumer thread exits gracefully.

The BlockingQueue interface and its implementations provide robust solutions for thread-safe communication between producer and consumer tasks in concurrent applications.

4.9 PriorityBlockingQueue

The PriorityBlockingQueue class is part of the java.util.concurrent package and implements a concurrent, unbounded, thread-safe priority queue. Internally, it uses a priority heap to order the elements according to their natural ordering or by a comparator provided at queue construction time. This class allows concurrent access and offers thread safety without the need for additional synchronization, making it highly useful in concurrent programming.

The PriorityBlockingQueue implements the BlockingQueue interface, which means it provides operations that wait for the queue to become non-empty when retrieving an element and wait for space to become available when storing an element. It is important to understand both the API and the underlying mechanisms to leverage its full potential.

```
import java.util.concurrent.PriorityBlockingQueue;

public class PriorityBlockingQueueExample {
    public static void main(String[] args) throws InterruptedException {
        PriorityBlockingQueue<Integer> queue = new PriorityBlockingQueue<>();

        queue.add(4);
        queue.add(2);
```

```
        queue.add(1);
        queue.add(3);

        while (!queue.isEmpty()) {
            System.out.println(queue.take());
        }
    }
}
```

The given example demonstrates the use of a PriorityBlockingQueue to order integers naturally. The output is ordered in ascending fashion due to the natural ordering of integers.

```
1
2
3
4
```

PriorityBlockingQueue is not a bounded queue. This means it can grow as needed to accommodate an unbounded number of elements. However, it does not accept null elements, and attempting to add a null element to the queue will result in a NullPointerException.

Elements in PriorityBlockingQueue are ordered either according to their natural ordering by implementing the Comparable interface or according to a Comparator provided at the queue's construction time. When constructing a PriorityBlockingQueue with custom ordering, the following code can be employed:

```
import java.util.concurrent.PriorityBlockingQueue;
import java.util.Comparator;

public class CustomComparatorExample {
    public static void main(String[] args) throws InterruptedException {
        Comparator<Integer> customComparator = (x, y) -> y - x;

        PriorityBlockingQueue<Integer> customOrderedQueue =
            new PriorityBlockingQueue<>(11, customComparator);

        customOrderedQueue.add(4);
        customOrderedQueue.add(2);
        customOrderedQueue.add(1);
        customOrderedQueue.add(3);

        while (!customOrderedQueue.isEmpty()) {
            System.out.println(customOrderedQueue.take());
        }
    }
}
```

In this example, the customOrderedQueue orders integers in descending order using a custom comparator.

4
3
2
1

Key Operations

- offer(E e): Inserts the specified element into the queue. If the element cannot be added immediately due to capacity restrictions, it may be queued later.
- poll(): Retrieves and removes the head of the queue. This method returns null if the queue is empty.
- take(): Retrieves and removes the head of the queue, waiting if necessary until an element becomes available.
- peek(): Retrieves, but does not remove, the head of this queue, or returns null if this queue is empty.
- size(): Returns the number of elements in the queue.

Threads attempting to retrieve an element will block until the queue is non-empty due to the blocking behavior of take(). Similarly, threads inserting elements will not block due to the queue's unbounded nature, ensuring high throughput in concurrent environments.

Performance Considerations

The PriorityBlockingQueue provides O(log n) time complexity for both insertion and extraction based on the priority heap structure. The main advantage is the concurrent access capability, wherein multiple threads can insert and retrieve elements concurrently without additional synchronization mechanisms. However, developers should consider whether the ordering criteria and blocking behaviors align with the application's specific requirements.

Use Cases

PriorityBlockingQueue is particularly suitable for scenarios requiring a prioritized task processing mechanism, such as:

- **Task Scheduling**: Prioritizing tasks based on urgency or priority levels.
- **Message Processing**: Handling messages in a priority-driven manner within messaging systems.

- **Job Queues**: Managing job queues where jobs with higher priority need to be processed first.

In essence, PriorityBlockingQueue serves as a robust utility in the java.util.concurrent package for handling priority-based operations in a concurrent setting.

4.10 ConcurrentHashMap

The ConcurrentHashMap is part of the java.util.concurrent package and provides a thread-safe variant of HashMap. Unlike Hashtable, which synchronizes each method individually, ConcurrentHashMap locks only portions of the underlying data structure (buckets), allowing higher concurrency and better performance in multi-threaded environments. This section delves into the internal mechanisms, design principles, and typical usage patterns of ConcurrentHashMap.

ConcurrentHashMap is designed using a technique known as lock striping, which segments the map into smaller portions (segments) and uses separate locks for each segment. This technique reduces contention because multiple threads can operate on different segments concurrently without interference. When a thread performs a retrieval operation, it accesses the underlying data directly without locking, while updates are controlled to ensure consistency.

To instantiate a ConcurrentHashMap, one can use the following constructors:

```
ConcurrentHashMap<K,V> map1 = new ConcurrentHashMap<>();
ConcurrentHashMap<K,V> map2 = new ConcurrentHashMap<>(int initialCapacity);
ConcurrentHashMap<K,V> map3 = new ConcurrentHashMap<>(int initialCapacity,
    float loadFactor);
ConcurrentHashMap<K,V> map4 = new ConcurrentHashMap<>(int initialCapacity,
    float loadFactor, int concurrencyLevel);
```

The parameters for the constructors are as follows:

- initialCapacity: The initial capacity of the hash table.
- loadFactor: The load factor threshold, used to control resizing.
- concurrencyLevel: An estimated number of concurrently updating threads. The implementation performs internal sizing based on this value.

In typical usage, ConcurrentHashMap provides methods such as put, get, remove, and compute, among others:

```
// Inserting a key-value pair
map1.put("key1", "value1");

// Retrieving a value
String value = map1.get("key1");

// Removing a key-value pair
map1.remove("key1");

// Computing a value for a given key
map1.compute("key1", (key, val) -> val == null ? "defaultValue" : val.concat("
    updated"));
```

The following characteristics define the behavior and performance of ConcurrentHashMap:

- Non-blocking Reads: Retrieval operations are generally non-blocking and do not require synchronization.

- Safe Publication: A put or remove operation ensures that any subsequent retrieval includes the latest updates.

- Atomic Operations: Compound operations such as putIfAbsent, remove(key, value), and compute are atomic.

- High Scalability: The internal structure is optimized for high concurrency with minimal lock contention.

Algorithm 4: Insert Key-Value Pair

Data: Key-Value pair (key, value)
Result: Inserts the key-value pair into the ConcurrentHashMap while ensuring concurrency safety

```
Function updateHashTable(map, key, value):
    hash ← hashCode(key);
    Segment ← getSegment(hash);
    lockSegment (Segment);
    data ← Segment.getData();
    if data.contains(key) then
        data.update(key, value);
    end
    else
        data.insert(key, value);
    end
    unlockSegment (Segment);
    return true;
```

Another essential feature of ConcurrentHashMap is its capacity to use thread-safe computing functions. The compute methods allow for atomic updates to the map entries, ensuring that functional transformations on values are executed safely in concurrent scenarios.

For example, consider the use of the compute method to update a value conditionally:

```
map1.compute("key1", (key, val) -> (val == null) ? "initialValue" : val + " suffix");
```

The compute method applies the provided function to the current value associated with the specified key, or to null if no value is present. The atomic nature of this method prevents race conditions commonly encountered in concurrent applications.

In scenarios needing iteration over a ConcurrentHashMap, specialized iterators provide thread-safe traversals. The iterators reflect the state of the map at the time of their creation and may be weakly consistent, i.e., they might not show modifications made to the map after the iterator was created but will never throw a ConcurrentModificationException. The following code demonstrates an iteration over a ConcurrentHashMap:

```
Iterator<Map.Entry<String, String>> iterator = map1.entrySet().iterator();
while (iterator.hasNext()) {
    Map.Entry<String, String> entry = iterator.next();
    System.out.println(entry.getKey() + ": " + entry.getValue());
```

```
}
```

Weak consistency in iterators ensures that even if the map changes during iteration, the iterator continues to reflect a consistent view without errors, promoting stability and predictability in multi-threaded applications.

ConcurrentHashMap provides a combination of optimal performance and reliable thread safety, making it indispensable for concurrent programming in Java. Proper understanding and utilization of this collection can significantly enhance the throughput and correctness of concurrent Java applications.

4.11 CopyOnWriteArrayList and CopyOnWriteArraySet

The CopyOnWriteArrayList and CopyOnWriteArraySet are part of the java.util.concurrent package and provide thread-safe variants of ArrayList and HashSet, respectively. These are designed for scenarios where the frequency of traversal operations significantly outweighs the frequency of mutative operations (e.g., insertion, removal, or update). The primary mechanism that ensures thread safety in these collections is the copy-on-write approach, where a new copy of the underlying array is created and updated for every mutative operation. This choice offers substantial benefits in terms of thread safety and concurrency management at the cost of increased memory consumption and update operation overhead.

The CopyOnWriteArrayList is implemented as follows:

```
public class CopyOnWriteArrayList<E> implements List<E>, RandomAccess,
    Cloneable, java.io.Serializable {
  private transient volatile Object[] array;

  // All mutative operations operate on a fresh copy of the array
  final void setArray(Object[] a) {
      array = a;
  }

  public boolean add(E e) {
      final ReentrantLock lock = this.lock;
      lock.lock();
      try {
          Object[] elements = getArray();
          int len = elements.length;
          Object[] newElements = Arrays.copyOf(elements, len + 1);
          newElements[len] = e;
```

```
            setArray(newElements);
            return true;
        } finally {
            lock.unlock();
        }
    }

    public E get(int index) {
        return getArrayUnchecked(index);
    }

    // Other methods such as remove, set, iterator etc.
}
```

The CopyOnWriteArraySet extends CopyOnWriteArrayList, utilizing the same underlying array mechanism but ensuring uniqueness of elements:

```
public class CopyOnWriteArraySet<E> implements Set<E>, Cloneable, java.io.
    Serializable {
    private final CopyOnWriteArrayList<E> al;

    public CopyOnWriteArraySet() {
        al = new CopyOnWriteArrayList<>();
    }

    public boolean add(E e) {
        return al.addIfAbsent(e);
    }

    public boolean contains(Object o) {
        return al.contains(o);
    }

    public boolean remove(Object o) {
        return al.remove(o);
    }

    // Other methods such as size, iterator etc.
}
```

These classes embody a distinct operational tradeoff by optimizing read operations through the use of a snapshot mechanism that each thread reads without interference, while write operations involve copying the entire array.

To better understand the practical application of CopyOnWriteArrayList, consider the following example, which demonstrates concurrent read and write operations:

```
import java.util.concurrent.CopyOnWriteArrayList;

public class CopyOnWriteArrayListExample {
    public static void main(String[] args) {
        CopyOnWriteArrayList<Integer> list = new CopyOnWriteArrayList<>();

        // Populate the list
```

```
        for (int i = 0; i < 100; i++) {
            list.add(i);
        }

        // Reader thread
        Thread readerThread = new Thread(() -> {
            for (int i : list) {
                System.out.println("Read value: " + i);
                try {
                    Thread.sleep(10);
                } catch (InterruptedException e) {
                    Thread.currentThread().interrupt();
                }
            }
        });

        // Writer thread
        Thread writerThread = new Thread(() -> {
            for (int i = 100; i < 200; i++) {
                list.add(i);
                System.out.println("Added value: " + i);
                try {
                    Thread.sleep(20);
                } catch (InterruptedException e) {
                    Thread.currentThread().interrupt();
                }
            }
        });

        // Start threads
        readerThread.start();
        writerThread.start();
    }
}
```

Executing the program yields the following type of interleaved output:

```
Read value: 0
Read value: 1
Added value: 100
Read value: 2
Read value: 3
Added value: 101
...
```

This demonstrates that CopyOnWriteArrayList guarantees thread-safe iteration without throwing ConcurrentModificationException. Each read operation sees a consistent snapshot of the list as it existed when the iterator was created, ensuring data visibility and safety.

Similarly, CopyOnWriteArraySet may be particularly useful in scenarios requiring a thread-safe set with minimal update operations, as shown below:

```
import java.util.concurrent.CopyOnWriteArraySet;

public class CopyOnWriteArraySetExample {
    public static void main(String[] args) {
        CopyOnWriteArraySet<String> set = new CopyOnWriteArraySet<>();
```

```
        // Add some elements
        set.add("A");
        set.add("B");
        set.add("C");

        // Reader thread
        Thread readerThread = new Thread(() -> {
            for (String s : set) {
                System.out.println("Read value: " + s);
                try {
                    Thread.sleep(50);
                } catch (InterruptedException e) {
                    Thread.currentThread().interrupt();
                }
            }
        });

        // Writer thread
        Thread writerThread = new Thread(() -> {
            String[] values = {"D", "E", "F"};
            for (String value : values) {
                set.add(value);
                System.out.println("Added value: " + value);
                try {
                    Thread.sleep(100);
                } catch (InterruptedException e) {
                    Thread.currentThread().interrupt();
                }
            }
        });

        // Start threads
        readerThread.start();
        writerThread.start();
    }
}
```

Expected output illustrates the concurrency safety and stability of read and write operations:

```
Read value: A
Read value: B
Added value: D
Read value: C
Read value: A
Added value: E
Read value: B
...
```

These classes, when used judiciously, facilitate robust and thread-safe collection manipulations in concurrent programming, especially suitable for read-heavy workloads.

4.12 ThreadLocal and InheritableThreadLocal

Thread-local variables provide a mechanism to maintain per-thread data, ensuring that each thread accessing a variable has its own, independent copy. Thread-local variables are particularly useful in scenarios where mutable state is not meant to be shared across different threads. The ThreadLocal and InheritableThreadLocal classes in the java.lang package facilitate such data encapsulation.

The ThreadLocal class isolates variables at the thread level. The lifecycle of a ThreadLocal variable is bound to the lifecycle of the thread that accesses it. The common methods provided by the ThreadLocal class include:

- get() - Retrieves the current thread's value of the variable.
- set(T value) - Sets the current thread's value of the variable to value.
- remove() - Removes the current thread's value for the variable.
- initialValue() - Returns the initial value for the current thread, optionally overridden.

Consider the following example that demonstrates how to use ThreadLocal:

```
public class ThreadLocalExample {
    private static final ThreadLocal<Integer> threadLocalValue = ThreadLocal.
        withInitial(() -> 0);

    public static void main(String[] args) {
        Thread thread1 = new Thread(new Task(), "Thread-1");
        Thread thread2 = new Thread(new Task(), "Thread-2");

        thread1.start();
        thread2.start();
    }

    static class Task implements Runnable {
        @Override
        public void run() {
            int currentValue = threadLocalValue.get();
            System.out.println(Thread.currentThread().getName() + " initial value: " +
                currentValue);
            threadLocalValue.set(currentValue + 1);
            System.out.println(Thread.currentThread().getName() + " incremented
                value: " + threadLocalValue.get());
            threadLocalValue.remove();
```

```
            System.out.println(Thread.currentThread().getName() + " final value after
                    remove: " + threadLocalValue.get());
        }
    }
}
```

When the program is executed, the output will be:

```
Thread-1 initial value: 0
Thread-1 incremented value: 1
Thread-1 final value after remove: 0
Thread-2 initial value: 0
Thread-2 incremented value: 1
Thread-2 final value after remove: 0
```

Each thread obtains and manipulates its own copy of the ThreadLocal variable, thus avoiding conflicts with other threads.

InheritableThreadLocal extends ThreadLocal to allow child threads to inherit the value of the variable from their parent thread. This is beneficial when thread-local variables are set in a parent thread and need to be accessible in child threads without having to set them explicitly.

The InheritableThreadLocal class provides similar methods to ThreadLocal, but it also overrides the childValue(T parentValue) method, which computes the child's initial value as a function of the parent thread's value. This functionality is illustrated in the following example:

```
public class InheritableThreadLocalExample {
    private static final InheritableThreadLocal<Integer> inheritableThreadLocalValue
            = new InheritableThreadLocal<>() {
        @Override
        protected Integer initialValue() {
            return 1;
        }

        @Override
        protected Integer childValue(Integer parentValue) {
            return parentValue + 1;
        }
    };

    public static void main(String[] args) {
        Thread parentThread = new Thread(() -> {
            System.out.println(Thread.currentThread().getName() + " initial value: " +
                    inheritableThreadLocalValue.get());
            inheritableThreadLocalValue.set(5);

            Thread childThread = new Thread(() -> {
                System.out.println(Thread.currentThread().getName() + " inherited
                        value: " + inheritableThreadLocalValue.get());
                inheritableThreadLocalValue.set(10);
                System.out.println(Thread.currentThread().getName() + " new value: "
                        + inheritableThreadLocalValue.get());
            }, "Child-Thread");
            childThread.start();

            try {
```

```
                childThread.join();
            } catch (InterruptedException e) {
                Thread.currentThread().interrupt();
            }

            System.out.println(Thread.currentThread().getName() + " final value: " +
                    inheritableThreadLocalValue.get());
        }, "Parent-Thread");

        parentThread.start();
    }
}
```

On executing the program, you might obtain an output similar to:

```
Parent-Thread initial value: 1
Child-Thread inherited value: 6
Child-Thread new value: 10
Parent-Thread final value: 5
```

This demonstrates that the child thread inherited the modified InheritableThreadLocal value (which was set to 5 in the parent thread), and incremented it as per the childValue method logic. Finally, each thread maintains its values independently after the inheritance has been established.

While both ThreadLocal and InheritableThreadLocal provide ways to handle thread-confined data, they must be used judiciously to prevent memory leaks, primarily when threads are part of a thread pool. It's crucial to call remove() to ensure that thread-local variables do not persist longer than necessary.

Chapter 5

Executors Framework

This chapter introduces the Executors Framework, which provides a high-level mechanism for managing thread execution. It outlines how to create and manage threads using ExecutorService, and the differences between FixedThreadPool, CachedThreadPool, SingleThreadExecutor, and ScheduledThreadPool. The chapter explores the Callable and Future interfaces for asynchronous task management, including task submission and handling exceptions. Additionally, it covers shutting down executors and using ScheduledExecutorService for timed and periodic tasks, highlighting a comparison between ForkJoinPool and ExecutorService to optimize thread management.

5.1 Introduction to Executors Framework

The Executors Framework in Java serves as a highly versatile toolset for managing and controlling thread execution. Grounded in the java.util.concurrent package, this framework abstracts many low-level threading complexities, allowing developers to focus on higher-level application logic rather than the intricacies of thread management.

At its core, the Executors Framework decouples the task submission from the mechanics of how each task is executed, including thread use, scheduling, and lifecycle management. This high-level approach streamlines multi-threaded programming by providing a collection of executor services that handle the execution details on behalf of the programmer.

The Executors Framework offers various types of executor services, each tailored for specific concurrency usage patterns:

- Executor: A simple interface providing a method to execute Runnable tasks.
- ExecutorService: An extension of Executor, providing lifecycle methods for managing tasks and applications.
- ScheduledExecutorService: Extends ExecutorService to provide methods for scheduling tasks to run periodically or after a specified delay.

A pivotal part of the Executors Framework is the ExecutorService interface, which provides a comprehensive suite of methods for task management:

```
public interface ExecutorService extends Executor {
    void shutdown();
    List<Runnable> shutdownNow();
    boolean isShutdown();
    boolean isTerminated();
    boolean awaitTermination(long timeout, TimeUnit unit)
        throws InterruptedException;
    <T> Future<T> submit(Callable<T> task);
    <T> Future<T> submit(Runnable task, T result);
    Future<?> submit(Runnable task);
    <T> List<Future<T>> invokeAll(Collection<? extends Callable<T>> tasks)
        throws InterruptedException;
    <T> List<Future<T>> invokeAll(Collection<? extends Callable<T>> tasks,
        long timeout, TimeUnit unit) throws InterruptedException;
    <T> T invokeAny(Collection<? extends Callable<T>> tasks)
        throws InterruptedException, ExecutionException;
    <T> T invokeAny(Collection<? extends Callable<T>> tasks,
        long timeout, TimeUnit unit) throws InterruptedException,
        ExecutionException, TimeoutException;
}
```

The ExecutorService implementation manages a pool of worker threads internally, which simplifies task submission and execution. Developers generally leverage factory methods from the Executors utility class to create suitable executor instances, such as:

- newFixedThreadPool(int nThreads): Creates a thread pool that reuses a fixed number of threads operating off a shared, unbounded queue.

- newCachedThreadPool(): Creates a thread pool that creates new threads as needed, but will reuse previously constructed threads when they are available.
- newSingleThreadExecutor(): Creates an executor that uses a single worker thread operating off an unbounded queue.
- newScheduledThreadPool(int corePoolSize): Creates a thread pool that can schedule commands to run after a given delay or periodically.

Using these factory methods, a common pattern to instantiate a fixed thread pool looks like this:

```
ExecutorService executorService = Executors.newFixedThreadPool(10);
```

In this example, the executorService will manage a pool of 10 threads, ensuring that no more than 10 tasks are executed concurrently.

Once tasks are assigned to an ExecutorService, they can be submitted using methods like submit(Runnable task) and submit(Callable<T> task).

```
Runnable task = () -> System.out.println("Task executed");
executorService.submit(task);

Callable<Integer> callableTask = () -> {
   return 123;
};
Future<Integer> future = executorService.submit(callableTask);
```

In this block, a Runnable task simply prints a message, while a Callable task returns an integer. The result of the Callable is encapsulated in a Future object, providing a reference to retrieve the computation result when it becomes available.

Proper resource management is crucial when working with executors. After tasks are completed, it is vital to shut down the executor to free resources and prevent potential memory leaks. This can be achieved by invoking the shutdown or shutdownNow methods.

```
executorService.shutdown();
```

The shutdown() method initiates an orderly shutdown in which previously submitted tasks are executed, but no new tasks will be accepted. In contrast, shutdownNow() attempts to stop all actively executing tasks and halts processing of waiting tasks.

By abstracting task execution, threading details, and resource management, the Executors Framework significantly simplifies building robust concurrent applications in Java. Understanding these concepts will enable more efficient and effective utilization of Java's concurrency capabilities in development projects.

5.2 Creating and Managing Threads with ExecutorService

The ExecutorService is a higher-level replacement for working with threads directly. It provides various methods to manage termination and methods that can produce a Future for tracking the progress of one or more asynchronous tasks. The ExecutorService can be used to create a thread pool, which manages a number of reusable threads for executing tasks.

To utilize the ExecutorService, the java.util.concurrent package must be imported.

```
import java.util.concurrent.ExecutorService;
import java.util.concurrent.Executors;
import java.util.concurrent.TimeUnit;
```

The Executors class provides factory methods to create different kinds of thread pools.

```
ExecutorService executor = Executors.newFixedThreadPool(4);
```

In the example above, newFixedThreadPool(4) creates a thread pool that reuses a fixed number of threads (4). At any point, there can be at most 4 active threads processing tasks. If additional tasks are submitted when all threads are active, they will wait in a queue until a thread becomes available.

To manage threads using ExecutorService, tasks are typically defined as Runnable or Callable objects.

Example of submitting a Runnable task:

```
executor.submit(() -> {
    // Task to be executed by thread pool
    System.out.println("Task executed by: " + Thread.currentThread().getName());
});
```

The submit method is used to submit a task for execution, which returns a Future representing that task. If a result is required, a Callable can be used instead of Runnable.

Example of submitting a Callable task:

```
Future<String> result = executor.submit(() -> {
    return "Task executed by: " + Thread.currentThread().getName();
});

try {
    System.out.println(result.get());
} catch (Exception e) {
    e.printStackTrace();
}
```

The Callable interface is similar to Runnable, but it can return a result and throw a checked exception. The get method of Future can be used to retrieve the result once the task has completed.

It is essential to properly shut down the ExecutorService to release system resources and avoid memory leaks. The shutdown method initiates an orderly shutdown, in which previously submitted tasks are executed, but no new tasks will be accepted.

```
executor.shutdown();
try {
    if (!executor.awaitTermination(60, TimeUnit.SECONDS)) {
        executor.shutdownNow();
    }
} catch (InterruptedException e) {
    executor.shutdownNow();
    Thread.currentThread().interrupt();
}
```

In the code above, the awaitTermination method blocks until all tasks have completed execution after a shutdown request or if the timeout occurs, whichever happens first. If the executor does not terminate within the specified timeout, the shutdownNow method is invoked to stop all active tasks and halt the executor immediately.

Using ExecutorService significantly simplifies thread management by abstracting the complexity of thread lifecycle management and task scheduling. This allows developers to focus on defining tasks, thus promoting better application scalability and reliability.

5.3 FixedThreadPool vs CachedThreadPool

The FixedThreadPool and the CachedThreadPool are two key variants of thread pools provided by the java.util.concurrent.Executors framework. Both aim to manage thread execution efficiently, but they have different strategies for thread reuse and different use cases. Understanding their characteristics and appropriate application scenarios is crucial for effective thread management.

FixedThreadPool is designed to create a fixed number of threads that are reused for executing tasks. The number of threads in the pool is determined at creation time and does not change. If additional tasks are submitted when all threads are active, the tasks are queued until a thread becomes available.

```
ExecutorService fixedThreadPool = Executors.newFixedThreadPool(4);
```

In this example, the fixedThreadPool is created with a fixed size of four threads. Each thread will be reused to execute tasks, ensuring bounded resource usage.

Advantages of FixedThreadPool:

- **Predictable Resource Usage:** The maximum number of threads is known and fixed, providing predictable memory and CPU usage.
- **Control Over Concurrency:** The number of concurrent tasks is limited to the number of threads, providing control over the degree of parallelism.
- **Simplicity:** It is simple to implement and manage.

Disadvantages of FixedThreadPool:

- **Potential Task Queuing:** If all threads are busy, additional tasks must wait in the queue, potentially leading to latency.
- **Static Size:** The number of threads is fixed and cannot adapt to varying workloads.

Use Cases for FixedThreadPool:

- **Limited Concurrency Requirements:** When there is a need to limit resource usage and control the number of concurrent tasks.
- **Stable Workload:** Applications with a steady and predictable workload where the number of threads can be predefined.

In contrast, the **CachedThreadPool** is designed to create new threads as needed but reuse previously constructed threads when available. If a thread is idle for a certain amount of time (default is 60 seconds), it is terminated and removed from the pool.

```
ExecutorService cachedThreadPool = Executors.newCachedThreadPool();
```

In this example, the cachedThreadPool can dynamically adjust the number of threads according to the workload, offering greater flexibility.

Advantages of CachedThreadPool:

- **Dynamic Flexibility:** The pool can expand or shrink based on the number of tasks, providing better resource utilization.
- **Reduced Task Latency:** New tasks do not have to wait if idle threads are available or new threads can be created immediately.

Disadvantages of CachedThreadPool:

- **Unbounded Resource Usage:** There is no upper limit on the number of threads, which can lead to resource exhaustion under heavy load.
- **Potential Overhead:** Creating and managing a large number of threads can introduce performance overhead.

Use Cases for CachedThreadPool:

- **Bursting Workloads:** Suitable for applications with intermittent heavy workloads where the demand for threads can vary significantly.
- **Short-Lived Tasks:** Ideal for scenarios where tasks are short-lived and can benefit from rapid scaling of thread count.

Selecting between FixedThreadPool and CachedThreadPool depends on the specific requirements of the application. For applications where resource use needs to be predictable and controlled, FixedThreadPool is more appropriate. For applications that experience variable workloads and can handle dynamic thread management, CachedThreadPool offers greater flexibility.

Understanding these two thread pool configurations aids in optimizing performance and resource management in concurrent Java applications. Each pool type presents trade-offs and choosing the right type involves considering factors such as workload characteristics, resource constraints, and performance requirements.

5.4 SingleThreadExecutor and ScheduledThreadPool

Single-thread executors and scheduled thread pools are integral components of the Executors Framework, offering distinct functionalities for managing tasks. Both of these executors serve specific use cases and scenarios, which can enhance the efficiency and control of thread management within an application.

SingleThreadExecutor ensures that tasks are executed sequentially in a single worker thread. This can be particularly useful when tasks are required to be performed one at a time. Here is how to create and use a SingleThreadExecutor:

```
import java.util.concurrent.ExecutorService;
import java.util.concurrent.Executors;

public class SingleThreadExecutorExample {
    public static void main(String[] args) {
        ExecutorService executor = Executors.newSingleThreadExecutor();
        for (int i = 0; i < 5; i++) {
            executor.submit(() -> {
                String threadName = Thread.currentThread().getName();
                System.out.println("Executing task in: " + threadName);
            });
        }
        executor.shutdown();
    }
}
```

The output will demonstrate that all tasks are executed by a single thread:

```
Executing task in: pool-1-thread-1
Executing task in: pool-1-thread-1
Executing task in: pool-1-thread-1
Executing task in: pool-1-thread-1
Executing task in: pool-1-thread-1
```

SingleThreadExecutor guarantees a strong ordering of task execution, which is vital in applications where tasks must not run concurrently to avoid shared resource conflicts.

ScheduledThreadPool is used when tasks need to be executed periodically or after a certain delay. The ScheduledExecutorService interface extends ExecutorService and provides methods for scheduling commands to run after a given delay or periodically.

To create a scheduled thread pool, you can use the factory method:

```
import java.util.concurrent.Executors;
import java.util.concurrent.ScheduledExecutorService;
import java.util.concurrent.TimeUnit;

public class ScheduledThreadPoolExample {
    public static void main(String[] args) {
        ScheduledExecutorService scheduler = Executors.newScheduledThreadPool(1);

        Runnable task = () -> System.out.println("Executing at " + System.
            currentTimeMillis());

        // Schedule task to run after 3 seconds
        scheduler.schedule(task, 3, TimeUnit.SECONDS);

        // Schedule task to run at a fixed rate
        scheduler.scheduleAtFixedRate(task, 1, 3, TimeUnit.SECONDS);

        // Schedule task to run with fixed delay
        scheduler.scheduleWithFixedDelay(task, 1, 3, TimeUnit.SECONDS);
    }
}
```

Each of the scheduling methods provided by ScheduledExecutorService fulfills a different requirement:

- schedule(Runnable command, long delay, TimeUnit unit): Schedules a one-time task to run after the given delay.
- scheduleAtFixedRate(Runnable command, long initialDelay, long period, TimeUnit unit): Schedules a task to run initially after the given initial delay and subsequently with a fixed period between the start of each execution.
- scheduleWithFixedDelay(Runnable command, long initialDelay, long delay, TimeUnit unit): Schedules a task to run initially after the given initial delay and subsequently with the given delay between the termination of one execution and the commencement of the next execution.

The sample application schedules tasks using these methods, and the output will indicate their execution times. Here is a potential output snippet focusing on periodic execution:

```
Executing at 1609459203000
Executing at 1609459204000
Executing at 1609459207000
Executing at 1609459210000
```

In practice, ScheduledThreadPool is instrumental in scenarios such as:

- Periodically polling resources or services.
- Timeout management.
- Periodic maintenance tasks (e.g., clearing caches, updating status).

Both SingleThreadExecutor and ScheduledThreadPool exhibit deterministic behavior by adhering to thread invocation policies, ensuring that developers can meticulously manage the execution context of their tasks.

5.5 Callable and Future Interfaces

The Callable and Future interfaces play crucial roles in managing asynchronous task execution within the Java concurrency framework. The Callable interface is a functional interface that represents a task that returns a result and may throw a checked exception. This is in contrast to the Runnable interface, which represents tasks that do not return a result and cannot throw a checked exception.

A task implemented using the Callable interface must implement the call() method. The call() method is analogous to the run() method defined by the Runnable interface but with notable differences in its signature:

```
import java.util.concurrent.Callable;

public class MyCallableTask implements Callable<String> {
    @Override
    public String call() throws Exception {
        // Perform some computation
        return "Result of the computation";
    }
}
```

An instance of MyCallableTask can be submitted to an ExecutorService for execution. Upon submission, the ExecutorService returns an instance of the Future interface. This Future object acts as a placeholder for the result of the Callable task. The Future interface provides methods to check the status of the task, retrieve the result, and cancel the execution of the task.

Key methods provided by the Future interface include:

- get() - Retrieves the result of the computation, waiting if necessary for the task to complete.
- cancel(boolean mayInterruptIfRunning) - Attempts to cancel the execution of the task.
- isCancelled() - Returns true if the task was cancelled before it completed normally.
- isDone() - Returns true if the task completed.

Consider the following example that demonstrates the usage of Callable and Future interfaces:

```
import java.util.concurrent.Callable;
import java.util.concurrent.ExecutionException;
import java.util.concurrent.ExecutorService;
import java.util.concurrent.Executors;
import java.util.concurrent.Future;

public class CallableFutureExample {
    public static void main(String[] args) {
        ExecutorService executorService = Executors.newSingleThreadExecutor();
        Callable<String> callableTask = new MyCallableTask();

        Future<String> future = executorService.submit(callableTask);

        try {
            // Perform other tasks if needed
            String result = future.get(); // Blocking call, waits if necessary
            System.out.println("Result from callableTask: " + result);
        } catch (InterruptedException | ExecutionException e) {
            e.printStackTrace();
        } finally {
            executorService.shutdown();
        }
    }
}
```

In the above example, the CallableFutureExample class submits an instance of MyCallableTask to the ExecutorService. The submit() method returns a Future instance representing the pending result of the task. The get() method of the Future instance blocks until the computation completes and the result can be retrieved.

It is essential to handle the InterruptedException and ExecutionException that may be thrown by the get() method. InterruptedException is thrown if the current thread is interrupted while waiting for the computation to complete. ExecutionException is thrown if the computation threw an exception.

The Future interface also provides additional control over the task execution. For instance, one can cancel the task using the cancel(boolean mayInterruptIfRunning) method. When mayInterruptIfRunning is set to true, the task is interrupted if it is currently running. Otherwise, if mayInterruptIfRunning is false, the task is allowed to complete if it has already started. The cancellation status can be checked using the isCancelled() method, which returns true if the task was cancelled before it completed.

The isDone() method is useful for polling purposes. It returns true if the task has completed, regardless of whether it completed successfully or was cancelled.

The combination of Callable and Future interfaces enables more flexible task management, allowing tasks to return results and support exception handling and cancellation. This is particularly useful in applications where tasks may need to report significant computation results or when managing a pool of tasks with varying priorities and execution times.

5.6 Submitting Tasks to ExecutorService

When working with the ExecutorService, tasks can be submitted for execution in various ways, primarily through the execute and submit methods. Understanding these mechanisms is crucial for efficient task management and execution in concurrent applications.

The execute Method

The execute method is part of the Executor interface, which ExecutorService extends. This method accepts a single Runnable argument and is typically used for tasks that do not return a result. Tasks submitted using execute are run asynchronously.

```
ExecutorService executorService = Executors.newFixedThreadPool(5);
executorService.execute(new Runnable() {
    @Override
    public void run() {
        System.out.println("Task executed using execute");
    }
});
executorService.shutdown();
```

In this example, a fixed thread pool of five threads is created. The execute method submits a Runnable task that prints a message to the console. Once the task is submitted, shutdown is called to prevent new tasks from being submitted.

The submit Method

The submit method, belonging to the ExecutorService interface, is more versatile. It accepts both Runnable and Callable tasks, offering greater flexibility by enabling tasks that return a result or throw a checked exception. The submit method returns a Future object, allowing further interaction with the task's execution and result.

- submit(Runnable task): Submits a Runnable task and returns a Future<?>. The Future's get method will return null upon successful completion.
- submit(Runnable task, T result): Submits a Runnable task and returns a Future<T> representing the given result upon completion.
- submit(Callable<T> task): Submits a Callable<T> task and returns a Future<T> representing the task's computations.

```
Runnable task = new Runnable() {
    @Override
    public void run() {
        System.out.println("Runnable task executed using submit");
    }
};
Future<?> runnableResult = executorService.submit(task);

Callable<Integer> callableTask = new Callable<Integer>() {
    @Override
    public Integer call() {
        return 42;
    }
};
Future<Integer> callableResult = executorService.submit(callableTask);

try {
    runnableResult.get(); // Returns null if task completed successfully
    Integer result = callableResult.get(); // Returns the result of the Callable
    System.out.println("Callable task result: " + result);
} catch (InterruptedException | ExecutionException e) {
    e.printStackTrace();
}
executorService.shutdown();
```

In the above code snippet, a Runnable task and a Callable<Integer> task are submitted to the ExecutorService. The submit method is used, which returns Future objects enabling synchronous waiting for task completions and retrieving results. The get method of Future is then invoked to block until the tasks are complete and their results are available.

Handling Properties of Future

The Future interface provides several key methods to interact with the asynchronous task execution.

- isCancelled(): Returns true if the task was cancelled before it completed normally.
- isDone(): Returns true if the task is completed.
- cancel(boolean mayInterruptIfRunning): Attempts to cancel execution of the task.
- get(): Waits if necessary for the computation to complete and then retrieves its result.
- get(long timeout, TimeUnit unit): Waits if necessary for at most the given time for the computation to complete and then retrieves its result.

```
Future<Integer> futureTask = executorService.submit(callableTask);

if (!futureTask.isDone()) {
    System.out.println("Task is not yet done.");
}

Integer result = null;
try {
    result = futureTask.get(1, TimeUnit.SECONDS);
} catch (TimeoutException e) {
    System.out.println("Task timed out.");
}

if (result != null) {
    System.out.println("Task completed with result: " + result);
}

if (!futureTask.isCancelled()) {
    futureTask.cancel(true);
}
executorService.shutdown();
```

This example illustrates the use of isDone, get with timeout, and cancel methods of Future. It checks if the task is done, waits for a result with a timeout, prints the result if available, and attempts to cancel the task if it is still running. This approach ensures efficient handling and monitoring of task execution within an ExecutorService.

These mechanisms of task submission and management via the ExecutorService are critical for effective concurrency control and resource management in Java, facilitating robust multi-threaded application development.

5.7 Shutting Down Executors

Effectively shutting down executors is crucial to ensure that all tasks are completed, system resources are efficiently reclaimed, and the application terminates gracefully. The ExecutorService provides several methods for shutting down executors programmatically.

Shutdown Methods: The ExecutorService interface offers two primary shutdown methods:

- shutdown()
- shutdownNow()

```
ExecutorService executor = Executors.newFixedThreadPool(2);
executor.submit(() -> {
    // Task details here
});
executor.shutdown();
```

The shutdown() method initiates an orderly shutdown in which previously submitted tasks are executed, but no new tasks will be accepted. Tasks that are already in the queue will continue to run, but any attempt to submit new tasks will result in a RejectedExecutionException. This method does not block the calling thread; the shutdown process is asynchronous.

```
ExecutorService executor = Executors.newFixedThreadPool(2);
executor.submit(() -> {
    // Task details here
});
List<Runnable> notExecutedTasks = executor.shutdownNow();
```

The shutdownNow() method attempts to stop all actively executing tasks, halts the processing of waiting tasks, and returns a list of the tasks that were waiting to be executed. It uses the interrupt mechanism to attempt to stop tasks that are currently being executed. However, there is no guarantee that a task can be terminated successfully, especially if it is not responding to interrupts.

Awaiting Termination: It is often necessary to wait for the executor to complete its shutdown process. This can be done using the awaitTermination method. This method blocks the calling thread until either the executor has completed the shutdown process or the given timeout period elapses.

```
executor.shutdown();
try {
```

```
    if (!executor.awaitTermination(60, TimeUnit.SECONDS)) {
        executor.shutdownNow();
    }
} catch (InterruptedException e) {
    executor.shutdownNow();
    Thread.currentThread().interrupt();
}
```

In the provided code snippet, awaitTermination(60, TimeUnit.SECONDS) waits up to 60 seconds for the executor to terminate. If it does not terminate within this time frame, the shutdownNow() method is invoked to forcefully terminate the executor. It is critical to handle InterruptedException appropriately to ensure that the current thread's interrupt status is not lost.

Best Practices for Executor Shutdown:

- Always shut down executors when they are no longer needed to free system resources.
- Prefer shutdown() over shutdownNow() to allow for an orderly shutdown when possible.
- Use awaitTermination() after shutdown() to ensure that all tasks are completed before proceeding.
- Handle InterruptedException properly to maintain thread interrupt status.

Example: Graceful Shutdown with ExecutorService

```
public class GracefulShutdownExample {
    public static void main(String[] args) {
        ExecutorService executor = Executors.newFixedThreadPool(2);

        for (int i = 0; i < 5; i++) {
            executor.submit(new Task(i));
        }

        executor.shutdown();

        try {
            if (!executor.awaitTermination(60, TimeUnit.SECONDS)) {
                executor.shutdownNow();
                if (!executor.awaitTermination(60, TimeUnit.SECONDS)) {
                    System.err.println("Executor did not terminate");
                }
            }
        } catch (InterruptedException e) {
            executor.shutdownNow();
            Thread.currentThread().interrupt();
        }
    }
```

```
    static class Task implements Runnable {
        private final int taskId;

        Task(int id) {
            this.taskId = id;
        }

        @Override
        public void run() {
            try {
                System.out.println("Executing task " + taskId);
                Thread.sleep(2000);
            } catch (InterruptedException e) {
                System.out.println("Task " + taskId + " was interrupted");
                Thread.currentThread().interrupt();
            }
        }
    }
}
```

This example creates a fixed thread pool with two threads and submits five tasks. The tasks simulate long-running operations using Thread.sleep(). After submitting the tasks, the executor is shut down gracefully. The awaitTermination() method ensures the main thread waits for up to 60 seconds for the executor to terminate. If the executor does not terminate within this period, shutdownNow() is called followed by a second awaitTermination().

Handling Exceptions during Shutdown: Exception handling during shutdown is crucial to dealing with interrupted tasks. Proper handling ensures that tasks can safely handle interrupts and that the main thread's interrupt status is preserved when it encounters an InterruptedException during shutdown.

By following the recommended practices for shutting down executors, applications can manage threads more effectively, ensuring that resources are properly cleaned up and that the application terminates as expected.

5.8 Handling Exceptions in Executors

When working with the Executors Framework, handling exceptions effectively is crucial to ensure robust and reliable concurrent applications. This section delves into how exceptions can be managed when tasks are executed within an ExecutorService.

In Java, when a task submitted to an ExecutorService throws an exception, it is important to handle that exception correctly to avoid unintended application behavior. The primary mechanisms for dealing with exceptions in the Executors Framework involve using the Future interface and customizing ThreadPoolExecutor.

Consider a scenario where a Callable task throws an exception. When the task is submitted to an ExecutorService, the exception can be captured and processed using Future. The following example demonstrates this:

```
import java.util.concurrent.*;

public class ExceptionHandlingExample {
    public static void main(String[] args) {
        ExecutorService executor = Executors.newFixedThreadPool(2);

        Callable<String> callableTask = () -> {
            if (true) {
                throw new IllegalArgumentException("Task Exception");
            }
            return "Task Completed";
        };

        Future<String> future = executor.submit(callableTask);

        try {
            String result = future.get();
        } catch (InterruptedException | ExecutionException e) {
            System.out.println("Exception: " + e.getCause().getMessage());
        }

        executor.shutdown();
    }
}
```

In this example, the Callable task throws an IllegalArgumentException. When the task is executed, the exception is encapsulated within an ExecutionException. By calling Future.get(), the exception is propagated to the calling thread, where it can be handled appropriately. The use of e.getCause().getMessage() helps in identifying the underlying exception cause.

In addition to handling exceptions through Future, the ThreadPoolExecutor allows for more granular exception handling by customizing its afterExecute method. This method provides a hook for processing any exceptions thrown by tasks. Here's a demonstration:

```
import java.util.concurrent.*;

public class CustomThreadPoolExecutor extends ThreadPoolExecutor {
    public CustomThreadPoolExecutor(int corePoolSize, int maximumPoolSize, long
            keepAliveTime, TimeUnit unit, BlockingQueue<Runnable> workQueue) {
        super(corePoolSize, maximumPoolSize, keepAliveTime, unit, workQueue);
    }

    @Override
```

```
    protected void afterExecute(Runnable r, Throwable t) {
        super.afterExecute(r, t);
        if (t != null) {
            System.out.println("Runnable Task Exception: " + t.getMessage());
        }

        if (r instanceof Future<?>) {
            try {
                ((Future<?>) r).get();
            } catch (CancellationException ce) {
                System.out.println("Task was cancelled");
            } catch (ExecutionException ee) {
                System.out.println("Execution Exception: " + ee.getCause().getMessage
                    ());
            } catch (InterruptedException ie) {
                Thread.currentThread().interrupt();
            }
        }
    }

    public static void main(String[] args) {
        BlockingQueue<Runnable> queue = new ArrayBlockingQueue<>(10);
        CustomThreadPoolExecutor executor = new CustomThreadPoolExecutor(2, 4,
             1, TimeUnit.MINUTES, queue);

        Callable<String> callableTask = () -> {
            if (true) {
                throw new IllegalArgumentException("Task Exception");
            }
            return "Task Completed";
        };

        executor.submit(callableTask);
        executor.shutdown();
    }
}
```

In this tailored ThreadPoolExecutor class, the afterExecute method overrides the default behavior. By inspecting the Runnable parameter and checking if it is an instance of Future, the method can attempt to call Future.get() and handle any resulting exceptions such as CancellationException, ExecutionException, or InterruptedException.

Additionally, exception handling strategies need to consider proper logging for debugging and operational monitoring. Using logging frameworks like Log4j or SLF4J ensures that exception details are appropriately captured.

Another approach to managing exceptions in Runnable tasks involves wrapping tasks in a try-catch block within the Runnable. This approach allows you to handle exceptions within the task body explicitly:

```
import java.util.concurrent.ExecutorService;
import java.util.concurrent.Executors;

public class ExceptionHandlingRunnableExample {
    public static void main(String[] args) {
```

```
        ExecutorService executor = Executors.newFixedThreadPool(2);

        Runnable runnableTask = () -> {
            try {
                if (true) {
                    throw new IllegalArgumentException("Task Exception");
                }
                System.out.println("Task Completed");
            } catch (Exception e) {
                System.out.println("Caught Exception in Runnable: " + e.getMessage());
            }
        };

        executor.submit(runnableTask);
        executor.shutdown();
    }
}
```

Here, the Runnable task itself manages exceptions by wrapping its content in a try-catch block. This localized exception handling is suitable for simpler error processing needs and ensures that exceptions are handled close to their point of origin.

Properly handling exceptions within the Executors Framework not only improves application reliability but also aids in debugging. By identifying and managing exceptions effectively, applications can recover from errors gracefully or alert developers and operations teams to issues requiring attention.

5.9 ScheduledExecutorService for Timed and Periodic Tasks

The ScheduledExecutorService extends the ExecutorService interface and provides the ability to schedule tasks to execute after a given delay or to execute periodically. This feature is particularly useful for situations requiring repeated execution of tasks at fixed intervals or for tasks that should start execution after a specific time delay. The ScheduledExecutorService can be created using factory methods available in the Executors class.

The following code example demonstrates how to create a ScheduledExecutorService:

```
ScheduledExecutorService scheduledExecutorService = Executors.
    newScheduledThreadPool(5);
```

In the above code, a ScheduledExecutorService is created with a pool of 5 threads. This pool can handle concurrent execution of scheduled tasks.

ScheduledExecutorService provides methods like schedule, scheduleAtFixedRate, and scheduleWithFixedDelay for scheduling tasks:

- schedule: Executes a one-shot action that becomes enabled after a given delay.
- scheduleAtFixedRate: Repeatedly executes a task with a fixed period between consecutive executions.
- scheduleWithFixedDelay: Repeatedly executes a task with a fixed delay between the termination of one execution and the commencement of the next.

Here are the method signatures:

```
<V> ScheduledFuture<V> schedule(Callable<V> callable, long delay, TimeUnit unit)
    ;

ScheduledFuture<?> schedule(Runnable command, long delay, TimeUnit unit);

ScheduledFuture<?> scheduleAtFixedRate(Runnable command, long initialDelay, long
    period, TimeUnit unit);

ScheduledFuture<?> scheduleWithFixedDelay(Runnable command, long initialDelay,
    long delay, TimeUnit unit);
```

Example of Delayed Task Execution

To schedule a task with a one-time delay, the schedule method can be used as follows:

```
ScheduledExecutorService scheduler = Executors.newScheduledThreadPool(1);

Runnable task = () -> System.out.println("Executing task after delay");
scheduler.schedule(task, 5, TimeUnit.SECONDS);
```

In this example, the task will execute after a delay of 5 seconds. The delay is specified in the TimeUnit.SECONDS.

Scheduling a Task at Fixed Rate

To schedule a task that executes periodically with a fixed rate, use the scheduleAtFixedRate method. This method starts the task after an initial delay and subsequently with a fixed period:

```
ScheduledExecutorService scheduler = Executors.newScheduledThreadPool(1);

Runnable periodicTask = () -> System.out.println("Periodic task execution");
scheduler.scheduleAtFixedRate(periodicTask, 0, 10, TimeUnit.SECONDS);
```

In this example, the task begins execution immediately (initial delay of 0) and repeats every 10 seconds. Note that if the task execution exceeds the period duration, the next execution will still wait for the current task to complete.

Scheduling a Task with Fixed Delay

To schedule a task that executes with a fixed delay between the end of one execution and the start of the next, use the scheduleWithFixedDelay method:

```
ScheduledExecutorService scheduler = Executors.newScheduledThreadPool(1);

Runnable delayedTask = () -> System.out.println("Delayed task execution");
scheduler.scheduleWithFixedDelay(delayedTask, 0, 5, TimeUnit.SECONDS);
```

In this example, the task starts immediately and then repeats with a 5-second delay between the end of one execution and the start of the next.

Handling Exceptions in Scheduled Tasks

Scheduled tasks can also throw exceptions during their execution. It is essential to handle these exceptions to prevent thread termination within the pool. The ScheduledExecutorService will attempt to re-execute tasks that have failed due to runtime exceptions. To manage exceptions, wrapping the task in a try-catch block is advisable:

```
ScheduledExecutorService scheduler = Executors.newScheduledThreadPool(1);

Runnable exceptionTask = () -> {
    try {
        System.out.println("Executing task");
        // Task implementation that might throw an exception
    } catch (Exception e) {
        System.err.println("Task encountered an exception: " + e.getMessage());
    }
};
scheduler.scheduleAtFixedRate(exceptionTask, 0, 10, TimeUnit.SECONDS);
```

Cancelling Scheduled Tasks

Tasks scheduled with ScheduledExecutorService can be cancelled or interrupted. The methods cancel and shutdown are used for these purposes. The shutdown method will prevent new tasks from being submitted, but previously submitted tasks will continue to execute:

```
ScheduledExecutorService scheduler = Executors.newScheduledThreadPool(1);

Runnable task = () -> System.out.println("Running scheduled task");
ScheduledFuture<?> future = scheduler.scheduleAtFixedRate(task, 0, 10, TimeUnit.
    SECONDS);
```

```
try {
    TimeUnit.SECONDS.sleep(30);
} catch (InterruptedException e) {
    e.printStackTrace();
}

future.cancel(true); // Cancel the scheduled task
scheduler.shutdown(); // Shutdown the scheduler
```

In this code snippet, the scheduled task is cancelled after 30 seconds, and the ScheduledExecutorService is shut down, ensuring no new tasks are accepted, but all ongoing tasks are allowed to finish.

By effectively utilizing ScheduledExecutorService, developers can manage timed and periodic task execution with precision and reliability, essential for tasks requiring scheduled intervals or specific delay timings.

5.10 ForkJoinPool vs ExecutorService

The distinction between ForkJoinPool and ExecutorService is pivotal for optimizing concurrent task management. Both are part of the java.util.concurrent framework, each tailored to specific scenarios.

ForkJoinPool is designed for tasks that can be recursively broken down into smaller subtasks, adhering to the divide-and-conquer paradigm. This is particularly effective for algorithms that exhibit recursive characteristics, such as those found in parallel computing and multi-core processors optimization. On the other hand, ExecutorService provides a higher-level API for managing a pool of threads, suitable for general task execution without inherent parallelism knowledge.

Task Decomposition in ForkJoinPool

ForkJoinPool utilizes work-stealing algorithms, where idle workers can "steal" tasks from busy workers, thereby optimizing CPU utilization. Tasks are represented by RecursiveTask<V> or RecursiveAction. The former returns a result, while the latter does not. For example, consider a recursive task for computing Fibonacci numbers:

```
import java.util.concurrent.RecursiveTask;

public class FibonacciTask extends RecursiveTask<Integer> {
    private final int n;

    public FibonacciTask(int n) {
        this.n = n;
    }

    @Override
```

```
    protected Integer compute() {
        if (n <= 1) {
            return n;
        }
        FibonacciTask task1 = new FibonacciTask(n - 1);
        task1.fork(); // Forks the task into a separate thread
        FibonacciTask task2 = new FibonacciTask(n - 2);
        int result = task2.compute() + task1.join(); // Joins the first forked task
        return result;
    }
}
```

In this example, the compute method checks if the task is simple enough to solve directly (n <= 1), otherwise, it splits the task into smaller subtasks. The fork method asynchronously executes one subtask, while the other is handled by the current thread. The join method waits for and retrieves the result of the forked task.

Executions in ForkJoinPool leverage work-stealing to balance the load among worker threads, efficiently utilizing available processors.

Thread Management in ExecutorService

ExecutorService provides mechanisms to manage a pool of threads and task execution without explicitly handling thread lifecycle. It supports different thread pool implementations, such as FixedThreadPool, CachedThreadPool, SingleThreadExecutor, and ScheduledThreadPool. For instance, a fixed-size thread pool can be created as follows:

```
import java.util.concurrent.ExecutorService;
import java.util.concurrent.Executors;
import java.util.concurrent.TimeUnit;

public class FixedThreadPoolExample {
    public static void main(String[] args) {
        ExecutorService executor = Executors.newFixedThreadPool(4); // Create
            thread pool with 4 threads
        for (int i = 0; i < 10; i++) {
            Runnable task = new Task(i);
            executor.execute(task);
        }
        executor.shutdown(); // Initiates an orderly shutdown
        try {
            if (!executor.awaitTermination(60, TimeUnit.SECONDS)) {
                executor.shutdownNow(); // Force termination if tasks do not complete
            }
        } catch (InterruptedException ex) {
            executor.shutdownNow();
        }
    }
}
```

Here, tasks are submitted to the ExecutorService, which allocates them to a fixed pool of threads. The shutdown() method ensures proper termination, and awaitTermination() waits for tasks to complete within a given timeout.

Comparative Analysis

The primary distinction between ForkJoinPool and ExecutorService lies in their usage patterns and internal mechanisms:

- ForkJoinPool is specialized for recursive task decomposition. It is best applied in scenarios where tasks can recursively split themselves into smaller tasks, leveraging the work-stealing algorithm for efficiency.
- ExecutorService, on the other hand, provides a versatile framework for managing threads. It is ideal for tasks that do not necessarily involve parallel recursive decomposition but benefit from concurrent execution.
- ForkJoinPool allows tasks to dynamically steal work, thereby adapting to varying workloads dynamically. ExecutorService requires predefined thread management strategies, such as fixed or cached thread pools.
- In terms of performance, ForkJoinPool may outperform ExecutorService in divide-and-conquer scenarios due to reduced contention and enhanced load balancing through work-stealing. Conversely, ExecutorService offers straightforward and flexible task management without the intricacies of load balancing logic.

The decision between ForkJoinPool and ExecutorService should be guided by the nature of the tasks at hand. For recursive, parallelizable tasks, ForkJoinPool offers significant performance gains. For broader task management needs, ExecutorService delivers a more general-purpose solution. Both frameworks are integral to the java.util.concurrent package, enabling robust and scalable concurrency models in Java applications.

Chapter 6

Fork/Join Framework

This chapter explores the Fork/Join Framework, which is designed for parallel processing by recursively breaking down tasks into smaller subtasks. It covers creating a ForkJoinPool and utilizing RecursiveTask and RecursiveAction for splitting tasks. The chapter explains the lifecycle of ForkJoinTask and the strategies for efficient split/join operations. It includes performance optimizations, real-world use cases, and examples, as well as guidance on monitoring and tuning Fork/Join applications to achieve high scalability and efficiency.

6.1 Introduction to Fork/Join Framework

The Fork/Join Framework is a powerful tool in Java designed specifically for parallel processing by decomposing tasks into smaller, manageable subtasks. This approach not only leverages multi-core processors but also maximizes the efficiency and scalability of applications. At its core, the Fork/Join Framework is predicated on the divide-and-conquer algorithmic paradigm, which recursively breaks down a problem into subproblems until they are simple enough to be solved directly. These solutions are then combined to address the initial problem.

The Fork/Join Framework comprises three key components: ForkJoinPool, ForkJoinTask, and the two abstract classes RecursiveTask and RecursiveAction. Understanding these components is crucial for mastering the framework. Each plays a distinct role in simplifying the parallelization of computational tasks.

A ForkJoinPool is a specialized implementation of the ExecutorService interface. It manages a pool of worker threads responsible for executing instances of ForkJoinTask. The pool dynamically adjusts the number of threads based on the workload, aiming to maintain an optimal level of parallelism. The pool uses a work-stealing algorithm, where idle threads can 'steal' tasks from busy threads, thus balancing the load and enhancing performance.

ForkJoinTask is the base class for tasks executed within a ForkJoinPool. It provides methods for checking the status of tasks, joining tasks to aggregate results, and handling exceptions. It is important to note that ForkJoinTask itself is an abstract class, necessitating the use of its concrete subclasses: RecursiveTask and RecursiveAction.

RecursiveTask is an abstract class used for tasks that return a result. When implementing RecursiveTask, the compute() method must be overridden to define the logic for splitting tasks and joining results.

```
public class CustomRecursiveTask extends RecursiveTask<Integer> {
    @Override
    protected Integer compute() {
        // Task splitting and execution logic
    }
}
```

RecursiveAction is the counterpart to RecursiveTask, designed for tasks that do not return a result. Like RecursiveTask, it requires overriding the compute() method.

```
public class CustomRecursiveAction extends RecursiveAction {
    @Override
    protected void compute() {
        // Task splitting and execution logic
    }
}
```

The compute() method in both RecursiveTask and RecursiveAction is where the task is divided into subtasks. The fork() method is used to asynchronously execute a subtask, and join() is used to wait for the completion of a subtask and retrieve its result. By repeatedly forking and joining subtasks, the framework ensures that work is efficiently distributed among the available threads.

An essential aspect of the Fork/Join Framework is its approach to dividing tasks. A common strategy involves setting a threshold, a problem size small enough to be solved sequentially. If the task size exceeds this threshold, it is split into smaller subtasks. This recursive splitting continues until the task size falls below the threshold. The threshold value significantly affects performance and must be carefully chosen based on the specific problem and system architecture.

```
private static final int THRESHOLD = 10;

public class CustomRecursiveTask extends RecursiveTask<Integer> {
    private final int[] array;
    private final int start, end;

    public CustomRecursiveTask(int[] array, int start, int end) {
        this.array = array;
        this.start = start;
        this.end = end;
    }

    @Override
    protected Integer compute() {
        if (end - start <= THRESHOLD) {
            return computeDirectly();
        } else {
            int mid = (start + end) / 2;
            CustomRecursiveTask leftTask = new CustomRecursiveTask(array, start,
                 mid);
            CustomRecursiveTask rightTask = new CustomRecursiveTask(array, mid,
                 end);
            leftTask.fork(); // asynchronously execute leftTask
            int rightResult = rightTask.compute(); // directly execute rightTask
            int leftResult = leftTask.join(); // wait and retrieve result of leftTask
            return leftResult + rightResult; // combine results of subtasks
        }
    }

    private Integer computeDirectly() {
        int sum = 0;
        for (int i = start; i < end; i++) {
            sum += array[i];
        }
        return sum;
    }
}
```

The provided code snippet illustrates a typical implementation of RecursiveTask. The task is to sum elements of an integer array. If the task size is below the threshold, it is computed directly using the computeDirectly() method. Otherwise, the task is split into two subtasks, each handling a portion of the array. The left subtask is forked and executed asynchronously, while the right subtask is executed synchronously. Finally, the results of both subtasks are joined and combined.

Understanding the intricacies of the Fork/Join Framework forms the foundation for mastering parallel computing in Java. The subsequent sections will delve deeper into the lifecycle of ForkJoinTask, efficient split/join strategies, performance optimizations, and real-world examples to consolidate your knowledge and skills in leveraging this powerful framework.

6.2 Parallelism vs Concurrency

Parallelism and concurrency are key concepts in computer science that, although related, have distinct characteristics and applications. Their understanding is crucial when working with the Fork/Join Framework, as it utilizes both to achieve efficient task execution. This section aims to clarify these concepts, elucidating their implications and importance within the context of the Fork/Join Framework.

Parallelism involves performing multiple operations simultaneously, leveraging multiple cores or processors to speed up computational tasks. This is most beneficial in situations where tasks are independent and can run simultaneously without interdependency. Parallelism exploits the hardware's ability to execute multiple threads or processes in parallel, thereby reducing computation time significantly.

For example, consider a task that involves sorting a large array. By breaking the array into smaller sub-arrays and sorting each sub-array in parallel using multiple processors, the overall sorting time can be reduced. The Fork/Join Framework facilitates this by enabling the task to be divided (forked) into smaller subtasks, each of which can be processed concurrently, and then combining (joining) the results.

On the other hand, concurrency refers to the ability of a program to deal with multiple tasks by managing their execution without necessarily running them simultaneously. Concurrency involves task scheduling and context switching, ensuring that multiple tasks make progress over time. It's a higher-level concept where the focus is on structuring a program to handle multiple operations, possibly overlapping in duration, but not necessarily executing at the same instant.

To illustrate concurrency, consider a web server handling multiple client requests. The server may not process each request in parallel but will interleave processing steps to handle multiple connections effectively. This involves suspending one task, switching to another, and eventually resuming the suspended task. Concurrency is essential in scenarios where tasks might need to wait for external resources, such as I/O operations, allowing other tasks to utilize the CPU during these wait times.

In the context of Java's Fork/Join Framework, understanding the distinction between parallelism and concurrency is pivotal. The Fork/Join

Framework primarily aims at parallelism by breaking down tasks into subtasks that are processed in parallel using a pool of worker threads managed by a 'ForkJoinPool'. However, it also needs to handle concurrency to manage the execution of these subtasks efficiently, ensuring elasticity and scalability.

Consider the implementation using RecursiveTask and RecursiveAction in the Fork/Join Framework. These classes encapsulate the tasks that are designed to be split into smaller units recursively. Below is an example of a simple fork/join task using RecursiveTask:

```
import java.util.concurrent.RecursiveTask;

public class SumTask extends RecursiveTask<Integer> {
    private static final int THRESHOLD = 10;
    private final int[] array;
    private final int start, end;

    public SumTask(int[] array, int start, int end) {
        this.array = array;
        this.start = start;
        this.end = end;
    }

    @Override
    protected Integer compute() {
        if (end - start <= THRESHOLD) {
            int sum = 0;
            for (int i = start; i < end; i++) {
                sum += array[i];
            }
            return sum;
        } else {
            int mid = (start + end) / 2;
            SumTask leftTask = new SumTask(array, start, mid);
            SumTask rightTask = new SumTask(array, mid, end);
            leftTask.fork();
            int rightResult = rightTask.compute();
            int leftResult = leftTask.join();
            return leftResult + rightResult;
        }
    }
}
```

In this code snippet, the SumTask class demonstrates parallelism by dividing the array into smaller chunks and processing these chunks in parallel once the threshold condition is met. The framework automatically handles the task splitting and merging, leveraging the underlying hardware for parallel processing.

To execute this task, a ForkJoinPool is employed:

```
import java.util.concurrent.ForkJoinPool;

public class Main {
    public static void main(String[] args) {
```

```
        int[] array = new int[100];
        for (int i = 0; i < array.length; i++) {
            array[i] = i + 1;
        }

        ForkJoinPool forkJoinPool = new ForkJoinPool();
        SumTask sumTask = new SumTask(array, 0, array.length);
        int result = forkJoinPool.invoke(sumTask);

        System.out.println("Sum: " + result);
    }
}
```

```
Sum: 5050
```

The above execution showcases parallelism in action, where the sum of an array is computed by partitioning and processing sub-arrays concurrently.

Recognizing the distinctions between parallelism and concurrency allows for better optimization of the Fork/Join Framework. Parallelism focuses on decomposing tasks to leverage multi-core processors optimally. Meanwhile, concurrency deals with the organization and management of these tasks to ensure efficient execution. Effective utilization of both enables the development of robust and high-performance applications.

6.3 Creating a ForkJoinPool

The ForkJoinPool is central to achieving efficient parallelism in Java's Fork/Join Framework. This class is a specialized implementation of the ExecutorService designed to accommodate the execution of large numbers of small tasks.

Creating a ForkJoinPool can be done either by using its default constructor, which creates a pool with a parallelism level equal to the number of available processors, or by specifying the desired level of parallelism directly.

```
ForkJoinPool pool = new ForkJoinPool();
```

This will create a ForkJoinPool instance that uses a parallelism level determined by Runtime.getRuntime().availableProcessors(). The parallelism level indicates the number of worker threads that will be utilized by the pool.

Alternatively, you can create a ForkJoinPool with a specific parallelism level by passing the level as an argument to the constructor.

```
int parallelismLevel = 4; // Adjust according to workload
ForkJoinPool customPool = new ForkJoinPool(parallelismLevel);
```

It's essential to choose an appropriate parallelism level based on the workload and the number of available CPU cores. A higher level may lead to excessive context switching, while a lower level might not fully utilize the available processing power.

The ForkJoinPool can execute subclasses of ForkJoinTask, namely RecursiveTask and RecursiveAction. To submit a ForkJoinTask to the pool, you can use methods such as invoke(), submit(), or execute().

```
class MyRecursiveTask extends RecursiveTask<Integer> {
    @Override
    protected Integer compute() {
        // Task logic here
        return 1;
    }
}

ForkJoinPool pool = new ForkJoinPool();
MyRecursiveTask task = new MyRecursiveTask();
int result = pool.invoke(task);
```

In the above example, the invoke() method is used to submit the task to the ForkJoinPool and wait for its completion. This method blocks until the task is finished, returning the result.

Another method, execute(), can be used to submit tasks non-blockingly.

```
ForkJoinPool pool = new ForkJoinPool();
MyRecursiveAction action = new MyRecursiveAction();
pool.execute(action);
```

The execute() method does not return a result since it is designed for tasks that do not produce a specific outcome (as RecursiveAction).

Furthermore, the submit() method, which can handle both Callable and Runnable tasks, offers a compromise between invoke() and execute().

```
ForkJoinPool pool = new ForkJoinPool();
MyRecursiveTask task = new MyRecursiveTask();
Future<Integer> future = pool.submit(task);
int result = future.get(); // Blocking call to get the result
```

In this case, submit() allows the task to be executed asynchronously, and the Future.get() method can be used to retrieve the result, blocking if necessary until the computation is complete.

Managing tasks in a ForkJoinPool also includes handling potential exceptions. The ForkJoinTask subclasses have built-in mechanisms to propagate exceptions to the caller, ensuring robust error handling.

```
ForkJoinPool pool = new ForkJoinPool();
MyRecursiveTask task = new MyRecursiveTask();

try {
    int result = pool.invoke(task);
} catch (Exception e) {
    e.printStackTrace();
}
```

The ForkJoinWorkerThreadFactory allows customization of the worker threads in the ForkJoinPool. By default, the common pool uses a factory that creates ForkJoinWorkerThread instances.

```
ForkJoinWorkerThreadFactory factory = pool -> {
    ForkJoinWorkerThread worker = ForkJoinPool.
            defaultForkJoinWorkerThreadFactory.newThread(pool);
    // Customize worker if necessary
    return worker;
};

ForkJoinPool customPool = new ForkJoinPool(parallelismLevel, factory, null, false);
```

Creating a customized factory allows tweaking thread properties such as naming, priorities, and other specific behaviors required for certain applications and the control over common thread-pool usage patterns.

A significant feature of the ForkJoinPool is the support for managed blocking. This feature allows tasks to declare that they might block, informing the pool to compensate by temporarily increasing the parallelism level if needed.

```
class BlockingTask implements ForkJoinPool.ManagedBlocker {
    boolean done = false;

    @Override
    public boolean block() throws InterruptedException {
        // Perform blocking operation here
        done = true;
        return true;
    }

    @Override
    public boolean isReleasable() {
        return done;
    }
}

ForkJoinPool pool = new ForkJoinPool();
BlockingTask blocker = new BlockingTask();
ForkJoinPool.managedBlock(blocker);
```

In the example above, a class implementing ForkJoin-

Pool.ManagedBlocker interface provides the block() and isReleasable() methods to handle blocking operations effectively. By using ForkJoinPool.managedBlock(), the pool knows about the blocking situation and can manage resources accordingly.

Building scalable and efficient parallel applications requires a good understanding of ForkJoinPool creation, task submission, exception handling, and managing custom worker threads. Future sections will delve deeper into the lifecycle and performance considerations, ensuring a comprehensive mastery of the Java Fork/Join Framework.

6.4 RecursiveTask and RecursiveAction

The Fork/Join framework leverages two primary abstractions for task decomposition: RecursiveTask and RecursiveAction, which facilitate handling tasks that return results and those that do not, respectively.

RecursiveTask is an abstract class that, when extended, allows for the creation of tasks that produce a result. The subclass must implement the compute() method, where the logic for task execution and splitting into subtasks resides.

```
import java.util.concurrent.RecursiveTask;

public class SumArrayTask extends RecursiveTask<Integer> {
    private static final int THRESHOLD = 10;
    private int[] array;
    private int start;
    private int end;

    public SumArrayTask(int[] array, int start, int end) {
        this.array = array;
        this.start = start;
        this.end = end;
    }

    @Override
    protected Integer compute() {
        if (end - start <= THRESHOLD) {
            int sum = 0;
            for (int i = start; i < end; i++) {
                sum += array[i];
            }
            return sum;
        } else {
            int mid = (start + end) / 2;
            SumArrayTask leftTask = new SumArrayTask(array, start, mid);
            SumArrayTask rightTask = new SumArrayTask(array, mid, end);
            leftTask.fork();
            int rightResult = rightTask.compute();
            int leftResult = leftTask.join();
            return leftResult + rightResult;
```

```
        }
    }
}
```

Key elements include checking if the task size is below a certain *threshold*, at which a direct computation is performed. Otherwise, the task is split into subtasks. The fork() method initiates a background subtask, while join() synchronizes and retrieves its result.

Conversely, RecursiveAction is an abstract class utilized for tasks that do not return a value. The compute() method in the subclass carries out the operation required by the task.

```
import java.util.concurrent.RecursiveAction;

public class IncrementArrayAction extends RecursiveAction {
    private static final int THRESHOLD = 10;
    private int[] array;
    private int start;
    private int end;

    public IncrementArrayAction(int[] array, int start, int end) {
        this.array = array;
        this.start = start;
        this.end = end;
    }

    @Override
    protected void compute() {
        if (end - start <= THRESHOLD) {
            for (int i = start; i < end; i++) {
                array[i]++;
            }
        } else {
            int mid = (start + end) / 2;
            IncrementArrayAction leftTask = new IncrementArrayAction(array, start,
                 mid);
            IncrementArrayAction rightTask = new IncrementArrayAction(array, mid,
                 end);
            invokeAll(leftTask, rightTask);
        }
    }
}
```

In this instance, if the task workload is manageable, it performs the operation directly; otherwise, it decomposes into two subtasks and synchronizes their completion using invokeAll(), an efficient way to fork and join tasks simultaneously.

Although invokeAll() is a simpler method to handle multiple subtasks, it is important not to cause large numbers of small tasks, which could degrade performance due to excessive overhead. An ideal workload size must be determined to balance task granularity and processing efficiency.

The *fork-join* approach's primary advantage is its ability to harness multiple processor cores efficiently. The ForkJoinPool manages worker threads, dynamically redistributing tasks especially with its work-stealing algorithm where idle threads can "steal" tasks from busy threads' queues to maximize resource utilization.

```
import java.util.concurrent.ForkJoinPool;

public class ForkJoinExample {
    public static void main(String[] args) {
        int[] array = {1, 2, 3, ..., 100};
        ForkJoinPool pool = new ForkJoinPool();
        SumArrayTask task = new SumArrayTask(array, 0, array.length);
        int result = pool.invoke(task);
        System.out.println("Sum: " + result);
    }
}
```

This demonstrates the practical execution of SumArrayTask. The ForkJoinPool's invoke() method initiates and returns the result of the task. For non-returning tasks, execute() is used instead.

Understanding the subtle nuances of RecursiveTask and RecursiveAction will enable efficient parallel computations, essential for applications requiring intensive data processing.

6.5 Executing ForkJoinTasks

The execution of ForkJoinTasks within the Fork/Join Framework is an essential process for achieving parallelism in Java applications. Understanding how to effectively execute these tasks involves grasping the underlying mechanisms of task submission, processing, and completion.

ForkJoinTasks are instances of ForkJoinTask<V>, where V indicates the result type of the computation. They can be directly submitted to a ForkJoinPool for execution. The framework provides two types of tasks: RecursiveTask<V>, which returns a result, and RecursiveAction, which does not return a result.

One starts by defining a class that extends either RecursiveTask<V> or RecursiveAction. The primary method to implement is compute(), which contains the logic for splitting the task and merging results if necessary.

Example RecursiveTask:

```
import java.util.concurrent.RecursiveTask;

public class SumTask extends RecursiveTask<Integer> {
    private static final int THRESHOLD = 10;
    private final int[] array;
    private final int start;
    private final int end;

    public SumTask(int[] array, int start, int end) {
        this.array = array;
        this.start = start;
        this.end = end;
    }

    @Override
    protected Integer compute() {
        if ((end - start) <= THRESHOLD) {
            int sum = 0;
            for (int i = start; i < end; i++) {
                sum += array[i];
            }
            return sum;
        } else {
            int mid = (start + end) / 2;
            SumTask leftTask = new SumTask(array, start, mid);
            SumTask rightTask = new SumTask(array, mid, end);
            leftTask.fork();
            int rightResult = rightTask.compute();
            int leftResult = leftTask.join();
            return leftResult + rightResult;
        }
    }
}
```

In this example, a SumTask calculates the sum of elements in an array. If the segment of the array is small enough (below the THRESHOLD), it computes the sum directly. If the segment is larger, it splits the task into two subtasks: leftTask and rightTask. The fork() method asynchronously executes leftTask, while the current thread computes rightTask. The result of leftTask is obtained via join().

RecursiveAction follows the same principles but omits result handling:

```
import java.util.concurrent.RecursiveAction;

public class PrintTask extends RecursiveAction {
    private static final int THRESHOLD = 5;
    private final int[] array;
    private final int start;
    private final int end;

    public PrintTask(int[] array, int start, int end) {
        this.array = array;
        this.start = start;
        this.end = end;
    }

    @Override
    protected void compute() {
```

```
        if ((end - start) <= THRESHOLD) {
            for (int i = start; i < end; i++) {
                System.out.println(array[i]);
            }
        } else {
            int mid = (start + end) / 2;
            PrintTask leftTask = new PrintTask(array, start, mid);
            PrintTask rightTask = new PrintTask(array, mid, end);
            invokeAll(leftTask, rightTask);
        }
    }
}
```

In PrintTask, the implementation for splits and execution is similar. The method invokeAll() replaces explicit calls to fork() and join(), allowing a concise delegation of subtasks.

Once defined, these tasks are executed by creating an instance of ForkJoinPool and invoking the invoke() method:

```
import java.util.concurrent.ForkJoinPool;

public class Main {
    public static void main(String[] args) {
        int[] array = {1, 2, 3, 4, 5, 6, 7, 8, 9, 10};
        ForkJoinPool pool = new ForkJoinPool();

        // Executing SumTask
        SumTask sumTask = new SumTask(array, 0, array.length);
        int result = pool.invoke(sumTask);
        System.out.println("Sum: " + result);

        // Executing PrintTask
        PrintTask printTask = new PrintTask(array, 0, array.length);
        pool.invoke(printTask);
    }
}
```

The ForkJoinPool manages threads and their workloads to optimize CPU usage. The method invoke() blocks until the task completes and returns the result. For tasks that do not need to return a result, such as PrintTask, it efficiently handles execution and synchronization.

Execution utilizing ForkJoinTasks must consider exceptions. If an exception is thrown during computation, it propagates back through methods like join() and invoke(). Ensuring robust error handling in the compute() method is crucial.

```
@Override
protected Integer compute() {
    try {
        // Task logic
    } catch (Exception e) {
        throw new RuntimeException("Task execution failed", e);
    }
}
```

Incorporating these principles ensures that ForkJoinTasks are efficiently executed, leveraging parallelism for computationally intensive tasks.

6.6 ForkJoinTask Lifecycle

The lifecycle of a ForkJoinTask within the Fork/Join Framework is critical for understanding how parallel tasks are managed and executed efficiently. Each phase of the lifecycle has specific characteristics and operations that affect task execution and resource utilization. Here, we outline and explain the various stages that contribute to the complete lifecycle of a ForkJoinTask.

A ForkJoinTask passes through the following stages:

- Construction
- Forking
- Execution
- Completion
- Joining
- Finalization

Construction: The lifecycle of a ForkJoinTask begins with its construction. A ForkJoinTask can be instantiated as either a RecursiveTask or a RecursiveAction, depending on whether the operation returns a result.

```
// Example of creating a RecursiveTask
public class SumTask extends RecursiveTask<Integer> {
  private final int[] array;
  private final int start;
  private final int end;

  public SumTask(int[] array, int start, int end) {
    this.array = array;
    this.start = start;
    this.end = end;
  }

  @Override
  protected Integer compute() {
    // Implementation of compute logic
  }
}
```

In this phase, the initialization parameters such as input arrays, start and end indices, or other computation-specific variables are set up.

Forking: Once a ForkJoinTask is created, it can be forked, which means it is scheduled to run asynchronously in a ForkJoinPool. The fork() method is used to initiate this process.

```
// Forking the task
SumTask task = new SumTask(array, 0, array.length);
task.fork();
```

The fork() method internally registers the task with the ForkJoinPool, placing it in the worker queue of the pool for execution.

Execution: The actual execution of the ForkJoinTask occurs when the compute() method is called. This method is responsible for defining the recursive splitting of the task and the concrete computation that each split carries out.

```
@Override
protected Integer compute() {
  if (end - start <= THRESHOLD) {
    return computeDirectly();
  } else {
    int middle = (start + end) / 2;
    SumTask leftTask = new SumTask(array, start, middle);
    SumTask rightTask = new SumTask(array, middle, end);

    leftTask.fork();
    int rightResult = rightTask.compute(); // Direct call
    int leftResult = leftTask.join();

    return leftResult + rightResult;
  }
}
```

In this example, the task recursively splits itself into smaller subtasks until reaching a base case (when the problem size is below a certain threshold).

Completion: Following the execution, a ForkJoinTask transitions to a completed state. This can happen either by successfully finishing the task's computation or through exceptional completion if an error occurs. The framework ensures that appropriate mechanisms are in place for handling exceptions.

Joining: Joining is the phase where the results of subtasks are collected and combined. The join() method is called to wait for the completion of a forked task and retrieve its result. Proper use of join is essential for avoiding performance bottlenecks.

```
int result = task.join();
System.out.println("Sum: " + result);
```

The method join() blocks the current task until the target task is completed, ensuring that the computation is synchronized and all results are collated.

Finalization: After the reproduction stage of the task, any necessary finalization tasks, such as resource deallocation or cleanup actions, should be performed. Though the Java garbage collector handles most memory management concerns, developers might need to implement specific cleanup logic.

The entire lifecycle of the ForkJoinTask is a sequence of well-defined stages that allow the Fork/Join Framework to manage, execute, and optimize parallel tasks efficiently. Understanding the operational flow, from construction to finalization, is fundamental for developing high-performing parallel applications within the Fork/Join framework.

6.7 Split/Join Strategy for RecursiveTasks

Effective utilization of the Fork/Join Framework necessitates a well-thought-out strategy for splitting tasks into subtasks and subsequently joining the results. This section details the split/join strategy when working with RecursiveTasks, which return a result, and elaborates on best practices to enhance performance and scalability.

A RecursiveTask represents a task that computes a value and is designed to split a large task into smaller pieces recursively. Each piece is processed in parallel, and the results are combined to form the final outcome.

Understanding the components is essential to mastering the split/join strategy:

Threshold Determination: The threshold, or the base case, is a critical component determining the granularity of the task splitting. If the task size falls below this threshold, the task should be processed se-

---

Algorithm 5: Example RecursiveTask for Summing Array Elements

---

Data: Workload threshold, array of data, start index, end index
Result: Sum of the array elements within the given range

```
if (end - start) < threshold then
    return sum of array elements from start to end;
end
else
    mid = (start + end) / 2;
    // Create subtasks
    leftTask = new SumTask(array, start, mid);
    rightTask = new SumTask(array, mid, end);
    // Fork left task
    leftTask.fork();
    // Compute right task
    rightResult = rightTask.compute();
    // Join left task
    leftResult = leftTask.join();
    // Combine results
    return leftResult + rightResult;
end
```

quentially. This avoids overhead associated with excessive task creation and context switching.

The selection of the threshold depends on the nature of the computation and the underlying hardware. A smaller threshold increases parallelism but may lead to higher overhead. Conversely, a larger threshold reduces overhead but limits parallelism. Profiling and empirical analysis are necessary to determine the optimal threshold.

```
// Example Java class for SumTask extending RecursiveTask<Integer>
class SumTask extends RecursiveTask<Integer> {
    private final int[] array;
    private final int start;
    private final int end;
    private static final int THRESHOLD = 1000;

    public SumTask(int[] array, int start, int end) {
        this.array = array;
        this.start = start;
        this.end = end;
    }

    @Override
    protected Integer compute() {
        if (end - start < THRESHOLD) {
            int sum = 0;
            for (int i = start; i < end; i++) {
                sum += array[i];
            }
            return sum;
        } else {
            int mid = (start + end) / 2;
            SumTask leftTask = new SumTask(array, start, mid);
            SumTask rightTask = new SumTask(array, mid, end);
            leftTask.fork();
            int rightResult = rightTask.compute();
            int leftResult = leftTask.join();
            return leftResult + rightResult;
        }
    }
}
```

Forking Subtasks: The method fork() is invoked to start the execution of the subtask asynchronously. It schedules the subtask for execution in the ForkJoinPool but does not wait for its completion. This allows the parent task to proceed with other computations or to fork additional subtasks.

In the example, leftTask.fork() schedules the left subtask, while the parent task processes the right subtask sequentially using rightTask.compute().

Joining Subtasks: The method join() is used to wait for the completion of the subtask and retrieve its result. If the subtask is not yet completed, the join operation blocks the parent task until the result is available.

In the example, once the right subtask is computed, the parent task calls leftTask.join() to obtain the result of the left subtask. Subsequently, the results of the left and right subtasks are combined to produce the final result for the parent task.

```
Sample Output:
Input Array: [1, 2, 3, 4, 5, ..., 1000]
Sum of Array Elements: 500500
```

This approach ensures efficient utilization of computational resources by leveraging parallelism, while also maintaining a balance between task granularity and overhead associated with task creation and synchronization.

Load Balancing: The choice of split point (in the example, mid) significantly impacts load balancing across the ForkJoinPool. A good split point ensures that each subtask has an approximately equal workload, avoiding scenarios where one subtask might finish quickly while another takes significantly longer.

Work-Stealing Algorithm: The ForkJoinPool employs a work-stealing algorithm for load balancing. Under this scheme, idle threads attempt to "steal" tasks from busy threads' queues to maximize resource utilization and minimize idle times.

Continuous monitoring and fine-tuning are essential to maintain an optimal split/join strategy. Profiling tools and metrics can help identify bottlenecks, allowing adjustments in the threshold and other parameters to achieve superior performance and scalability.

6.8 Performance Optimizations

To optimize performance in the Fork/Join Framework, it is crucial to understand both the underlying principles and practical techniques that can significantly enhance the overall efficiency and scalability of your parallel applications. The key strategies revolve around optimizing task granularity, minimizing synchronization overhead, and efficiently leveraging system resources.

Task Granularity: One of the core principles for optimizing performance is selecting the appropriate granularity for tasks. Granularity refers to the size of the tasks into which the main problem is divided. Fine-grained tasks offer greater parallelism but may introduce higher overhead due to the increased number of tasks. Coarse-grained tasks reduce overhead but might underutilize the available processing cores. The optimal balance lies in ensuring tasks are neither too fine nor too coarse.

The following code snippet demonstrates calculating the optimal threshold for task granularity in a RecursiveTask:

```
private static final int THRESHOLD = 1000;

@Override
protected Long compute() {
    if (end - start < THRESHOLD) {
        return sequentialSum();
    } else {
        int middle = (start + end) / 2;
        RecursiveTask<Long> leftTask = new SumTask(start, middle);
        RecursiveTask<Long> rightTask = new SumTask(middle, end);

        leftTask.fork(); // asynchronously execute the left task
        long rightResult = rightTask.compute(); // synchronously execute the right task
        long leftResult = leftTask.join(); // wait for the left task to complete

        return leftResult + rightResult;
    }
}
```

Minimizing Synchronization Overhead: Excessive synchronization can significantly degrade performance by necessitating frequent context switches and causing contention among threads. When using shared resources, it is preferable to use concurrent collections like ConcurrentHashMap or atomic variables such as AtomicInteger to reduce locking overhead. Using ReentrantLock or synchronized blocks sparingly and only when absolutely required will minimize contention and maximize efficient execution.

The following snippet demonstrates replacing synchronized blocks with atomic operations:

```
import java.util.concurrent.atomic.AtomicInteger;

public class Counter {
    private AtomicInteger count = new AtomicInteger(0);

    public void increment() {
        count.getAndIncrement();
    }

    public int getCount() {
        return count.get();
    }
}
```

Efficient Memory Usage: The Fork/Join Framework extensively uses worker threads that maintain their own specific work queues. Efficient memory usage and avoiding memory leaks are critical for optimal performance. Utilize primitives where possible, avoid creating unnecessary intermediate objects, and ensure proper handling of task objects.

The efficient use of memory can also be monitored by profiling tools such as VisualVM or YourKit, which help in identifying memory bottlenecks and leaks. Managing heap size and garbage collection using appropriate JVM flags can further enhance performance.

Work Stealing: The Fork/Join Framework uses a work-stealing algorithm where idle worker threads can "steal" tasks from the queue of busy threads. Proper task partitioning helps in better distribution of load among threads. Balancing load across worker threads ensures minimal idle time and maximizes resource utilization for faster task completion.

Avoiding Blocking Operations: Blocking operations such as I/O should be minimized within Fork/Join tasks. Compute-bound tasks benefit from non-blocking algorithms or using asynchronous I/O operations where applicable. Utilizing non-blocking constructs ensures worker threads remain active and productive.

```
import java.util.concurrent.CompletableFuture;

public class NonBlockingTask {
    public void performTask() {
        CompletableFuture.supplyAsync(() -> {
            // Non-blocking operation
            return computeResult();
        }).thenAccept(result -> {
            processResult(result);
        });
    }
}
```

Profiling and Monitoring: Real-time monitoring of the Fork/Join pool and tasks can provide invaluable insights into performance bottlenecks and task distribution. Using tools like Java Mission Control or JVisualVM, developers can profile thread usage, task execution times, and memory consumption. Fine-tuning based on profiling data enables targeted optimizations.

Adaptive Task Sizing: Dynamic adjustment of task size based on workload characteristics can lead to better performance. Implementing adaptive strategies where task granularity is adjusted in real-time based on the observed performance metrics ensures optimal utilization of resources under varying workloads.

Continual performance optimization in the Fork/Join Framework demands a solid understanding of parallel algorithms, meticulous profiling, and adjusting JVM and application-level parameters according to observed patterns and specific use-case requirements.

6.9 Using Fork/Join with RecursiveTasks

The Fork/Join framework in Java provides a powerful mechanism for parallelizing tasks by extending the RecursiveTask class. When a task returns a result upon execution, RecursiveTask<V> should be utilized, where V denotes the type of the result. The process involves splitting the main task into smaller subtasks that can be processed concurrently, and then combining the results of these subtasks. This ensures efficient parallel processing and effective use of system resources.

Implementing a RecursiveTask involves extending the RecursiveTask<V> class and overriding its compute method. This method defines the core logic for splitting the task, processing the subtasks, and then combining the results. Below is a typical implementation pattern for a RecursiveTask.

```
import java.util.concurrent.RecursiveTask;

public class FibonacciTask extends RecursiveTask<Long> {
    private final long number;

    public FibonacciTask(long number) {
        this.number = number;
    }

    @Override
    protected Long compute() {
        if (number <= 1) {
            return number;
        }
        FibonacciTask smallerTask1 = new FibonacciTask(number - 1);
        FibonacciTask smallerTask2 = new FibonacciTask(number - 2);
        smallerTask1.fork();
        Long result2 = smallerTask2.compute();
        Long result1 = smallerTask1.join();
        return result1 + result2;
    }
}
```

In the implementation above, the provided FibonacciTask calculates the Fibonacci number for a given input number. If the number is less than or equal to 1, the computation is trivial and the task returns the number itself. Otherwise, the task is split into two subtasks: smallerTask1 and smallerTask2, which are then recursively computed. The fork() method asynchronously executes smallerTask1, while the current task computes smallerTask2. After computing smallerTask2, the result of smallerTask1 is obtained by calling the join() method. The final result is the sum of the results from the two subtasks.

Next, it's essential to understand how to execute these tasks using the ForkJoinPool. The ForkJoinPool manages and schedules the tasks for parallel execution. Here's how to create and execute a FibonacciTask using ForkJoinPool.

```
import java.util.concurrent.ForkJoinPool;

public class FibonacciCalculator {
    public static void main(String[] args) {
        ForkJoinPool forkJoinPool = new ForkJoinPool();
        FibonacciTask task = new FibonacciTask(30);
        Long result = forkJoinPool.invoke(task);
        System.out.println("Fibonacci number at position 30 is " + result);
    }
}
```

In this example, a ForkJoinPool instance is created, and the FibonacciTask is instantiated with the input value 30. The invoke() method of ForkJoinPool is used to execute the task. This calls the compute() method, which eventually returns the calculated Fibonacci number, and the result is printed.

It's important to note that while the example provided uses a simple recursive algorithm, RecursiveTasks can be applied to more complex problem domains. The real power of RecursiveTask comes into play in scenarios where the tasks can be divided into many independent smaller tasks, each requiring significant computation time. Examples include parallel array processing, matrix multiplications, sorting algorithms like Merge Sort, and other divide-and-conquer algorithms.

When defining the logic for splitting tasks, consider the granularity of the subdivision. Tasks should be large enough to justify the overhead of managing multiple threads but small enough to still provide concurrency benefits. For instance, too fine-grained tasks might lead to excessive context switching and overhead, whereas too coarse-grained tasks might not fully utilize the available processors.

Thresholding is a common technique used in recursive task split strategies. A threshold determines when a task should stop splitting further and solve the problem directly. This approach provides a trade-off between parallelism overhead and the benefits of breaking tasks into smaller units. Implementing a threshold involves deciding an optimal point where the costs of splitting and managing smaller tasks outweigh the gains from further parallelism.

Below is an enhanced version of the FibonacciTask utilizing a threshold for better efficiency:

```
import java.util.concurrent.RecursiveTask;

public class FibonacciTaskWithThreshold extends RecursiveTask<Long> {
    private static final long THRESHOLD = 10;
    private final long number;

    public FibonacciTaskWithThreshold(long number) {
        this.number = number;
    }

    @Override
    protected Long compute() {
        if (number <= THRESHOLD) {
            return sequentialFibonacci(number);
        }
        FibonacciTaskWithThreshold subtask1 = new FibonacciTaskWithThreshold(
                number - 1);
        FibonacciTaskWithThreshold subtask2 = new FibonacciTaskWithThreshold(
                number - 2);
        subtask1.fork();
        Long result2 = subtask2.compute();
        Long result1 = subtask1.join();
        return result1 + result2;
    }

    private long sequentialFibonacci(long n) {
        if (n <= 1) {
            return n;
        }
        long fib = 1, prevFib = 1;
        for (long i = 2; i < n; i++) {
            long temp = fib;
            fib += prevFib;
            prevFib = temp;
        }
        return fib;
    }
}
```

In this refined implementation, the task performs a sequential computation of the Fibonacci number if the input is below a predefined THRESHOLD, enhancing performance by reducing the overhead of task splitting managing smaller tasks.

A practical understanding of using RecursiveTask with the Fork/Join framework involves experimenting with different split strategies, thresholds, and problem domains, striking a balance between computational intensity and parallelism overhead, leading to effective and highly scalable applications.

6.10 Real-World Use Case and Examples

The application of the Fork/Join framework is demonstrated in a variety of real-world scenarios where efficient parallel processing can significantly enhance performance. The following use case illustrates how the Fork/Join framework can be employed to speed up a data-intensive computation. This example involves processing large-scale datasets, such as those used in scientific research or complex modeling.

Use Case: Parallel Matrix Multiplication

Matrix multiplication is a fundamental operation in various computational fields, including scientific computing, machine learning, and computer graphics. When dealing with large matrices, the computation can be extremely time-consuming. The Fork/Join framework can be utilized to parallelize this task, thereby reducing the computation time.

Consider two matrices A and B, where A is of size $m \times n$ and B is of size $n \times p$. The product matrix C will have the dimensions $m \times p$. The operation can be described as follows:

$$C[i][j] = \sum_{k=0}^{n-1} A[i][k] \times B[k][j]$$

The Fork/Join framework will allow us to split this task into smaller subtasks. Specifically, each element of the resultant matrix C can be computed independently of the others, making it an ideal candidate for parallel processing.

```
import java.util.concurrent.RecursiveTask;
import java.util.concurrent.ForkJoinPool;

public class MatrixMultiplicationTask extends RecursiveTask<double[][]> {

    private static final int THRESHOLD = 64;
    private double[][] A;
    private double[][] B;
    private double[][] C;
    private int rowStart, rowEnd, colStart, colEnd;

    public MatrixMultiplicationTask(double[][] A, double[][] B, double[][] C,
                                    int rowStart, int rowEnd, int colStart, int colEnd) {
        this.A = A;
        this.B = B;
        this.C = C;
        this.rowStart = rowStart;
        this.rowEnd = rowEnd;
        this.colStart = colStart;
        this.colEnd = colEnd;
    }
```

```
    @Override
    protected double[][] compute() {
        if ((rowEnd - rowStart) <= THRESHOLD && (colEnd - colStart) <=
            THRESHOLD) {
            for (int i = rowStart; i < rowEnd; i++) {
                for (int j = colStart; j < colEnd; j++) {
                    C[i][j] = 0;
                    for (int k = 0; k < A[0].length; k++) {
                        C[i][j] += A[i][k] * B[k][j];
                    }
                }
            }
            return C;
        } else {
            int rowMid = (rowStart + rowEnd) / 2;
            int colMid = (colStart + colEnd) / 2;

            MatrixMultiplicationTask task1 = new MatrixMultiplicationTask(A, B, C,
                rowStart, rowMid, colStart, colMid);
            MatrixMultiplicationTask task2 = new MatrixMultiplicationTask(A, B, C,
                rowStart, rowMid, colMid, colEnd);
            MatrixMultiplicationTask task3 = new MatrixMultiplicationTask(A, B, C,
                rowMid, rowEnd, colStart, colMid);
            MatrixMultiplicationTask task4 = new MatrixMultiplicationTask(A, B, C,
                rowMid, rowEnd, colMid, colEnd);

            invokeAll(task1, task2, task3, task4);
            task1.join();
            task2.join();
            task3.join();
            task4.join();
            return C;
        }
    }

    public static double[][] multiplyMatrices(double[][] A, double[][] B) {
        int rowsA = A.length;
        int colsA = A[0].length;
        int colsB = B[0].length;
        double[][] C = new double[rowsA][colsB];

        ForkJoinPool pool = new ForkJoinPool();
        MatrixMultiplicationTask task = new MatrixMultiplicationTask(A, B, C, 0,
            rowsA, 0, colsB);
        pool.invoke(task);
        return C;
    }
}
```

Explanation of the Code

The class MatrixMultiplicationTask extends RecursiveTask<double[][]>, which signifies that it will return a 2D array of type double upon completion. The class includes:

- A, B, C: Matrices used for multiplication and storing the result.
- rowStart, rowEnd, colStart, colEnd: The range of rows and columns to be processed by each task.

- THRESHOLD: A predefined constant determining the maximum chunk size for which the task will not be further split.

When the compute() method is called, the task either computes the product directly if the matrix chunk is small enough or splits the task into four subtasks, thereby dividing the work further until the base condition is met.

Output of the Program

To verify the correctness and performance of our parallel matrix multiplication, consider matrices A and B initialized with specific values. The resulting matrix C is expected to be:

```
[ [sum1, sum2, ...],
  [sum3, sum4, ...],
  ...
]
```

This solution lends itself well to parallelization due to the data-independent nature of matrix element computations, making the Fork/Join framework efficient for this use case.

Performance Evaluation

Assessing the performance involves comparing the execution time of the parallel approach against a sequential matrix multiplication implementation. The metrics of interest include:

- Execution Time: Time taken to compute the product matrix.
- Speedup: Ratio of the execution time of the sequential approach to the parallel approach.
- Scalability: The efficiency of the program as the number of processors increases.

This is conducted by measuring the computation time using both methods and analyzing the results.

```
public class SequentialMatrixMultiplication {

    public static double[][] multiplyMatrices(double[][] A, double[][] B) {
        int rowsA = A.length;
        int colsA = A[0].length;
        int colsB = B[0].length;
        double[][] C = new double[rowsA][colsB];

        for (int i = 0; i < rowsA; i++) {
            for (int j = 0; j < colsB; j++) {
                C[i][j] = 0;
```

```
                for (int k = 0; k < colsA; k++) {
                    C[i][j] += A[i][k] * B[k][j];
                }
            }
        }
        return C;
    }
}
```

Analyzing timing results and speedup achieved with increasing numbers of processors helps in understanding the efficiency and applicability of the Fork/Join framework to real-world problems.

This example demonstrates the practical application and benefits of the Fork/Join framework in computationally intensive tasks. The detailed implementation serves as an educational reference for leveraging parallel processing to enhance performance.

6.11 Monitoring and Tuning Fork/Join Applications

Monitoring and tuning Fork/Join applications are pivotal for maximizing the efficiency and scalability of parallel processing tasks. Understanding how to analyze the performance metrics and applying appropriate tuning techniques can significantly enhance the execution of your applications. This section delves into the practical aspects of monitoring Fork/Join tasks, interpreting various performance indicators, and optimizing the applications for superior performance.

Monitoring Fork/Join applications begins with the utilization of tools and metrics provided by the Java platform. The Java Management Extensions (JMX) and Java Flight Recorder (JFR) are instrumental in gathering performance data.

Enabling JMX Monitoring

Java provides built-in support for JMX, which can be enabled through JVM options. This can be achieved by adding the following JVM options at the application startup:

```
-Dcom.sun.management.jmxremote
-Dcom.sun.management.jmxremote.port=9010
-Dcom.sun.management.jmxremote.authenticate=false
-Dcom.sun.management.jmxremote.ssl=false
```

These options enable remote JMX monitoring on port 9010 without authentication and SSL, allowing tools like VisualVM or JConsole to connect and monitor the application in real-time.

ForkJoinPool exposes various management interfaces that can be accessed through JMX. Key metrics include:

- PoolSize: The number of worker threads.
- ActiveThreadCount: The number of active threads executing tasks.
- StealCount: The total number of tasks stolen from other threads.
- QueuedTaskCount: The number of tasks currently awaiting execution.
- Parallelism: The targeted parallelism level of the pool.

Understanding these metrics provides insight into the workload distribution, thread utilization, and task efficiency within the ForkJoinPool.

Using Java Flight Recorder (JFR)

Java Flight Recorder is a JVM-integrated monitoring and profiling tool that captures low-level details about the application's performance. To enable JFR:

```
-XX:StartFlightRecording=duration=60s,filename=recording.jfr
```

This command starts a flight recording for 60 seconds and saves the data to recording.jfr. Analysis of this file can be carried out using Java Mission Control (JMC), which provides deep insights into thread states, method execution times, garbage collection events, and more.

Tuning Fork/Join Applications

Effective tuning of Fork/Join applications involves several strategies aimed at optimizing task partitions and thread management. Key aspects include:

1. Adjusting Parallelism

The ForkJoinPool constructor allows setting the desired parallelism level, which controls the number of worker threads. This can be done as follows:

```
ForkJoinPool customPool = new ForkJoinPool(8); // Setting parallelism to 8
```

The optimal parallelism is typically related to the number of available processor cores, ideally set to the number of cores - 1 to reserve some capacity for other system operations.

2. Optimizing Task Granularity

Granularity refers to the size of the tasks into which the main problem is subdivided. A balance must be struck as excessively coarse tasks lead to suboptimal parallelism, while overly fine tasks result in overhead due to excessive task management. The ideal approach is to perform empirical testing, starting with a moderate task size and adjusting based on performance metrics such as total execution time and thread utilization.

RecursiveTask and RecursiveAction subclasses should implement the compute method in a manner that efficiently splits work:

```
protected List<SubTask> createSubTasks() {
    List<SubTask> subTasks = new ArrayList<>();
    int mid = thisWork.length() / 2;
    subTasks.add(new SubTask(this.work.substring(0, mid)));
    subTasks.add(new SubTask(this.work.substring(mid)));
    return subTasks;
}

@Override
protected void compute() {
    if (this.work.length() <= THRESHOLD) {
        process(this.work);
    } else {
        ForkJoinTask.invokeAll(createSubTasks());
    }
}
```

This code snippet illustrates dividing the work only if it exceeds a predefined THRESHOLD, optimizing for both task management overhead and parallel efficiency.

3. Managing Task Workloads

Unbalanced workloads can lead to a situation where some threads are idle while others are overwhelmed. To monitor and debug these scenarios, track the StealCount. A low StealCount might indicate efficient load distribution, while a high count signifies frequent task stealing due to imbalanced workloads. Adjust the task partitioning strategy to reduce such imbalances.

4. Avoiding Deadlocks and Reducing Contention

Deadlocks and contention can degrade the performance of Fork/Join applications. Analyze Thread Dumps and Lock Contention using JFR. Avoid synchronized blocks or locks within the compute method where possible, as they severely restrict parallel execution. Apply non-blocking synchronization alternatives like java.util.concurrent.atomic classes where feasible.

```
AtomicInteger counter = new AtomicInteger(0);

void updateCounter() {
    counter.incrementAndGet();
}
```

This ensures non-blocking updates, thereby enhancing performance under concurrent workloads.

Lastly, empirical validation remains crucial. Visualize different performance aspects using tools like VisualVM, JFR, and custom logging to iteratively refine the strategies. Detailed performance logs and profiling data are indispensable for nuanced tuning and optimization of Fork/Join applications. This analytical approach leads to the identification and rectification of bottlenecks, ensuring optimal scalability and efficiency.

Chapter 7

Atomic Variables and Lock-Free Programming

This chapter focuses on atomic variables and lock-free programming techniques that enable high-performance concurrent applications. It introduces various atomic classes such as AtomicInteger, AtomicLong, AtomicBoolean, AtomicReference, and AtomicStampedReference, along with atomic field updaters. The chapter details the concept of Compare-And-Swap (CAS) operations, the advantages of lock-free programming, and designing lock-free algorithms. Challenges in lock-free programming are discussed, along with performance considerations and practical examples of using atomic variables in real-world scenarios.

7.1 Introduction to Atomic Variables

Concurrent programming poses significant challenges due to the necessity of managing multiple threads that manipulate shared data. Traditional synchronization techniques like locks, while commonly used, can lead to several issues such as deadlocks, contention, and performance bottlenecks. Atomic variables, introduced in the java.util.concurrent.atomic package, offer an alternative that allows for lock-free and thread-safe manipulation of variables.

Atomic variables leverage hardware-level atomic operations to achieve synchronization at a finer granularity. These variables eliminate the need for explicit locks, minimizing the risk of thread contention and improving performance in highly concurrent programs.

The primary classes for atomic variables in Java include:

- AtomicInteger
- AtomicLong
- AtomicBoolean
- AtomicReference
- AtomicStampedReference

Each of these classes provides methods to perform atomic operations on their encapsulated values. These classes rely on low-level atomic hardware instructions, such as Compare-And-Swap (CAS), to achieve their lock-free properties.

Consider the following example demonstrating the usage of AtomicInteger:

```
import java.util.concurrent.atomic.AtomicInteger;

public class AtomicExample {
    private static final AtomicInteger counter = new AtomicInteger(0);

    public static void main(String[] args) {
        Runnable incrementTask = () -> {
            for (int i = 0; i < 1000; i++) {
                counter.incrementAndGet();
            }
        };

        Thread thread1 = new Thread(incrementTask);
        Thread thread2 = new Thread(incrementTask);

        thread1.start();
        thread2.start();

        try {
            thread1.join();
            thread2.join();
        } catch (InterruptedException e) {
            Thread.currentThread().interrupt();
        }

        System.out.println("Counter value: " + counter.get());
    }
}
```

In this example, two threads concurrently increment the AtomicInteger 1000 times each. The incrementAndGet() method is atomic and guarantees that each increment operation is thread-safe without explicit locking.

The output for the given example will be:

```
Counter value: 2000
```

The atomic classes allow for various atomic operations, including:

- get(): Returns the current value.
- set(int newValue): Sets to the given value.
- lazySet(int newValue): Eventually sets to the given value.
- compareAndSet(int expect, int update): Atomically sets the value to the given update value if the current value equals the expected value.
- getAndIncrement(): Atomically increments by one the current value.
- incrementAndGet(): Atomically increments by one the current value and returns the updated value.
- addAndGet(int delta): Atomically adds the given value to the current value.

Among these, the compareAndSet() method is particularly crucial as it underpins many lock-free algorithms. It attempts to update the value only if it matches a specified expected value. This method embodies the concept of optimistic concurrency control—performing an update assuming no other thread has modified the value in the interim, and retrying if the assumption proves false.

```
import java.util.concurrent.atomic.AtomicInteger;

public class CompareAndSetExample {
    private static final AtomicInteger value = new AtomicInteger(0);

    public static void main(String[] args) {
        boolean updated = value.compareAndSet(0, 1);

        if (updated) {
            System.out.println("Value updated to 1");
        } else {
            System.out.println("Update failed");
        }

        System.out.println("Current value: " + value.get());
    }
}
```

When executed, this code will output:

```
Value updated to 1
Current value: 1
```

This occurs because the initial value is 0, and the compareAndSet() method successfully updates it to 1.

The atomic classes also provide variants for references and stamped references. An AtomicReference allows for atomic operations on object references, while an AtomicStampedReference adds a stamp (typically a version number) to the value, providing a mechanism to avoid the ABA problem, a common concurrency issue where a value is changed from A to B and back to A by another thread.

The introduction of atomic variables marks a significant improvement in writing concurrent programs by providing:

- Improved performance due to reduced contention.
- Simplified code by eliminating complex lock management.
- Increased scalability for applications involving high throughput of atomic operations.

Understanding the principles and proper usage of atomic variables is foundational for mastering lock-free programming and designing robust, high-performance concurrent applications.

7.2 AtomicInteger, AtomicLong, and AtomicBoolean

The introduction of atomic classes such as AtomicInteger, AtomicLong, and AtomicBoolean in the java.util.concurrent.atomic package marks a significant advancement in the development of concurrent applications in Java. These classes provide a set of atomic operations that enable efficient and thread-safe updates to single variables. Atomic variables eliminate the need for synchronization using locks, thereby avoiding potential drawbacks such as thread contention and context switching.

The AtomicInteger class encapsulates an integer value that can be updated atomically. The following code snippet demonstrates the use of AtomicInteger:

```
import java.util.concurrent.atomic.AtomicInteger;
```

```
public class AtomicIntegerExample {
    private AtomicInteger counter = new AtomicInteger(0);

    public void incrementCounter() {
        counter.incrementAndGet();
    }

    public int getCounter() {
        return counter.get();
    }

    public static void main(String[] args) {
        AtomicIntegerExample example = new AtomicIntegerExample();
        example.incrementCounter();
        System.out.println("Counter: " + example.getCounter());
    }
}
```

In this example, the incrementCounter() method uses the incrementAndGet() method to atomically increment the counter. The getCounter() method returns the current value of the counter.

The incrementAndGet() method not only increments the value atomically but also returns the updated value. This method, along with other atomic operations such as decrementAndGet(), addAndGet(int delta), and compareAndSet(int expect, int update), leverages hardware-level atomic instructions to ensure thread-safe operations.

Similarly, AtomicLong supports atomic operations on long values:

```
import java.util.concurrent.atomic.AtomicLong;

public class AtomicLongExample {
    private AtomicLong counter = new AtomicLong(0L);

    public void incrementCounter() {
        counter.incrementAndGet();
    }

    public long getCounter() {
        return counter.get();
    }

    public static void main(String[] args) {
        AtomicLongExample example = new AtomicLongExample();
        example.incrementCounter();
        System.out.println("Counter: " + example.getCounter());
    }
}
```

In AtomicLong, the incrementAndGet() method serves the same purpose as in AtomicInteger, providing an atomic increment operation for long values.

The AtomicBoolean class, on the other hand, supports atomic updates to boolean values. The following code demonstrates its usage:

```
import java.util.concurrent.atomic.AtomicBoolean;

public class AtomicBooleanExample {
    private AtomicBoolean flag = new AtomicBoolean(false);

    public void setFlagTrue() {
        flag.set(true);
    }

    public boolean getFlag() {
        return flag.get();
    }

    public static void main(String[] args) {
        AtomicBooleanExample example = new AtomicBooleanExample();
        example.setFlagTrue();
        System.out.println("Flag: " + example.getFlag());
    }
}
```

In this example, setFlagTrue() sets the flag to true atomically. The getFlag() method retrieves the current value of flag.

The compareAndSet() method is a crucial part of these classes, enabling compare-and-swap (CAS) operations. It sets the variable to a new value if the current value equals the expected value, otherwise fails. This ensures that updates to a variable are applied only if it remains unchanged since the last operation, preventing race conditions. Here's an example of compareAndSet in action:

```
import java.util.concurrent.atomic.AtomicInteger;

public class AtomicCompareAndSetExample {
    private AtomicInteger counter = new AtomicInteger(0);

    public boolean compareAndSetCounter(int expected, int update) {
        return counter.compareAndSet(expected, update);
    }

    public int getCounter() {
        return counter.get();
    }

    public static void main(String[] args) {
        AtomicCompareAndSetExample example = new
                AtomicCompareAndSetExample();
        boolean result = example.compareAndSetCounter(0, 1);
        System.out.println("Compare and Set Result: " + result);
        System.out.println("Counter: " + example.getCounter());
    }
}
```

In this example, compareAndSetCounter() attempts to set the counter from 0 to 1. If counter is 0, the operation succeeds, and compareAndSet() returns true. Otherwise, it returns false.

Understanding and utilizing atomic classes like AtomicInteger, AtomicLong, and AtomicBoolean allows developers to design highly concurrent and thread-safe algorithms. Atomic operations reduce the overhead of synchronization and mitigate the risks associated with lock-based mechanisms, promoting robust and efficient concurrent programming practices.

7.3 AtomicReference and AtomicStampedReference

The AtomicReference and AtomicStampedReference classes are part of the java.util.concurrent.atomic package, providing support for atomic operations on objects and pairs of objects and integer stamps, respectively. Unlike the primitive atomic classes such as AtomicInteger and AtomicLong, these classes handle references to objects, offering a broader range of use cases in complex applications.

AtomicReference

AtomicReference permits atomic operations on object references. These operations include get, set, lazySet, compareAndSet, weakCompareAndSet, and getAndSet. Here is an example illustrating the usage of AtomicReference:

```
import java.util.concurrent.atomic.AtomicReference;

public class AtomicReferenceExample {
    private static AtomicReference<String> atomicString = new AtomicReference<>("
        initial value");

    public static void main(String[] args) {
        System.out.println("current value: " + atomicString.get());

        // Attempt to change the value atomically
        boolean isUpdated = atomicString.compareAndSet("initial value", "new value");
        System.out.println("updated: " + isUpdated);
        System.out.println("current value: " + atomicString.get());

        // Attempt to change the value atomically with an incorrect expected value
        isUpdated = atomicString.compareAndSet("incorrect value", "another new value
            ");
        System.out.println("updated: " + isUpdated);
        System.out.println("current value: " + atomicString.get());
    }
}
```

Below is what you would see when executing the above code:

```
current value: initial value
updated: true
current value: new value
updated: false
current value: new value
```

AtomicReference provides a simple interface for performing atomic operations on object references without explicit locking. However, it is not suitable for objects that might have been concurrently mutated or need version control to handle specific concurrency issues. For such use cases, AtomicStampedReference is utilized.

AtomicStampedReference

AtomicStampedReference addresses a more sophisticated scenario where a reference should be associated with an integer value, often representing versioning or timestamps. It is instrumental in preventing the ABA problem, wherein a location holds the value A, is changed to value B, and then back to value A, leading the typical compareAndSet operations to falsely succeed.

The AtomicStampedReference class provides atomic operations on pairs of objects and an integer "stamp." Here is an example showcasing its usage:

```
import java.util.concurrent.atomic.AtomicStampedReference;

public class AtomicStampedReferenceExample {
    private static final AtomicStampedReference<String> stampedReference =
        new AtomicStampedReference<>("initial value", 0);

    public static void main(String[] args) {
        int[] stampHolder = new int[1];

        // Get the current reference and stamp
        String currentReference = stampedReference.get(stampHolder);
        System.out.println("current reference: " + currentReference + ", stamp: " +
             stampHolder[0]);

        // Attempt to change the reference and stamp atomically
        boolean isUpdated = stampedReference.compareAndSet("initial value", "new
             value", stampHolder[0], stampHolder[0] + 1);
        System.out.println("updated: " + isUpdated);
        System.out.println("current reference: " + stampedReference.get(stampHolder)
             + ", stamp: " + stampHolder[0]);

        // Attempt to change with an incorrect stamp
        isUpdated = stampedReference.compareAndSet("new value", "another new
             value", stampHolder[0], stampHolder[0] + 1);
        System.out.println("updated: " + isUpdated);
        System.out.println("current reference: " + stampedReference.get(stampHolder)
             + ", stamp: " + stampHolder[0]);

        // Direct manipulation of the reference without altering the stamp (risky)
        stampedReference.set("force set value", stampHolder[0]);
        System.out.println("current reference: " + stampedReference.get(stampHolder)
             + ", stamp: " + stampHolder[0]);
```

```
    }
}
```

The program executed would provide the following output:

```
current reference: initial value, stamp: 0
updated: true
current reference: new value, stamp: 1
updated: true
current reference: another new value, stamp: 2
current reference: force set value, stamp: 2
```

Utilizing AtomicStampedReference ensures that changes to the reference are accompanied by the correct version (stamp) changes, preventing scenarios where the ABA problem would cause undesired behavior.

Both AtomicReference and AtomicStampedReference increase the granularity at which concurrent updates can be managed effectively. They are pivotal in scenarios where object references need to be handled atomically in a concurrent context, ensuring system stability and robustness without necessitating synchronized blocks.

7.4 AtomicFieldUpdater Classes

The AtomicFieldUpdater classes provide a mechanism to perform atomic updates on designated fields of specified classes. This is achieved through the use of reflection. The AtomicFieldUpdater variants include AtomicIntegerFieldUpdater, AtomicLongFieldUpdater, and AtomicReferenceFieldUpdater. These classes are particularly useful when updating non-static fields of objects where the cost of creating atomic wrapper objects is prohibitive.

AtomicFieldUpdater classes are a part of the java.util.concurrent.atomic package and offer a low-level means of manipulating the fields of objects in a thread-safe manner. Each updater can only operate on a single field of a class. Consequently, these updaters are instantiated with a target class and a specific field name.

Creating an AtomicIntegerFieldUpdater

Here is an example of how to create and use an AtomicIntegerFieldUpdater:

```
import java.util.concurrent.atomic.AtomicIntegerFieldUpdater;

class Person {
```

```
    volatile int age;
}

public class AtomicFieldUpdaterExample {
    // Create an AtomicIntegerFieldUpdater for the field 'age' in Person class
    private static final AtomicIntegerFieldUpdater<Person> ageUpdater =
            AtomicIntegerFieldUpdater.newUpdater(Person.class, "age");

    public static void main(String[] args) {
        Person person = new Person();
        person.age = 25;

        // Increment the age atomically
        ageUpdater.incrementAndGet(person);
        System.out.println("Updated age: " + person.age);
    }
}
```

```
Updated age: 26
```

In this example, the AtomicIntegerFieldUpdater for the age field of the Person class is created using the newUpdater method. This updater ensures that updates to the age field are atomic. The field must be volatile to ensure visibility of updates across threads.

AtomicLongFieldUpdater and AtomicReferenceFieldUpdater

Similarly, AtomicLongFieldUpdater and AtomicReferenceFieldUpdater can be created for operating on long and reference types respectively. Below is an example using AtomicLongFieldUpdater:

```
import java.util.concurrent.atomic.AtomicLongFieldUpdater;

class Account {
    volatile long balance;
}

public class AtomicLongFieldUpdaterExample {
    private static final AtomicLongFieldUpdater<Account> balanceUpdater =
            AtomicLongFieldUpdater.newUpdater(Account.class, "balance");

    public static void main(String[] args) {
        Account account = new Account();
        account.balance = 1000L;

        // Add 500 to the balance atomically
        balanceUpdater.addAndGet(account, 500L);
        System.out.println("Updated balance: " + account.balance);
    }
}
```

```
Updated balance: 1500
```

For the AtomicReferenceFieldUpdater, the usage pattern remains the same:

```
import java.util.concurrent.atomic.AtomicReferenceFieldUpdater;

class Node {
    volatile Node next;
}

public class AtomicReferenceFieldUpdaterExample {
    private static final AtomicReferenceFieldUpdater<Node, Node> nextUpdater =
            AtomicReferenceFieldUpdater.newUpdater(Node.class, Node.class, "next");

    public static void main(String[] args) {
        Node node1 = new Node();
        Node node2 = new Node();

        // Set node2 as the next node of node1 atomically
        nextUpdater.set(node1, node2);
        System.out.println("Node1's next is node2: " + (node1.next == node2));
    }
}
```

```
Node1's next is node2: true
```

Use Cases and Advantages

The use of AtomicFieldUpdater classes is advantageous in various contexts, mainly when dealing with performance-sensitive code. Key use cases include:

- **Reducing object contention**: By directly manipulating fields rather than encapsulating them within atomic wrapper objects, you reduce the overhead of additional object creation and contention.
- **Memory efficiency**: These classes are preferable when you have multiple objects requiring updates to fields, as it negates the need for each object to have its atomic wrapper instance.
- **Improving cache locality**: Direct field manipulation can provide better cache performance compared to manipulating values through additional levels of indirection.

Security restrictions are crucial when using AtomicFieldUpdater. Only fields that can be accessed by standard Java access control (private, protected, and package-private fields) can be updated via these updaters. Moreover, both the field and the updater must be declared through the same class loader to prevent incorrect visibility or security violations.

Limitations and Considerations

Despite the advantages, there are several limitations and considerations to bear in mind:

- Initialization: The target fields must be declared as volatile.
- Type Safety: There is no compile-time checking to ensure that the provided field name matches the expected field type.
- Reflection Overhead: Using reflection introduces a certain level of overhead, and improper use can lead to performance degradation.

Here is an algorithm illustrating the typical usage of AtomicIntegerFieldUpdater:

Algorithm 6: Usage of AtomicIntegerFieldUpdater

```
Data: Class with volatile integer field
Result: Atomic updates to integer field
SetupUpdater() begin
    Initialize updater with target class and field name;
UpdateField(obj, value) begin
    atomically update the field of obj with value;
Main() begin
    Create an instance of target class;
    Set initial value of the field;
    Call UpdateField();
```

This structured approach ensures thread-safe manipulation of object fields while leveraging concurrent programming capabilities of the Java platform effectively. The use of AtomicFieldUpdater aligns closely with the principles of lock-free programming, promoting high-performance concurrent application design.

7.5 Compare-And-Swap (CAS) Operations

Compare-And-Swap (CAS) is a pivotal concept in the realm of lock-free programming. CAS operations enable atomicity in concurrent environments without relying on traditional synchronization mechanisms like locks. The CAS paradigm is crucial for the implementation of various atomic classes in Java and supports building high-performance, non-blocking algorithms.

A CAS operation involves three essential components:

- Expected Value: The value that the variable is expected to hold.
- New Value: The value to be set if the expected value matches the current value.
- Memory Location: The specific memory location of the variable being modified.

The CAS operation verifies if the value at the given memory location equals the expected value. If true, the value is updated to the new value. If false, no change occurs. This entire sequence is performed atomically, ensuring that no other thread intervenes during the process.

The Java programming language provides native support for CAS operations through the sun.misc.Unsafe class. However, for higher-level and safer usage, the java.util.concurrent.atomic package offers several classes that abstract the complexity of direct CAS operations.

Below is a simple example using the sun.misc.Unsafe class to perform a CAS operation:

```
import sun.misc.Unsafe;
import java.lang.reflect.Field;

public class CASExample {
    private static final Unsafe unsafe;
    private static final long valueOffset;
    private volatile int value;

    static {
        try {
            Field f = Unsafe.class.getDeclaredField("theUnsafe");
            f.setAccessible(true);
            unsafe = (Unsafe) f.get(null);
            valueOffset = unsafe.objectFieldOffset(CASExample.class.getDeclaredField("
                value"));
        } catch (Exception ex) {
            throw new Error(ex);
        }
    }

    public CASExample(int initialValue) {
        value = initialValue;
    }

    public boolean compareAndSwap(int expectedValue, int newValue) {
        return unsafe.compareAndSwapInt(this, valueOffset, expectedValue, newValue);
    }
```

```
    public int getValue() {
        return value;
    }

    public void setValue(int newValue) {
        value = newValue;
    }

    public static void main(String[] args) {
        CASExample casExample = new CASExample(5);
        boolean result = casExample.compareAndSwap(5, 10);
        System.out.println("CAS Result: " + result); // should print true
        System.out.println("New Value: " + casExample.getValue()); // should print 10
    }
}
```

```
CAS Result: true
New Value: 10
```

In this example, an object of CASExample is created with an initial value of 5. The compareAndSwap method attempts to compare the current value with the expected value 5 and, if they match, updates the value to 10. The operations are performed atomically using the unsafe.compareAndSwapInt() method.

The concept of CAS can be more seamlessly utilized with the atomic classes in the java.util.concurrent.atomic package. Below is an example using AtomicInteger:

```
import java.util.concurrent.atomic.AtomicInteger;

public class AtomicIntegerExample {
    public static void main(String[] args) {
        AtomicInteger atomicInteger = new AtomicInteger(5);

        boolean result = atomicInteger.compareAndSet(5, 10);
        System.out.println("CAS Result: " + result); // should print true
        System.out.println("New Value: " + atomicInteger.get()); // should print 10
    }
}
```

```
CAS Result: true
New Value: 10
```

In this example, the compareAndSet method of AtomicInteger is effectively wrapping the CAS operation, providing a more user-friendly interface.

CAS operations are not just confined to integers. Java provides atomic classes for other primitive types and objects, such as AtomicBoolean, AtomicLong, AtomicReference, and AtomicStampedReference. Each of these classes relies on CAS operations to provide atomic updates.

The CAS algorithm can be described as follows:

Algorithm 7: CAS Algorithm

Data: Expected value E, New Value N, Memory Location M
Result: Returns true if successful, false otherwise

while *is not interrupted* **do**
    Load the current value from memory location M into C;
    if $C == E$ **then**
        Set memory location M to N;
        return true;
    else
        return false;

CAS forms the foundation of various lock-free data structures, such as concurrent queues, stacks, and counters. It significantly reduces the risk of contention and deadlock, common issues in lock-based synchronization techniques. However, one must consider that CAS can have its own challenges, such as the ABA problem, where the value in memory can change from A to B, and back to A again, leading to erroneous behavior in some scenarios.

Java addresses the ABA problem using the AtomicStampedReference, which pairs the reference with a stamp (version number). By checking both the reference and the stamp, you can detect changes and avoid certain anomalies.

Here is an example of using AtomicStampedReference to solve the ABA problem:

```
import java.util.concurrent.atomic.AtomicStampedReference;

public class AtomicStampedReferenceExample {
    public static void main(String[] args) {
        String initialValue = "foo";
        int initialStamp = 0;

        AtomicStampedReference<String> atomicStampedReference = new
            AtomicStampedReference<>(initialValue, initialStamp);

        int[] stampHolder = new int[1];

        String value = atomicStampedReference.get(stampHolder);
        int currentStamp = stampHolder[0];

        boolean result = atomicStampedReference.compareAndSet(value, "bar",
            currentStamp, currentStamp + 1);
        System.out.println("CAS Result: " + result); // should print true
        System.out.println("New Value: " + atomicStampedReference.getReference());
            // should print bar
```

```
        System.out.println("New Stamp: " + atomicStampedReference.getStamp()); //
            should print 1
    }
}
```

```
CAS Result: true
New Value: bar
New Stamp: 1
```

Understanding CAS operations is critical for developing lock-free and wait-free algorithms. They provide a powerful means to achieve atomicity in concurrent programming without the overhead and complexities associated with traditional locking mechanisms.

7.6 Advantages of Lock-Free Programming

Lock-free programming offers a compelling set of advantages crucial for developing high-performance concurrent applications. Herein, we examine these advantages with a focus on practical implications and underlying mechanisms that contribute to them.

Improved Scalability: One of the primary benefits of lock-free programming is its enhanced scalability. Traditional locking mechanisms, such as synchronized blocks or explicit locks, can become bottlenecks in multi-threaded applications. When multiple threads compete for the same lock, contention arises, and some threads may be forced to wait, significantly reducing performance. Lock-free algorithms, by contrast, allow threads to proceed independently without waiting for locks, thereby reducing contention and improving scalability.

Reduced Deadlock Risk: Deadlocks occur when two or more threads are unable to proceed because each is waiting for the other to release a lock. Deadlock prevention and resolution can be complex and costly. Lock-free programming inherently avoids deadlocks as threads do not acquire locks to perform operations. Instead, they use atomic operations and Compare-And-Swap (CAS) techniques to ensure data consistency, which, by design, eliminates the possibility of deadlocks.

Consistency under High Contention: In environments with high contention, traditional locking can lead to significant performance degradation due to the frequent blocking and unblocking of threads. Lock-free algorithms maintain consistency without suspending threads, making them particularly effective in such scenarios. The following pseudocode illustrates the difference:

```
synchronized void increment() {
    counter++;
}
```

```
void lockFreeIncrement() {
    int temp;
    do {
        temp = atomicCounter.get();
    } while (!atomicCounter.compareAndSet(temp, temp + 1));
}
```

The lock-free implementation using compareAndSet ensures that the increment operation is performed atomically without blocking other threads.

Higher Throughput: Lock-based mechanisms can significantly reduce throughput due to context switching, especially under high load conditions. Context switching is an expensive operation where the state of a currently running thread is saved and the state of the next thread is loaded. Lock-free operations are typically single CAS instructions executed directly by the hardware, thus minimizing context switching and increasing throughput.

Fault-Tolerance and Robustness: Systems employing lock-free programming demonstrate better fault tolerance. When a thread is paused or terminated unexpectedly in a lock-free system, other threads can continue executing without waiting for the release of locks. This ensures higher availability and reliability of the system.

Minimized Latency: In low-latency systems, waiting for locks can introduce unacceptable delays. Lock-free techniques leverage atomic operations that complete in a bounded amount of time. This predictability is crucial for applications where response time is critical, such as real-time trading systems or interactive applications.

Avoidance of Priority Inversion: Priority inversion occurs when higher-priority threads are blocked by lower-priority ones holding a necessary lock. Lock-free programming avoids this scenario entirely as higher-priority threads never have to wait for lower-priority threads to release locks. This ensures that system resources are optimally used in accordance with thread priorities.

Simplicity and Maintenance: Though lock-free algorithms can be more complex to implement initially, they often simplify maintenance. Conventional lock-based systems can suffer from subtle bugs like deadlocks and priority inversions, which are notoriously difficult to diagnose and fix. Once a lock-free algorithm is correctly implemented, it tends to be easier to understand and maintain due to the absence of these concurrency issues.

Energy Efficiency: Systems that employ idle spinning or blocking mechanisms tend to consume more energy due to frequent context switching and processor activity. Lock-free techniques, by reducing idle time and improving processing efficiency, contribute to lower power consumption. This is particularly beneficial in mobile and embedded systems where energy efficiency is paramount.

Enhanced Performance Metrics: Finally, practical implementations and benchmarking often show that lock-free algorithms outperform their lock-based counterparts across multiple metrics, including throughput, latency, and CPU utilization. This is due to their ability to facilitate greater parallelism and minimize overhead associated with traditional locking.

By leveraging atomic variables and lock-free programming techniques, developers can design systems that are not only high-performing but also reliable and scalable, addressing many of the concurrency issues faced in modern multi-threaded applications. The reduction in locking overhead and contention leads to more efficient resource utilization and optimal execution of concurrent tasks.

7.7 Designing Lock-Free Algorithms

Designing lock-free algorithms necessitates a thorough understanding of atomic operations and the underlying hardware mechanisms such as Compare-And-Swap (CAS). Lock-free data structures are devised to ensure that some thread will complete its operation in a finite number of steps, regardless of the progress of other threads.

Concept of Lock-Free Structures: Lock-free structures employ a methodology where threads cooperate and make progress without mutually-exclusive locks. Each thread operates independently, with atomic variables ensuring data integrity without the use of traditional locks, thus enhancing parallelism and reducing contention.

AtomicReference assists in implementing lock-free algorithms by enabling the atomic comparison and setting of references. Consider a lock-free stack:

```
import java.util.concurrent.atomic.AtomicReference;

public class LockFreeStack<T> {
```

```
    private static class Node<T> {
        final T value;
        Node<T> next;

        Node(T value) {
            this.value = value;
        }
    }

    private final AtomicReference<Node<T>> top = new AtomicReference<>();

    public void push(T value) {
        Node<T> newNode = new Node<>(value);
        Node<T> currentTop;
        do {
            currentTop = top.get();
            newNode.next = currentTop;
        } while (!top.compareAndSet(currentTop, newNode));
    }

    public T pop() {
        Node<T> currentTop;
        Node<T> newTop;
        do {
            currentTop = top.get();
            if (currentTop == null) return null;
            newTop = currentTop.next;
        } while (!top.compareAndSet(currentTop, newTop));
        return currentTop.value;
    }
}
```

In this implementation, the push method creates a new node and places it at the top of the stack. It uses compareAndSet to ensure the top reference is updated atomically. The pop method reads the current top, retrieves the value, and attempts to update the top reference using compareAndSet.

Advantages of Lock-Free Algorithms: 1. Increased parallelism: Threads are not blocked, allowing multiple operations to occur simultaneously. 2. Reduced contention: Since there are no locks, the contention points that could slow down the threads are minimized. 3. Prevent deadlocks: Lock-free algorithms cannot encounter deadlocks, as they do not hold locks.

Design Considerations: When designing lock-free algorithms, consider:

- Atomicity: Use atomic variables and operations to ensure that intermediate states are not visible to other threads.
- Correctness: Ensure the correctness through rigorous testing and validation of the algorithm.

- Fairness: Design the algorithm such that every thread gets a fair opportunity to make progress.
- Consistency: Ensure the algorithm maintains the consistency of the data structure.

Example: Lock-Free Queue

Here is an example of a lock-free queue using AtomicReference:

```
import java.util.concurrent.atomic.AtomicReference;

public class LockFreeQueue<T> {
    private static class Node<T> {
        final T value;
        final AtomicReference<Node<T>> next;

        Node(T value, Node<T> next) {
            this.value = value;
            this.next = new AtomicReference<>(next);
        }
    }

    private final AtomicReference<Node<T>> head;
    private final AtomicReference<Node<T>> tail;

    public LockFreeQueue() {
        Node<T> dummy = new Node<>(null, null);
        head = new AtomicReference<>(dummy);
        tail = new AtomicReference<>(dummy);
    }

    public void enqueue(T value) {
        Node<T> newNode = new Node<>(value, null);
        Node<T> curTail;
        Node<T> tailNext;
        while (true) {
            curTail = tail.get();
            tailNext = curTail.next.get();
            if (curTail == tail.get()) {
                if (tailNext == null) {
                    if (curTail.next.compareAndSet(null, newNode)) {
                        tail.compareAndSet(curTail, newNode);
                        return;
                    }
                } else {
                    tail.compareAndSet(curTail, tailNext);
                }
            }
        }
    }

    public T dequeue() {
        Node<T> curHead;
        Node<T> curTail;
        Node<T> next;
        while (true) {
            curHead = head.get();
            curTail = tail.get();
            next = curHead.next.get();
```

```
            if (curHead == head.get()) {
                if (curHead == curTail) {
                    if (next == null) {
                        return null;
                    }
                    tail.compareAndSet(curTail, next);
                } else {
                    if (head.compareAndSet(curHead, next)) {
                        return next.value;
                    }
                }
            }
        }
    }
}
```

In this queue, enqueue and dequeue methods employ compareAndSet to atomically manage the head and tail references, ensuring thread safety without locks.

Designing lock-free algorithms often requires leveraging lower-level primitives and can be challenging due to the complexity of ensuring correctness and avoiding subtle bugs. Despite the complexity, the benefits of improved performance and scalability in multi-core environments make lock-free algorithms a compelling area for concurrent programming.

7.8 Challenges in Lock-Free Programming

Lock-free programming presents several challenges that must be addressed to develop efficient and correct concurrent applications. Recognizing these challenges and understanding their implications is essential to mastering lock-free techniques. The main challenges include the complexity of algorithm design, difficulty in debugging, ensuring fairness, handling memory contention, and managing memory reclamation.

Complexity of Algorithm Design: Designing lock-free algorithms is inherently complex because it requires a deep understanding of concurrent changes to shared data structures without using locks. A fundamental operation used in lock-free programming is Compare-And-Swap (CAS), but relying solely on CAS to manage state transitions can lead to intricate code paths that are difficult to reason about.

A lock-free algorithm must ensure that every thread makes progress or, at the very least, prevents any thread from becoming permanently blocked. This requirement is known as the progress guarantee. Achieving this while handling all possible interleavings of threads, especially in systems with many processors, challenges the developer to think beyond the typical sequential logic.

Difficulty in Debugging: Lock-free programs are notoriously difficult to debug. Concurrency issues such as race conditions, data inconsistencies, and memory ordering problems can manifest in non-deterministic ways, making them hard to reproduce and analyze. Unlike traditional locking mechanisms where critical sections are clearly delineated, lock-free constructs interleave operations in a way that is less transparent.

A common debugging challenge is the subtle nature of heisenbugs, which are bugs that seem to vanish when one attempts to study them, often due to added debug output or changes in timing. Traditional debugging tools are often less effective because they can introduce delays that alter the timing of concurrent operations, masking the real problem. Advanced tools and techniques such as thread sanitizers and specialized tracing tools are necessary for effective debugging of lock-free programs.

Ensuring Fairness: Fairness in lock-free programming means that no single thread should continuously succeed at the expense of others due to faster execution or better scheduling. This scenario, often referred to as starvation, can occur when multiple threads compete for the same resource and the lock-free algorithm favors one thread consistently.

Ensuring fairness requires designing algorithms that allow all participants a fair chance to execute their critical sections. One strategy to mitigate starvation involves backoff mechanisms, where a thread that fails to acquire a resource waits for a randomized period before retrying. This approach helps distribute contention more evenly over time.

Handling Memory Contention: Memory contention arises when multiple threads attempt to access or modify the same memory location simultaneously, leading to reduced performance. In lock-free programming, techniques such as spatial and temporal locality optimization are used to minimize contention. Spatial locality ensures that frequently accessed data are located close to each other in memory to take advantage of cache lines, whereas temporal locality tries to ensure data is accessed by each thread predictably.

A common solution to alleviate memory contention is employing padding. By adding extra space around critical data structures, false sharing—a performance-degrading scenario where two or more

Algorithm 8: Backoff algorithm to reduce contention

```
Function Backoff()
    base_wait ← initial_wait
    max_wait ← maximum_wait
    num_failed ← 0
    while true do
        if critical_section_available then
            acquire_critical_section()
            return
        wait_time ← calculate_wait_time(base_wait,
          num_failed, max_wait)
        sleep(wait_time)
        num_failed ← num_failed + 1
```

threads modify adjacent data fields causing an entire cache line to be invalidated—is reduced.

```
public class PaddedAtomicLong {
    private volatile long value;
    private long pad1, pad2, pad3, pad4, pad5, pad6, pad7; // Padding fields

    public long get() {
        return value;
    }

    public void set(long newValue) {
        value = newValue;
    }
}
```

Managing Memory Reclamation: When nodes or objects are removed in a lock-free data structure, such as a linked list or a queue, safely reclaiming memory without race conditions presents a significant challenge. Traditional memory reclamation strategies like garbage collection can lead to inefficiencies in real-time systems due to unpredictable pauses.

Hazard pointers and epochs are advanced techniques employed to manage memory reclamation in lock-free algorithms. Hazard pointers allow threads to safely indicate which nodes they are currently accessing, thus preventing other threads from reclaiming those nodes prematurely.

```
public class HazardPointer {
    private static int MAX_THREADS = 10;
```

```
    private static volatile Object[] hazardPointers = new Object[MAX_THREADS];

    public static void enter(int threadId, Object ptr) {
        hazardPointers[threadId] = ptr;
    }

    public static void exit(int threadId) {
        hazardPointers[threadId] = null;
    }

    public static boolean isPointerHazarded(Object ptr) {
        for (Object hPtr : hazardPointers) {
            if (hPtr == ptr) {
                return true;
            }
        }
        return false;
    }
}
```

Epoch-based reclamation segments operation durations into epochs, ensuring objects are not freed until all operations that might reference them are complete. An epoch counter keeps track of the latest safe point for memory reclamation, coordinating among threads to signal the completion of critical sections.

```
public class EpochManager {
    private AtomicLong currentEpoch = new AtomicLong(0);
    private final ThreadLocal<Long> threadEpoch = ThreadLocal.withInitial(() -> 0L)
        ;

    public void enterCriticalSection() {
        long epoch = currentEpoch.get();
        threadEpoch.set(epoch);
    }

    public void exitCriticalSection() {
        // Epoch leaving logic
    }

    public void advanceEpoch() {
        currentEpoch.incrementAndGet();
        // Reclaim memory logic
    }
}
```

Despite these challenges, advancements in tooling, methodologies, and the understanding of concurrency principles continue to facilitate the utilization of lock-free techniques in developing high-performance concurrent applications.

7.9 Atomic Arrays

Atomic arrays provide a scalable way to handle atomic variables in array structures, essential in concurrent programming scenarios where managing multiple variables atomically can otherwise lead to significant synchronization overhead. The java.util.concurrent.atomic package includes several classes designed for atomic operations on array elements, including AtomicIntegerArray, AtomicLongArray, and AtomicReferenceArray. These classes extend the atomicity guarantees from single variables to arrays, aiding in the creation of lock-free and thread-safe code.

AtomicIntegerArray

The AtomicIntegerArray class wraps an array of integers, allowing atomic operations to be performed on its elements. It uses a volatile array internally to ensure visibility of changes across threads. Common atomic operations include get, set, lazySet, compareAndSet, getAndIncrement, getAndDecrement, and getAndAdd. Consider the following code example:

```
AtomicIntegerArray atomicArray = new AtomicIntegerArray(10);

// Setting an element
atomicArray.set(0, 1);

// Getting an element
int value = atomicArray.get(0);

// Atomically incrementing an element
int oldValue = atomicArray.getAndIncrement(0);
```

The compareAndSet method is particularly useful for implementing non-blocking algorithms, as shown below:

```
boolean updated = atomicArray.compareAndSet(0, 1, 2);
```

In this snippet, compareAndSet compares the value at index 0 to the expected value (1) and sets it to the new value (2) if they are equal. The operation is atomic, ensuring no other thread interferes during the comparison and update.

AtomicLongArray

Similar to AtomicIntegerArray, the AtomicLongArray class is designed for arrays of long values. This class provides identical methods but operates on long integers.

```
AtomicLongArray atomicLongArray = new AtomicLongArray(10);

// Setting an element
atomicLongArray.set(0, 10L);

// Getting an element
long longValue = atomicLongArray.get(0);

// Atomically adding a value
long previousValue = atomicLongArray.getAndAdd(0, 5L);
```

compareAndSet in AtomicLongArray works the same way:

```
boolean longUpdated = atomicLongArray.compareAndSet(0, 10L, 15L);
```

This operation will atomically check if the current value at index 0 is 10L and, if so, update it to 15L.

AtomicReferenceArray

For non-primitive data types, AtomicReferenceArray allows atomic operations on an array of object references. This is highly beneficial for managing references concurrently, ensuring consistency without explicit synchronization.

```
AtomicReferenceArray<String> atomicReferenceArray = new AtomicReferenceArray
    <>(10);

// Setting an element
atomicReferenceArray.set(0, "Hello");

// Getting an element
String referencedValue = atomicReferenceArray.get(0);

// Atomically updating a value
boolean referenceUpdated = atomicReferenceArray.compareAndSet(0, "Hello", "World"
    );
```

Atomic reference arrays are leveraged for creating sophisticated non-blocking data structures such as concurrent linked lists, queue implementations, and other collections where reference integrity is paramount.

Practical Use Cases

Atomic arrays are especially useful in high-performance computing applications where large datasets need concurrent access and updates. For instance, consider a scenario involving parallel processing of sensor data where each sensor's readings are stored in atomic arrays and processed concurrently by multiple threads. Atomic arrays ensure that updates to sensor readings are correctly synchronized without the need for explicit locks, thus enhancing performance.

Another practical application involves implementing a concurrent hash table where each bucket is managed by an AtomicReferenceArray. This approach allows for fine-grained synchronization at the bucket level, avoiding global locks and reducing contention.

Performance Considerations

While atomic arrays offer significant advantages over explicit locking mechanisms by reducing contention and improving scalability, they are not a panacea. The performance benefits can be context-specific; in scenarios with low contention or where complex atomic operations are required, traditional locks might still be more efficient. Furthermore, excessive reliance on atomic operations can lead to challenges such as increased memory consumption due to internal padding to prevent false sharing, and higher algorithmic complexity.

Understanding these trade-offs and profiling concurrent applications to tailor atomic array usage appropriately is crucial for achieving optimal performance.

Atomic arrays represent a vital tool in the concurrent programming toolbox, bridging the gap between single atomic variables and more complex concurrent data structures. Their usage promotes lock-free programming paradigms, enabling the development of scalable and responsive multithreaded applications.

7.10 Performance Considerations in Lock-Free Programming

Lock-free programming offers significant advantages in terms of performance, especially in highly concurrent environments. However, these benefits come with various considerations that developers must account for when designing and implementing lock-free data structures and algorithms. Understanding these considerations is crucial for harnessing the full potential of lock-free techniques.

First, let us examine the cache coherence protocols and how they impact the performance of lock-free algorithms. Modern processors are equipped with multi-level caches to reduce the latency of memory accesses. These caches must stay coherent across multiple cores, meaning that when one core updates a variable, the changes must be visible to other cores promptly. This coherence is typically maintained through protocols such as MESI (Modified, Exclusive, Shared, Invalid).

Lock-free algorithms frequently operate with shared variables, invoking frequent cache coherence operations. Consequently, these cache operations can introduce overhead. For instance, the Compare-And-Swap (CAS) operation, fundamental in many lock-free structures, may result in multiple cache misses or invalidations, reflecting in the overall performance.

```
final AtomicInteger atomicInt = new AtomicInteger(0);
while (!atomicInt.compareAndSet(expectedValue, newValue)) {
    // Retry mechanism
}
```

Given this, the careful design of data structures to minimize contention is vital. False sharing, where independent variables share a cache line, can degrade performance since updates to one variable result in unnecessary invalidations of the other variable's cache line. A common practice to mitigate false sharing is to pad variables to ensure they occupy separate cache lines.

```
class PaddedAtomicInteger {
    private volatile int value;
    private long p1, p2, p3, p4, p5, p6, p7; // Padding fields
    public PaddedAtomicInteger(int initialValue) {
        value = initialValue;
    }
    ...
}
```

Additionally, the choice and implementation of atomic operations like CAS themselves introduce varying levels of performance impact. On some architectures, CAS operations can be highly optimized, while others may incur significant overhead. Understanding the specific hardware characteristics and leveraging processor-specific optimizations can make a notable difference. For example, on x86 architectures, LOCK_CMPXCHG can introduce a full memory barrier, which can be costly.

Algorithm 9: CAS Operation in x86 Architecture

```
Data: AtomicInteger atomicInt, int expectedValue, int newValue
while atomicInt.compareAndSet(expectedValue, newValue) ==
  False do
    retry;
end
```

Another critical consideration is the memory allocation patterns associated with lock-free data structures. Memory management strategies, such as garbage collection in languages like Java, must be taken into account. Lock-free algorithms frequently create and manage many short-lived objects, which can increase the garbage collector's workload and negatively impact performance. Employing object pools or other memory management techniques might alleviate this.

The scalability of lock-free algorithms is another aspect that necessitates attention. Although lock-free techniques often outperform traditional locking mechanisms in scenarios with high contention, their performance can still degrade under extreme concurrency levels. The contention on atomic variables, especially under high thread count, can lead to excessive retries in CAS loops, diminishing returns in performance.

For example, a lock-free stack implemented using an AtomicReference<Node> might perform well up to a certain number of threads but may experience performance bottlenecks as thread count increases:

```
class LockFreeStack<T> {
    private AtomicReference<Node> top = new AtomicReference<>(null);

    void push(T value) {
        Node newNode = new Node(value);
        Node currentTop;
        do {
            currentTop = top.get();
            newNode.next = currentTop;
        } while (!top.compareAndSet(currentTop, newNode));
    }

    T pop() {
        Node currentTop;
        Node newTop;
        do {
            currentTop = top.get();
            if (currentTop == null) return null; // Empty stack
            newTop = currentTop.next;
        } while (!top.compareAndSet(currentTop, newTop));
        return currentTop.value;
    }
```

```
    private static class Node {
        final T value;
        Node next;
        Node(T value) {
            this.value = value;
        }
    }
}
```

Lastly, developers must incorporate appropriate monitoring and profiling tools to effectively analyze the performance of lock-free algorithms. Tools that can measure CPU cycles, memory bandwidth, cache hits and misses, and synchronization costs are invaluable for this purpose. Profiling can reveal hidden bottlenecks and guide optimizations tailored to specific workloads and hardware configurations.

Understanding the nuanced interplay of factors such as cache coherence, false sharing, atomic operation overheads, memory management, scalability, and tools for profiling culminates in a comprehensive approach to optimizing lock-free programming. Each consideration is an essential piece in achieving performant and reliable concurrent applications.

7.11 Examples of Atomic Variables in Real-World Applications

Atomic variables are pivotal in crafting high-performance concurrent applications without the need for explicit synchronization mechanisms like mutexes or locks. By leveraging atomic variables, one can ensure thread-safe operations that are non-blocking, leading to refined control over shared resources. This section elucidates real-world examples demonstrating the utility and significance of atomic variables such as AtomicInteger, AtomicLong, AtomicBoolean, AtomicReference, and AtomicStampedReference.

1. Implementing a Thread-Safe Counter

Counters are fundamental components in numerous applications, ranging from statistical data collection to performance monitoring. A traditional counter can become a point of contention in a multi-threaded environment, leading to bottlenecks. Utilizing AtomicInteger ensures the counter remains thread-safe and highly performant.

```
import java.util.concurrent.atomic.AtomicInteger;
```

```
public class ThreadSafeCounter {
    private AtomicInteger counter = new AtomicInteger(0);

    public void increment() {
        counter.getAndIncrement();
    }

    public int getValue() {
        return counter.get();
    }
}
```

Execution of multiple threads incrementing the counter reliably increments the value atomically.

```
Thread 1: Incrementing counter to 1
Thread 2: Incrementing counter to 2
...
Final Counter Value: 1000
```

2. Enhancing a Shared Flag with AtomicBoolean

A shared flag often determines the status of a concurrent process. For example, in implementing a safe-shutdown mechanism, using AtomicBoolean helps ensure the flag is modified atomically across multiple threads.

```
import java.util.concurrent.atomic.AtomicBoolean;

public class SafeShutdown {
    private AtomicBoolean running = new AtomicBoolean(true);

    public void stop() {
        running.set(false);
    }

    public boolean isRunning() {
        return running.get();
    }
}
```

Thread-safe modification of the running flag prevents inconsistent states during shutdown.

```
Thread 1: Stopping service...
Service stopped safely.
```

3. Concurrent Stack Using AtomicReference

Implementing a concurrent stack involves managing references to nodes atomically to avoid race conditions. AtomicReference can be used to manage the stack's head node safely.

```
import java.util.concurrent.atomic.AtomicReference;

public class ConcurrentStack<E> {
```

```
    private static class Node<E> {
        final E item;
        Node<E> next;

        Node(E item) {
            this.item = item;
        }
    }

    private final AtomicReference<Node<E>> head = new AtomicReference<>();

    public void push(E item) {
        Node<E> newNode = new Node<>(item);
        Node<E> oldHead;
        do {
            oldHead = head.get();
            newNode.next = oldHead;
        } while (!head.compareAndSet(oldHead, newNode));
    }

    public E pop() {
        Node<E> oldHead;
        Node<E> newHead;
        do {
            oldHead = head.get();
            if (oldHead == null) {
                return null; // Stack is empty
            }
            newHead = oldHead.next;
        } while (!head.compareAndSet(oldHead, newHead));
        return oldHead.item;
    }
}
```

This stack implementation ensures atomic operations for push and pop, even with multiple concurrent threads.

```
Thread 1: Pushed value 10
Thread 2: Pushed value 20
Thread 3: Popped value 20
Thread 4: Popped value 10
```

4. Optimistic Locking with AtomicStampedReference

In scenarios where version control or timestamping of an object is required, AtomicStampedReference aids in managing both the object reference and metadata atomicity.

```
import java.util.concurrent.atomic.AtomicStampedReference;

public class VersionedReference<T> {
    private final AtomicStampedReference<T> ref;

    public VersionedReference(T initialRef, int initialStamp) {
        ref = new AtomicStampedReference<>(initialRef, initialStamp);
    }

    public T getReference() {
        return ref.getReference();
    }
```

```
    public int getStamp() {
        return ref.getStamp();
    }

    public boolean compareAndSet(T expectedReference, T newReference, int
            expectedStamp, int newStamp) {
        return ref.compareAndSet(expectedReference, newReference, expectedStamp,
                newStamp);
    }
}
```

Using AtomicStampedReference ensures version control consistency during concurrent modifications.

```
Current Reference: Object1, Version: 1
Updating to Object2, Version: 2
Update successful: true
```

5. Non-Blocking Counters with AtomicLong for High-Frequency Timestamps

Recording high-frequency timestamps requires a non-blocking counter mechanism. AtomicLong is an optimal choice to minimize contention and improve throughput in time-critical applications.

```
import java.util.concurrent.atomic.AtomicLong;

public class HighFrequencyTimestamp {
    private final AtomicLong timestamp = new AtomicLong();

    public long getNextTimestamp() {
        return timestamp.incrementAndGet();
    }
}
```

Atomic increment operations ensure each timestamp is unique and generated efficiently.

```
Timestamp: 1
Timestamp: 2
Timestamp: 3
...
Timestamp: 100000
```

These examples illuminate the practicality and effectiveness of atomic variables in solving concurrency challenges inherent in real-world applications. The non-blocking properties intrinsic to atomic variables foster scalable and performant designs.

Chapter 8

Working with Futures and CompletableFutures

This chapter covers the use of Future and CompletableFuture for asynchronous programming in Java. It explains how to create and manage Future objects, including cancelling and checking the status of asynchronous tasks. The chapter introduces CompletableFuture, detailing task creation, chaining, and combining CompletableFutures. It addresses exception handling, running asynchronous tasks, and provides real-world examples to illustrate practical usage. Emphasis is placed on improving application performance and responsiveness through effective use of these concurrency constructs.

8.1 Introduction to Future Interface

The Future interface in Java represents the result of an asynchronous computation. It provides a way to write multi-threaded programs where tasks are executed in parallel, and their results can be retrieved at a later point in time. The core idea of the Future interface is to abstract the concept of an operation that will complete in the future, allowing programmers to decouple the execution of a task from its result.

The Future interface is part of the java.util.concurrent package and defines several essential methods to manage the execution and retrieval of asynchronous task results. Below is the complete definition of the Future interface:

```
public interface Future<V> {
    boolean cancel(boolean mayInterruptIfRunning);
    boolean isCancelled();
    boolean isDone();
    V get() throws InterruptedException, ExecutionException;
    V get(long timeout, TimeUnit unit)
        throws InterruptedException, ExecutionException, TimeoutException;
}
```

Each method of the Future interface has a specific purpose:

- cancel(boolean mayInterruptIfRunning): Attempts to cancel the execution of the task. If the task has already completed or been cancelled, this method will return false. If cancellation is successful, it returns true. The mayInterruptIfRunning parameter determines if the thread executing the task should be interrupted.
- isCancelled(): Returns true if the task was cancelled before it completed normally.
- isDone(): Returns true if the task is completed, either by normal termination, an exception, or cancellation.
- get(): Retrieves the result of the task, blocking if necessary until the computation is done. This method throws InterruptedException if the current thread is interrupted while waiting, and ExecutionException if the computation threw an exception.
- get(long timeout, TimeUnit unit): Similar to get(), but allows specifying a timeout. If the timeout elapses before the result becomes available, a TimeoutException is thrown.

To better understand the Future interface, consider a simple example where a long-running computation is executed asynchronously using a Future:

```
import java.util.concurrent.*;

public class FutureExample {
    public static void main(String[] args) {
        ExecutorService executor = Executors.newFixedThreadPool(1);
        Future<Integer> future = executor.submit(() -> {
            Thread.sleep(3000); // Simulate long-running task
            return 42;
        });

        try {
```

```
            System.out.println("Doing other tasks while waiting for result...");
            Integer result = future.get(); // Wait and retrieve the result
            System.out.println("Result of computation: " + result);
        } catch (InterruptedException | ExecutionException e) {
            e.printStackTrace();
        } finally {
            executor.shutdown();
        }
    }
}
```

In this example, an ExecutorService is used to run a task that takes approximately 3 seconds to complete. The result of the task is an integer value (42), which is retrieved using the Future.get() method. While waiting for the task to complete, other operations can be performed, demonstrating the non-blocking nature of asynchronous programming.

The task of managing and retrieving results from the Future introduces several scenarios: 1. Proper handling of task cancellation scenarios where tasks need to be stopped gracefully. 2. Managing timeouts to avoid indefinitely waiting for slower tasks. 3. Handling exceptions properly to ensure system robustness against unexpected behaviors during the asynchronous computations.

Let's delve deeper into exception handling with Future: When the Future.get() method throws an ExecutionException, it wraps the actual exception thrown by the task. This requires the use of getCause() to retrieve the underlying cause:

```
try {
    Integer result = future.get();
    // Use result
} catch (ExecutionException e) {
    Throwable cause = e.getCause();
    if (cause instanceof SomeSpecificException) {
        // Handle specific exception
    } else {
        e.printStackTrace();
    }
} catch (InterruptedException e) {
    // Handle interruption
}
```

Efficient exception handling ensures that the system remains stable even when asynchronous tasks fail unexpectedly.

Understanding the Future interface is fundamental for working effectively with asynchronous programming in Java. As we proceed to explore the CompletableFuture, the concepts of task chaining and parallelism build on the basics provided by the Future interface, leading to more powerful and flexible concurrent programming paradigms.

8.2 Creating and Managing Futures

To utilize futures in Java effectively, understanding their creation and management is crucial. Java provides several means by which futures can be created, primarily through the ExecutorService interface and its implementing classes. This section will describe the creation and basic management of Future objects, focusing on essential methods and practices that ensure correct utilization in concurrent applications.

A Future represents the result of an asynchronous computation. Methods are provided to check if the computation is complete, wait for its completion, and retrieve the result of the computation. The core methods of the Future interface include isDone(), isCancelled(), cancel(), and get().

```
import java.util.concurrent.Callable;
import java.util.concurrent.ExecutionException;
import java.util.concurrent.ExecutorService;
import java.util.concurrent.Executors;
import java.util.concurrent.Future;

public class FutureExample {
    public static void main(String[] args) {
        ExecutorService executorService = Executors.newSingleThreadExecutor();

        Callable<Integer> task = () -> {
            // Some computation
            Thread.sleep(1000);
            return 123;
        };

        Future<Integer> future = executorService.submit(task);

        try {
            System.out.println("Future result: " + future.get()); // Blocks until result is
                 available
        } catch (InterruptedException | ExecutionException e) {
            e.printStackTrace();
        } finally {
            executorService.shutdown();
        }
    }
}
```

This example demonstrates creating a Future using the ExecutorService's submit() method. The submit() method accepts a Callable or Runnable task and returns a Future representing its pending completion. A Callable differs from a Runnable in that it can return a result and throw a checked exception.

The get() method of the Future interface blocks until the task is completed. If the computation has completed, get() method immediately returns the result. If the computation has not completed, the get() call waits for the computation to finish and then returns the result.

Checking Task Completion

To check if a task has completed without blocking, the isDone() method is used. This is particularly useful for polling or when tasks need to be periodically checked.

```
if (future.isDone()) {
    try {
        Integer result = future.get();
        System.out.println("Result obtained: " + result);
    } catch (InterruptedException | ExecutionException e) {
        e.printStackTrace();
    }
}
```

The isDone() method returns true if the task completed. This method can be called repeatedly in a loop to check the completion status. However, frequent polling can be inefficient and should be avoided if possible in favor of other mechanisms such as callbacks provided by CompletableFuture.

Cancelling a Future

A future can be cancelled using the cancel() method. This is useful when a task's result is no longer needed or if the task is taking too long to complete. The cancel() method attempts to stop the task from further execution and returns a boolean indicating if the cancellation was successful. The mayInterruptIfRunning parameter determines if the thread executing the task should be interrupted in an attempt to cancel the task.

```
boolean success = future.cancel(true); // Attempt to cancel the task, interrupt if
    running
if (success) {
    System.out.println("Task was cancelled");
} else {
    System.out.println("Task cancellation failed or already completed");
}
```

If the task associated with the future has completed, been cancelled, or could not be cancelled for some reason, cancel() returns false. Otherwise, it returns true. If the task is successfully cancelled, subsequent calls to isDone() will return true and isCancelled() will return true.

```
Task was cancelled
```

Handling InterruptedException and ExecutionException

When retrieving the result of an asynchronous task using get(), two exceptions need special attention: InterruptedException and ExecutionException.

InterruptedException indicates that the current thread was interrupted while waiting. The interrupted status of the thread is cleared when this exception is thrown, and it must be handled carefully to maintain thread interruption policies.

ExecutionException wraps an exception thrown during the task's execution, making it necessary to handle underlying causes separately. It provides an getCause() method to retrieve the original exception.

```
try {
    Integer result = future.get();
    System.out.println("Result: " + result);
} catch (InterruptedException e) {
    Thread.currentThread().interrupt(); // Reset interrupt status
    System.err.println("Task interrupted");
} catch (ExecutionException e) {
    Throwable cause = e.getCause();
    System.err.println("Execution exception: " + cause);
}
```

Properly handling these exceptions is vital to ensure the robustness of concurrent applications, preventing resource leaks, and allowing threads to react appropriately to interruptions.

This comprehensive understanding of creating and managing Future objects will serve as the foundation for further exploration of advanced asynchronous programming constructs in Java, such as CompletableFuture. This knowledge enhances the capability to build responsive, performant applications that leverage concurrency effectively.

8.3 Cancelling and Checking Status of Futures

Managing asynchronous tasks not only involves triggering and completing them but also ensuring that we can effectively control and monitor their state. An essential aspect of such control includes the ability to cancel tasks and check their status. In Java, the Future interface provides multiple methods to handle these aspects. The key methods for this purpose are cancel(), isCancelled(), and isDone().

cancel(boolean mayInterruptIfRunning): This method attempts to cancel the execution of the associated task. Depending on the boolean parameter mayInterruptIfRunning, the cancellation request can behave differently. If mayInterruptIfRunning is true, the task will be interrupted if it is running. Otherwise, if the task has not started, it will be prevented from starting. The method returns true if the task was successfully cancelled or if it was already completed before the cancellation request, otherwise it returns false.

```
Future<?> futureTask = executorService.submit(new CallableTask());

// Attempt to cancel the task
boolean wasCancelled = futureTask.cancel(true);

System.out.println("Task cancelled: " + wasCancelled);
```

isCancelled(): This method checks if the task was cancelled before completion. It returns true if the task was indeed cancelled, otherwise it returns false. Checking this status can provide more control over the task lifecycle and ensure that appropriate actions are taken if the task did not complete as expected.

```
if (futureTask.isCancelled()) {
    System.out.println("Task was cancelled.");
} else {
    System.out.println("Task was not cancelled.");
}
```

isDone(): This method verifies if the task has completed. It returns true if the task finished, regardless of whether it was normally completed, cancelled, or encountered an exception. This check is useful to determine if the outcome of an asynchronous task is ready to be retrieved or if further handling is necessary.

```
if (futureTask.isDone()) {
    System.out.println("Task is done.");
} else {
    System.out.println("Task is still running.");
}
```

To illustrate the practical application of these methods, consider a scenario where a long-running computation task must be executed, and depending on real-time conditions, it might need to be cancelled before completion. Let's examine a more comprehensive example:

```
public class FutureCancellationExample {
    public static void main(String[] args) throws InterruptedException {
        ExecutorService executorService = Executors.newSingleThreadExecutor();
        Future<?> future = executorService.submit(() -> {
            try {
                for (int i = 0; i < 10; i++) {
                    System.out.println("Task is running...");
                    Thread.sleep(1000);
                }
            } catch (InterruptedException e) {
```

```
                System.out.println("Task was interrupted");
            }
        });

        Thread.sleep(3000); // Let the task run for a while

        // Attempt to cancel the task
        boolean cancellationResult = future.cancel(true);

        if (cancellationResult) {
            System.out.println("Task was cancelled successfully.");
        } else {
            System.out.println("Task cancellation failed.");
        }

        // Check if the task is done
        if (future.isDone()) {
            System.out.println("Task has completed.");
        } else {
            System.out.println("Task is still running or was cancelled.");
        }

        executorService.shutdown();
    }
}
```

The output for this code can be observed as:

```
Task is running...
Task is running...
Task is running...
Task was interrupted
Task was cancelled successfully.
Task is still running or was cancelled.
```

By using Future's cancellation methods in conjunction with status checks, we can implement a robust mechanism to manage asynchronous tasks. This approach ensures that long-running tasks do not unnecessarily consume resources if they need to be stopped. Additionally, it offers a way to handle task statuses accurately, providing the necessary flexibility and control over asynchronous execution.

8.4 Timeouts with Future.get()

When working with asynchronous tasks in Java, it is crucial to manage potential delays effectively to maintain application responsiveness. The Future interface provides the get(long timeout, TimeUnit unit) method that allows a developer to specify a maximum wait time for retrieving the result of a computation. If the result is not available within the specified timeout duration, a TimeoutException is thrown. This section delves into the utilization of this method, presenting detailed insights and examples to solidify your understanding.

The get(long timeout, TimeUnit unit) method operates similarly to the get() method but includes an additional timeout parameter. The timeout parameter specifies the maximum time to wait for the result, and the unit parameter determines the time unit for the timeout duration. The possible units are defined in the java.util.concurrent.TimeUnit enum, which provides granularity from nanoseconds to days. Here is an example demonstrating the usage of the get method with a timeout:

```
import java.util.concurrent.*;

public class TimeoutExample {
    public static void main(String[] args) {
        ExecutorService executor = Executors.newCachedThreadPool();
        Future<Integer> future = executor.submit(new Callable<Integer>() {
            @Override
            public Integer call() throws Exception {
                // Simulate long-running task
                Thread.sleep(5000);
                return 123;
            }
        });

        try {
            // Attempt to retrieve the result within 2 seconds
            Integer result = future.get(2, TimeUnit.SECONDS);
            System.out.println("Result: " + result);
        } catch (TimeoutException e) {
            System.out.println("Timeout occurred, no result retrieved.");
        } catch (InterruptedException | ExecutionException e) {
            e.printStackTrace();
        } finally {
            executor.shutdown();
        }
    }
}
```

In this example, a task is submitted to an executor service that simulates a long-running computation by sleeping for 5 seconds. By calling future.get(2, TimeUnit.SECONDS), the main thread waits for up to 2 seconds to retrieve the result. Since the task does not complete within the specified timeout, a TimeoutException is thrown, and the catch block handles this scenario, printing a timeout message.

Effectively leveraging the timeout mechanism in Future.get() can prevent an application from becoming unresponsive due to prolonged asynchronous task execution. It is essential to handle TimeoutException appropriately to ensure the robustness of the application. Common strategies include retrying the operation, falling back to an alternative task, or logging the timeout event for further analysis.

Consider this example in a real-world application scenario, such as a web service that performs background data fetching. Suppose the data fetch task may sometimes take longer than usual due to network latency or server load. By using a timeout, the service can gracefully handle such delays without blocking the main processing flow. Here's an illustration of this scenario:

```
import java.util.concurrent.*;
import java.util.*;

public class DataService {
    private final ExecutorService executor = Executors.newFixedThreadPool(4);

    public List<String> fetchData() {
        Future<List<String>> future = executor.submit(this::fetchFromDatabase);

        try {
            // Specify a 3-second timeout for data fetching
            return future.get(3, TimeUnit.SECONDS);
        } catch (TimeoutException e) {
            System.err.println("Data fetch timeout, returning default data.");
            return Collections.emptyList();
        } catch (InterruptedException | ExecutionException e) {
            e.printStackTrace();
            return Collections.emptyList();
        }
    }

    private List<String> fetchFromDatabase() throws InterruptedException {
        // Simulate data fetch with delay
        Thread.sleep(5000);
        return Arrays.asList("Data1", "Data2", "Data3");
    }

    public void shutdown() {
        executor.shutdown();
    }

    public static void main(String[] args) {
        DataService dataService = new DataService();
        List<String> data = dataService.fetchData();
        System.out.println("Retrieved Data: " + data);
        dataService.shutdown();
    }
}
```

In this example, the DataService class contains a method fetchData() that attempts to fetch data from the database with a 3-second timeout. If the data fetch operation exceeds this period, a TimeoutException is caught, and an empty list is returned as a fallback. This showcases how timeouts can ensure responsiveness even when dealing with potentially slow operations.

Understanding and implementing timeouts with Future.get() is fundamental for maintaining the performance and responsiveness of applications that rely on asynchronous computations. It ensures that the application can gracefully handle delayed tasks, avoiding prolonged blocks in execution.

8.5 Introduction to CompletableFuture

The CompletableFuture class, part of the java.util.concurrent package, enhances Java's concurrency model by integrating a combination of the Future interface with additional capabilities to build and manage asynchronous computations. Unlike Future, which represents a single, one-shot asynchronous computation that can be checked for completion or cancelled, CompletableFuture is designed to handle more complex asynchronous workflows through chaining and combination of tasks.

CompletableFuture implements the Future interface, thereby retaining all functionalities provided by Future. It adds a more powerful toolset through the implementation of the CompletionStage interface, enabling functional-style programming with robust handling of asynchronous task composition, exception handling, and dependent task execution.

The creation of a CompletableFuture can be achieved through several static factory methods provided within the class. The primary methods include CompletableFuture::completedFuture, CompletableFuture::supplyAsync, CompletableFuture::runAsync, among others.

Creating a Completed CompletableFuture: The completedFuture method instantiates a CompletableFuture that is already completed with the provided value. This is useful in scenarios where a precomputed result is available and needs to be wrapped as a Future.

```
CompletableFuture<String> completedFuture = CompletableFuture.completedFuture("
    Hello");
```

The above code snippet creates a CompletableFuture that is already completed with the string value "Hello".

Executing Tasks Asynchronously: Two primary methods for executing tasks asynchronously are supplyAsync and runAsync.

- supplyAsync: This method is used when a task returns a result.
- runAsync: This method is used when a task does not return a result.

Both methods accept a Supplier or Runnable respectively, and optionally, an Executor to run the task. If an Executor is not provided, the default ForkJoinPool.commonPool() is used.

```
CompletableFuture<Void> runAsyncFuture = CompletableFuture.runAsync(() -> {
    // Perform some asynchronous processing
    System.out.println("Task executed asynchronously.");
});

CompletableFuture<String> supplyAsyncFuture = CompletableFuture.supplyAsync(()
    -> {
    // Simulate a long-running calculation, then return a result
    return "Task result";
});
```

Chaining Asynchronous Computations: A primary strength of CompletableFuture is its support for chaining asynchronous tasks. This can be achieved through its various then methods, such as thenApply, thenAccept, and thenRun.

The thenApply method transforms the result of a CompletableFuture by applying a function to it:

```
CompletableFuture<String> future = CompletableFuture.supplyAsync(() -> "Hello")
                                        .thenApply(result -> result + " World"
                                        );
```

The thenAccept method consumes the result of a CompletableFuture without returning any value:

```
CompletableFuture<Void> future = CompletableFuture.supplyAsync(() -> "Hello")
                                        .thenAccept(result -> System.out.println(
                                        result));
```

The thenRun method allows execution of a task after the current CompletableFuture completes without using its result:

```
CompletableFuture<Void> future = CompletableFuture.supplyAsync(() -> "Hello")
                                        .thenRun(() -> System.out.println("Task
                                        completed"));
```

Combining Multiple CompletableFutures: Tasks may involve multiple asynchronous operations whose results are needed together. The methods thenCombine, thenCompose, and allOf facilitate such scenarios.

The thenCombine method combines results from two CompletableFutures when both complete:

```
CompletableFuture<String> future1 = CompletableFuture.supplyAsync(() -> "Hello");
CompletableFuture<String> future2 = CompletableFuture.supplyAsync(() -> "World")
    ;

CompletableFuture<String> combinedFuture = future1.thenCombine(future2, (result1,
    result2) -> result1 + " " + result2);
```

The thenCompose method achieves sequential tasks where the outcome of one stage is used to invoke the next stage:

```
CompletableFuture<String> future = CompletableFuture.supplyAsync(() -> "Hello")
                                    .thenCompose(result ->
                                        CompletableFuture.supplyAsync(()
                                        -> result + " World"));
```

The allOf method runs multiple CompletableFutures concurrently and waits for all to complete. It returns a new CompletableFuture that completes when all provided CompletableFutures complete.

```
CompletableFuture<Void> allOfFuture = CompletableFuture.allOf(future1, future2);
```

Such operations empower the developer to create complex, non-blocking asynchronous workflows efficiently.

Exception Handling in CompletableFutures: CompletableFuture provides robust mechanisms for handling exceptions that occur during asynchronous processing. Methods like handle, exceptionally, and whenComplete allow handling and recovery from exceptions:

```
CompletableFuture<String> futureWithException = CompletableFuture.supplyAsync
    (() -> {
    if (Math.random() > 0.5) {
        throw new RuntimeException("Simulated exception");
    }
    return "Success";
});
```

exceptionally can specify a fallback action for exceptional cases:

```
CompletableFuture<String> handleException = futureWithException.exceptionally(ex
    -> "Fallback value");
```

handle provides a more flexible way to manage both normal and exceptional cases:

```
CompletableFuture<String> handleErrorsFuture = futureWithException.handle((result
    , ex) -> {
    if (ex != null) {
        return "Error handled";
    }
    return result;
});
```

Understanding and utilizing these advanced features of CompletableFuture can significantly improve application responsiveness and resource utilization in concurrent programming scenarios.

8.6 Creating CompletableFutures

The CompletableFuture class provides a powerful way to create and manage asynchronous computations in Java. Introduced in Java 8, it extends the capabilities of the Future interface by allowing the composition of complex asynchronous operations.

To create an instance of CompletableFuture, you can use several static methods provided by the class. Below, we will explore the most commonly used methods: completedFuture, runAsync, and supplyAsync.

- completedFuture
- runAsync
- supplyAsync

completedFuture

The completedFuture method is a straightforward way to create a CompletableFuture that is already completed with a given value. This is useful when a method needs to return a CompletableFuture but the computation has already been completed or the result is readily available.

```
CompletableFuture<String> future = CompletableFuture.completedFuture("Hello");
System.out.println(future.isDone()); // true
System.out.println(future.get()); // "Hello"
```

In this example, the CompletableFuture is immediately completed with the value "Hello". This can be confirmed by calling isDone, which returns true, and get, which returns the completed value.

runAsync

The runAsync method is used to run a task asynchronously without returning any result. It accepts a Runnable as a parameter and returns a CompletableFuture<Void>.

```
CompletableFuture<Void> future = CompletableFuture.runAsync(() -> {
    // Simulate long-running task
    try {
        Thread.sleep(2000);
    } catch (InterruptedException e) {
        throw new IllegalStateException(e);
    }
    System.out.println("Task over!");
});

System.out.println("Waiting for the task to complete...");
```

```
future.get(); // Waiting for task completion
System.out.println("Task Completed!");
```

Here, runAsync runs a simple task that simulates a long-running operation by sleeping for 2 seconds. The main thread will print "Waiting for the task to complete...", then block, waiting for the asynchronous task to complete before printing "Task Completed!".

supplyAsync

The supplyAsync method is similar to runAsync, but it allows returning a result from the asynchronous task. It accepts a Supplier<T> as a parameter and returns a CompletableFuture<T>.

```
CompletableFuture<String> future = CompletableFuture.supplyAsync(() -> {
    // Simulate long-running task
    try {
        Thread.sleep(2000);
    } catch (InterruptedException e) {
        throw new IllegalStateException(e);
    }
    return "Hello World!";
});

System.out.println("Waiting for the result...");
String result = future.get(); // Waiting for task completion and getting the result
System.out.println("Result: " + result);
```

In this code, supplyAsync executes a task that returns a string "Hello World!" after simulating a delay. The main thread will block until the computation is completed, then retrieve and print the result.

Executor Services for Better Control

While runAsync and supplyAsync run tasks using the common fork-join pool by default, you can specify a custom Executor to have better control over the threading behavior. Using a custom Executor can be advantageous for fine-tuning performance or adhering to application-specific constraints.

```
ExecutorService executorService = Executors.newFixedThreadPool(5);

CompletableFuture<Void> future = CompletableFuture.runAsync(() -> {
    // Task logic
    System.out.println("Task running in custom executor");
}, executorService);

future.get(); // Wait for task completion
executorService.shutdown();
```

In this example, a FixedThreadPool with 5 threads is created using Executors.newFixedThreadPool(5). The runAsync method then runs the task using this custom executor. After the task finishes, the ExecutorService is shut down to release resources.

Careful management of executor services is important to avoid resource leaks and ensure efficient utilization of system resources.

```
ExecutorService executorService = Executors.newCachedThreadPool();

CompletableFuture<String> future = CompletableFuture.supplyAsync(() -> {
    // Task logic
    return "Task executed with custom executor";
}, executorService);

String result = future.get(); // Wait for task completion and get the result
System.out.println("Result: " + result);
executorService.shutdown();
```

This code demonstrates the use of a CachedThreadPool for running an asynchronous task that returns a result. Similar to the previous example, the task runs using the specified executor, and the ExecutorService is shut down after task completion.

8.7 Chaining and Combining CompletableFuture Tasks

The CompletableFuture class provides powerful capabilities for chaining and combining asynchronous tasks, resulting in more concise and readable code compared to traditional callback-based approaches. Understanding how to effectively leverage these features is crucial for developing non-blocking applications that maintain high performance and responsiveness.

CompletableFuture chaining allows multiple dependent tasks to run sequentially. Two primary methods facilitate this chaining: thenApply and thenCompose. The thenApply method is used when the next step depends on the result of the previous step and returns a new CompletableFuture after applying a function to the result. In contrast, thenCompose is used when the next step involves another asynchronous computation. Here's an example that demonstrates their usage:

```
CompletableFuture<Integer> future = CompletableFuture.supplyAsync(() -> 50)
    .thenApply(result -> result * 2)
    .thenCompose(result -> CompletableFuture.supplyAsync(() -> result + 25));

future.thenAccept(finalResult -> System.out.println("Final result: " + finalResult));
```

In this example: - CompletableFuture.supplyAsync initializes the computation with a supplier that provides the integer value 50. - thenApply multiplies this result by 2. - thenCompose handles another asynchronous computation adding 25 to the intermediate result. - The thenAccept method is used to consume and print the final result once the computation chain completes.

In situations where multiple independent CompletableFuture tasks need to be combined, thenCombine and thenCombineAsync methods are pertinent. thenCombine combines the results of two independent CompletableFuture completions with a provided BiFunction. An example demonstrating this is shown below:

```
CompletableFuture<Integer> future1 = CompletableFuture.supplyAsync(() -> 30);
CompletableFuture<Integer> future2 = CompletableFuture.supplyAsync(() -> 70);

CompletableFuture<Integer> combinedFuture = future1.thenCombine(future2, (result1,
      result2) -> result1 + result2);

combinedFuture.thenAccept(finalResult -> System.out.println("Combined result: " +
      finalResult));
```

In this code snippet: - CompletableFuture.supplyAsync initiates two independent tasks producing results 30 and 70. - thenCombine merges these results into one computation that adds them together. - The result is consumed and printed by thenAccept.

Furthermore, when handling multiple CompletableFuture tasks that can complete in any order, allOf and anyOf methods facilitate waiting for the completion of all tasks or any one of the tasks respectively:

```
CompletableFuture<Void> allFutures = CompletableFuture.allOf(future1, future2);
allFutures.thenRun(() -> System.out.println("All tasks are done!"));

CompletableFuture<Object> anyFuture = CompletableFuture.anyOf(future1, future2);
anyFuture.thenAccept(result -> System.out.println("One of the tasks finished. Result: "
      + result));
```

- CompletableFuture.allOf creates a new CompletableFuture that completes when all provided futures complete. - CompletableFuture.anyOf completes as soon as any of the provided futures completes.

Composing these methods effectively enables managing complex asynchronous workflows. A practical scenario might involve fetching data from multiple services, processing the data, and aggregating the results. This can be elegantly handled with the chaining and combining capabilities of CompletableFuture.

Developers should be aware of handling exceptions in chained tasks, as any task in the chain can fail. Methods like handle and exceptionally allow defining recovery paths or error handling strategies when exceptions occur. For instance:

```
CompletableFuture<Integer> futureWithErrorHandling = CompletableFuture.
    supplyAsync(() -> {
    if (Math.random() > 0.5) throw new IllegalStateException("Random failure!");
    return 50;
}).exceptionally(ex -> {
    System.err.println("Exception: " + ex);
    return 0; // Default value on failure
});

futureWithErrorHandling.thenAccept(result -> System.out.println("Result after error
    handling: " + result));
```

- exceptionally provides a default value and logs the exception when an error occurs. - The pipeline can then proceed with the defined recovery strategy.

Understanding and utilizing these chaining and combining techniques enhances the design of non-blocking, efficient concurrent applications, ensuring both readability and robustness in asynchronous Java programming.

8.8 Handling Exceptions in CompletableFutures

Handling exceptions effectively is critical when working with asynchronous tasks using CompletableFuture. Java CompletableFuture provides several methods to manage exceptions. These methods ensure that any runtime anomalies do not cause the entire application to fail and allow developers to implement robust exception-handling strategies.

When a computation in a CompletableFuture completes exceptionally, methods such as exceptionally, handle, and whenComplete can be utilized to respond gracefully.

1. The exceptionally Method

The exceptionally method allows developers to return a default value if the CompletableFuture completes exceptionally. It takes a function that is called if an exception occurs. Here is a basic example:

```
CompletableFuture<String> future = CompletableFuture.supplyAsync(() -> {
    if (Math.random() > 0.5) {
        throw new RuntimeException("Random error!");
    }
    return "Success";
}).exceptionally(ex -> {
    System.out.println("An error occurred: " + ex.getMessage());
```

```
    return "Fallback result";
});

System.out.println(future.join());
```

In this code, if the RuntimeException occurs during the execution, the exceptionally method provides a fallback result and logs the error.

2. The handle Method

The handle method is a more flexible way to process both normal and exceptional results. It takes a BiFunction as an argument that receives the result or the exception, allowing developers to handle either case within one method:

```
CompletableFuture<String> future = CompletableFuture.supplyAsync(() -> {
    if (Math.random() > 0.5) {
        throw new RuntimeException("Random error!");
    }
    return "Success";
}).handle((result, ex) -> {
    if (ex != null) {
        System.out.println("An error occurred: " + ex.getMessage());
        return "Fallback result";
    } else {
        return result;
    }
});

System.out.println(future.join());
```

This method captures both success and error scenarios in a more unified manner, providing a comprehensive handling mechanism.

3. The whenComplete Method

Another option is the whenComplete method, which allows developers to execute some code after the computation completes, regardless of whether it completed normally or with an exception. This method does not alter the outcome but can log or further analyze it:

```
CompletableFuture<String> future = CompletableFuture.supplyAsync(() -> {
    if (Math.random() > 0.5) {
        throw new RuntimeException("Random error!");
    }
    return "Success";
}).whenComplete((result, ex) -> {
    if (ex != null) {
        System.out.println("An error occurred: " + ex.getMessage());
    } else {
        System.out.println("Completed successfully: " + result);
    }
});

System.out.println(future.join());
```

In this code snippet, whenComplete logs the computation result or the exception but does not change the outcome of the CompletableFuture.

Combining Exception Handling in Chained CompletableFutures

Exception handling in CompletableFuture can be more complex in task chains. It is critical to understand how an exception in one stage affects subsequent stages. For example:

```
CompletableFuture<String> future = CompletableFuture.supplyAsync(() -> {
    if (Math.random() > 0.5) {
        throw new RuntimeException("Initial Error!");
    }
    return "Initial Success";
}).thenApply(result -> {
    System.out.println("Processing result: " + result);
    return result + " after processing";
}).exceptionally(ex -> {
    System.out.println("Caught an exception: " + ex.getMessage());
    return "Fallback after exception";
}).thenAccept(result -> {
    System.out.println("Final result: " + result);
});
```

In this example, if the initial stage throws an exception, exceptionally handles it, providing a fallback, and the chain continues. Exception handling can be fine-tuned at each stage of the chain to ensure resilient task flows.

Exception Propagation and Custom Exceptions

If custom exceptions are needed, CompletableFuture can propagate these exceptions, allowing specific handling strategies at different points in the computation chain:

```
public class CustomException extends RuntimeException {
    public CustomException(String message) {
        super(message);
    }
}

CompletableFuture<String> future = CompletableFuture.supplyAsync(() -> {
    if (Math.random() > 0.5) {
        throw new CustomException("Custom error occurred!");
    }
    return "Success";
}).handle((result, ex) -> {
    if (ex != null) {
        if (ex.getCause() instanceof CustomException) {
            System.out.println("Handling custom exception: " + ex.getMessage());
            return "Handled CustomException";
        } else {
            System.out.println("Handling other exception: " + ex.getMessage());
            return "Fallback result";
        }
    } else {
        return result;
```

```
    }
});
System.out.println(future.join());
```

In this code, a custom exception CustomException is used and handled specifically, differentiating it from other exceptional conditions.

An understanding of these exception-handling techniques in CompletableFuture is crucial for developing robust, fault-tolerant asynchronous applications. The careful application of exceptionally, handle, and whenComplete methods ensures the smooth continuation and completion of complex asynchronous workflows.

8.9 Running Asynchronous Tasks with CompletableFutures

The CompletableFuture class in the java.util.concurrent package simplifies the execution of asynchronous tasks, allowing developers to write more concise and readable concurrent code. Asynchronous programming enables tasks to run independently of the main program flow, improving application responsiveness and performance.

CompletableFuture supports various methods to run tasks asynchronously. The primary methods are runAsync(Runnable runnable) and supplyAsync(Supplier<U> supplier).

The runAsync method is used for tasks that do not return a result:

```
CompletableFuture<Void> future = CompletableFuture.runAsync(() -> {
    // Simulating a long-running task
    try {
        TimeUnit.SECONDS.sleep(2);
    } catch (InterruptedException e) {
        throw new IllegalStateException(e);
    }
    System.out.println("Task executed in parallel");
});
```

The supplyAsync method is employed for tasks that return a result:

```
CompletableFuture<String> future = CompletableFuture.supplyAsync(() -> {
    // Simulating a long-running computation
    try {
        TimeUnit.SECONDS.sleep(2);
    } catch (InterruptedException e) {
        throw new IllegalStateException(e);
    }
    return "Result of the asynchronous computation";
```

```
});
```

Both methods execute tasks asynchronously using the common ForkJoinPool by default. To use a custom Executor, pass it as the second argument:

```
ExecutorService executorService = Executors.newFixedThreadPool(3);

CompletableFuture<Void> asyncFuture = CompletableFuture.runAsync(() -> {
    // Task code
}, executorService);

CompletableFuture<String> supplyFuture = CompletableFuture.supplyAsync(() -> {
    // Computation code
    return "Task result";
}, executorService);
```

CompletableFuture supports multiple methods to handle task completion, enhancing the ability to write expressive code. The thenApply method transforms the result of a completed CompletableFuture:

```
CompletableFuture<String> future = CompletableFuture.supplyAsync(() -> "Sample
    text");

CompletableFuture<Integer> lengthFuture = future.thenApply(text -> {
    // Transforming the result by computing the length
    return text.length();
});

lengthFuture.thenAccept(length -> System.out.println("Length: " + length));
```

Another useful method is thenAccept, which performs a further action upon completion without returning a result:

```
CompletableFuture<String> future = CompletableFuture.supplyAsync(() -> "Another
    text");

future.thenAccept(result -> System.out.println("Result: " + result));
```

For cases where a future task depends on another task's result, the thenCompose method is suitable to chain tasks:

```
CompletableFuture<String> future = CompletableFuture.supplyAsync(() -> "Async
    task result")
    .thenCompose(result -> CompletableFuture.supplyAsync(() -> "Dependent task
        using: " + result));

future.thenAccept(System.out::println);
```

Tasks can also be combined using thenCombine, which accepts a BiFunction to process the results of two futures:

```
CompletableFuture<String> firstTask = CompletableFuture.supplyAsync(() -> "First
    Task");
```

```
CompletableFuture<String> secondTask = CompletableFuture.supplyAsync(() -> "
    Second Task");

CompletableFuture<String> combinedFuture = firstTask.thenCombine(secondTask,
    (firstResult, secondResult) -> firstResult + " & " + secondResult);

combinedFuture.thenAccept(System.out::println);
```

In situations where multiple independent tasks need to be executed and a combined result is required, the allOf and anyOf methods come into play. allOf waits for all tasks to complete:

```
CompletableFuture<String> task1 = CompletableFuture.supplyAsync(() -> "Result of
    Task1");
CompletableFuture<String> task2 = CompletableFuture.supplyAsync(() -> "Result of
    Task2");
CompletableFuture<String> task3 = CompletableFuture.supplyAsync(() -> "Result of
    Task3");

CompletableFuture<Void> allOfFuture = CompletableFuture.allOf(task1, task2, task3)
    ;
allOfFuture.thenRun(() -> {
    try {
        System.out.println("Task1: " + task1.get());
        System.out.println("Task2: " + task2.get());
        System.out.println("Task3: " + task3.get());
    } catch (InterruptedException | ExecutionException e) {
        e.printStackTrace();
    }
});
```

Conversely, anyOf completes as soon as any one of the tasks completes:

```
CompletableFuture<String> task1 = CompletableFuture.supplyAsync(() -> {
    // Simulating delay
    try {
        TimeUnit.SECONDS.sleep(2);
    } catch (InterruptedException e) {
        e.printStackTrace();
    }
    return "Result of Task1";
});

CompletableFuture<String> task2 = CompletableFuture.supplyAsync(() -> "Result of
    Task2");

CompletableFuture<Object> anyOfFuture = CompletableFuture.anyOf(task1, task2);
anyOfFuture.thenAccept(result -> System.out.println("First to complete: " + result));
```

These methods enable robust handling and chaining of asynchronous tasks using CompletableFuture, thereby offering significant enhancements for performance and responsive behavior in concurrent Java applications.

8.10 Examples of CompletableFuture in Real-World Applications

Practical applications of CompletableFuture are abundant in contemporary software systems that necessitate asynchronous programming for improved performance and responsiveness. This section explores detailed examples showcasing how CompletableFuture can be utilized in real-world scenarios.

Consider an e-commerce application that processes customer orders, integrates with external payment services, and updates inventory data. Here, parallelism and asynchronous processing can significantly enhance performance. We will illustrate this with multiple CompletableFutures to handle each subtask.

```
import java.util.concurrent.CompletableFuture;

public class OrderProcessor {
    public static void main(String[] args) {
        CompletableFuture<Void> futureOrder = CompletableFuture.runAsync(() ->
              processOrder())
            .thenRunAsync(() -> integratePaymentService())
            .thenRunAsync(() -> updateInventory());

        // Wait for all tasks to complete
        futureOrder.join();
    }

    private static void processOrder() {
        System.out.println("Order processed");
        // Simulate order processing delay
        try { Thread.sleep(1000); } catch (InterruptedException e) { e.printStackTrace()
              ; }
    }

    private static void integratePaymentService() {
        System.out.println("External payment service integrated");
        // Simulate payment service delay
        try { Thread.sleep(1000); } catch (InterruptedException e) { e.printStackTrace()
              ; }
    }

    private static void updateInventory() {
        System.out.println("Inventory updated");
        // Simulate inventory update delay
        try { Thread.sleep(1000); } catch (InterruptedException e) { e.printStackTrace()
              ; }
    }
}
```

The code snippet demonstrates a sequence of asynchronous tasks using thenRunAsync() to chain the methods. CompletableFuture.runAsync() initiates the order processing, followed by payment service integration and inventory update. This approach ensures that each action runs asynchronously, independently harnessing system resources optimally.

Another real-world scenario is a web service that aggregates data from multiple microservices. Using CompletableFuture, we can parallelize HTTP requests to fetch data from various services concurrently, thus reducing overall response time.

```
import java.util.concurrent.CompletableFuture;

public class DataAggregator {
    public static void main(String[] args) {
        CompletableFuture<String> service1 = fetchFromService1();
        CompletableFuture<String> service2 = fetchFromService2();
        CompletableFuture<String> service3 = fetchFromService3();

        CompletableFuture<Void> allServices = CompletableFuture.allOf(service1,
             service2, service3);

        // Wait for all services to respond
        allServices.join();

        // Combine results
        String aggregatedResult = service1.join() + service2.join() + service3.join();
        System.out.println("Aggregated Result: " + aggregatedResult);
    }

    private static CompletableFuture<String> fetchFromService1() {
        return CompletableFuture.supplyAsync(() -> {
            // Simulate service call delay
            try { Thread.sleep(500); } catch (InterruptedException e) { e.
                 printStackTrace(); }
            return "Service1Data;";
        });
    }

    private static CompletableFuture<String> fetchFromService2() {
        return CompletableFuture.supplyAsync(() -> {
            // Simulate service call delay
            try { Thread.sleep(800); } catch (InterruptedException e) { e.
                 printStackTrace(); }
            return "Service2Data;";
        });
    }

    private static CompletableFuture<String> fetchFromService3() {
        return CompletableFuture.supplyAsync(() -> {
            // Simulate service call delay
            try { Thread.sleep(300); } catch (InterruptedException e) { e.
                 printStackTrace(); }
            return "Service3Data;";
        });
    }
}
```

In this example, data fetched from three services is aggregated. Each service request is initiated via supplyAsync(), enabling concurrent processing. The allOf() method waits for all requests to complete, and results are combined thereafter.

Another practical application is in financial services, where CompletableFuture can be used for executing and aggregating stock price queries. Financial applications rely on real-time data from multiple sources; using asynchronous tasks can ensure timely and efficient data processing.

```
import java.util.concurrent.CompletableFuture;

public class StockPriceAggregator {
    public static void main(String[] args) {
        CompletableFuture<Double> stockService1 = fetchStockPrice("AAPL", "
            Service1");
        CompletableFuture<Double> stockService2 = fetchStockPrice("AAPL", "
            Service2");
        CompletableFuture<Double> stockService3 = fetchStockPrice("AAPL", "
            Service3");

        CompletableFuture<Void> allServices = CompletableFuture.allOf(stockService1,
             stockService2, stockService3);

        // Wait for all services to respond
        allServices.join();

        // Aggregate results and calculate average price
        double avgPrice = (stockService1.join() + stockService2.join() + stockService3.
            join()) / 3;
        System.out.println("Average Stock Price: " + avgPrice);
    }

    private static CompletableFuture<Double> fetchStockPrice(String stock, String
         service) {
        return CompletableFuture.supplyAsync(() -> {
            // Simulate service call delay
            try { Thread.sleep(400); } catch (InterruptedException e) { e.
                printStackTrace(); }
            return Math.random() * 1000; // Simulated stock price
        });
    }
}
```

This code snippet showcases fetching stock prices from multiple services, averaging them to provide a reliable market price. Each stock price query executes asynchronously, significantly optimizing data retrieval times.

Furthermore, we can consider a machine learning application where asynchronous tasks are used for preprocessing data. Here, we demonstrate cleaning, validating, and normalizing data using CompletableFuture.

```
import java.util.concurrent.CompletableFuture;

public class DataPreprocessor {
```

```
    public static void main(String[] args) {
        CompletableFuture<Void> futureProcessing = CompletableFuture.runAsync(()
            -> cleanData())
            .thenRunAsync(() -> validateData())
            .thenRunAsync(() -> normalizeData());

        // Wait for all preprocessing tasks to complete
        futureProcessing.join();
    }

    private static void cleanData() {
        System.out.println("Data cleaned");
        // Simulate data cleaning delay
        try { Thread.sleep(1000); } catch (InterruptedException e) { e.printStackTrace()
            ; }
    }

    private static void validateData() {
        System.out.println("Data validated");
        // Simulate data validation delay
        try { Thread.sleep(1000); } catch (InterruptedException e) { e.printStackTrace()
            ; }
    }

    private static void normalizeData() {
        System.out.println("Data normalized");
        // Simulate data normalization delay
        try { Thread.sleep(1000); } catch (InterruptedException e) { e.printStackTrace()
            ; }
    }
}
```

In machine learning, preprocessing is crucial for preparing data for training models. By cleaning, validating, and normalizing the data asynchronously, the overall preprocessing time is reduced, leading to a faster training phase.

Through these examples, the utility and flexibility of CompletableFuture in real-world applications are evident. Applying asynchronous programming constructs can markedly enhance efficiency and responsiveness across various domains. Each code sample herein can serve as a foundation to build more complex, domain-specific solutions that leverage concurrent processing.

8.11 Improving Performance with CompletableFutures

Leveraging CompletableFuture can significantly enhance the performance and responsiveness of your applications by enabling efficient asynchronous programming. This section examines various strategies to maximize performance gains using CompletableFuture, considering aspects like task parallelism, optimal use of threads, and avoiding common pitfalls.

Parallelism with CompletableFuture

One of the primary advantages of CompletableFuture is its ability to run tasks in parallel, efficiently utilizing multiple CPU cores. To achieve parallelism, break down a large task into smaller, independent subtasks and execute them asynchronously. CompletableFuture provides methods such as thenCombine, allOf, and anyOf to manage and combine multiple asynchronous computations.

Consider the following example where multiple API calls are made concurrently:

```
import java.util.concurrent.CompletableFuture;
import java.util.concurrent.ExecutionException;

public class ParallelAPICalls {

    private static CompletableFuture<String> fetchUserDetails() {
        return CompletableFuture.supplyAsync(() -> {
            // Simulate API call to get user details
            return "User Details";
        });
    }

    private static CompletableFuture<String> fetchOrderHistory() {
        return CompletableFuture.supplyAsync(() -> {
            // Simulate API call to get order history
            return "Order History";
        });
    }

    private static CompletableFuture<String> fetchRecommendations() {
        return CompletableFuture.supplyAsync(() -> {
            // Simulate API call to get recommendations
            return "Recommendations";
        });
    }

    public static void main(String[] args) throws ExecutionException,
          InterruptedException {
        CompletableFuture<String> userDetailsFuture = fetchUserDetails();
        CompletableFuture<String> orderHistoryFuture = fetchOrderHistory();
        CompletableFuture<String> recommendationsFuture = fetchRecommendations
            ();

        CompletableFuture<Void> allFutures = CompletableFuture.allOf(
            userDetailsFuture, orderHistoryFuture, recommendationsFuture);

        allFutures.join();

        System.out.println("User Details: " + userDetailsFuture.get());
        System.out.println("Order History: " + orderHistoryFuture.get());
        System.out.println("Recommendations: " + recommendationsFuture.get());
    }
```

```
}
```

This code concurrently fetches user details, order history, and recommendations, ensuring that the overall task completes faster than if these calls were made sequentially.

Optimal Use of Threads

Using CompletableFuture.supplyAsync without specifying an executor uses the common ForkJoinPool, which might not always be optimal for specific applications. Customizing the thread pool allows better control over resource allocation and performance tuning.

Here is an example utilizing a custom thread pool:

```
import java.util.concurrent.CompletableFuture;
import java.util.concurrent.ExecutionException;
import java.util.concurrent.ExecutorService;
import java.util.concurrent.Executors;

public class CustomThreadPool {

    private static final ExecutorService customExecutor = Executors.
        newFixedThreadPool(10);

    private static CompletableFuture<String> fetchData() {
        return CompletableFuture.supplyAsync(() -> {
            // Simulate data fetching
            return "Fetched Data";
        }, customExecutor);
    }

    public static void main(String[] args) throws ExecutionException,
        InterruptedException {
        CompletableFuture<String> dataFuture = fetchData();
        System.out.println("Data: " + dataFuture.get());

        customExecutor.shutdown();
    }
}
```

A custom executor with a fixed thread pool optimizes resource utilization, allowing you to fine-tune the number of threads for specific workloads.

Avoiding Common Pitfalls

Efficient use of CompletableFuture involves avoiding common mistakes that can degrade performance. Some pitfalls include blocking calls, excessive chaining, and unhandled exceptions.

1. **Blocking Calls**: Avoid directly calling get() or join() within an asynchronous pipeline as it blocks the running thread and negates the benefits of asynchronous programming. Prefer non-blocking methods

like thenApply or handle.

```
CompletableFuture<String> future = CompletableFuture.supplyAsync(() -> "Result")
    .thenApply(result -> {
        // Perform non-blocking transformation
        return "Transformed " + result;
    });
```

2. **Excessive Chaining**: Deeply chained CompletableFuture pipelines can become complex and hard to debug. Maintain a balance between chaining and breaking down tasks into separate, manageable futures.

3. **Unhandled Exceptions**: Ensure robust exception handling to prevent undesirable thread termination. Use methods like handle, exceptionally, and whenComplete to handle exceptions gracefully.

```
CompletableFuture<String> future = CompletableFuture.supplyAsync(() -> {
    if (Math.random() > 0.5) {
        throw new RuntimeException("Failed");
    }
    return "Success";
}).handle((result, ex) -> {
    if (ex != null) {
        return "Error";
    }
    return result;
});
```

Combining Asynchronous Computations

Combining multiple asynchronous tasks can yield significant performance improvements. Use methods such as thenCombine to combine the results of two independent futures once both complete.

```
CompletableFuture<String> future1 = CompletableFuture.supplyAsync(() -> "Result
    1");
CompletableFuture<String> future2 = CompletableFuture.supplyAsync(() -> "Result
    2");

CompletableFuture<String> combinedFuture = future1.thenCombine(future2, (result1,
     result2) -> {
    return result1 + " and " + result2;
});

String combinedResult = combinedFuture.join();
System.out.println("Combined Result: " + combinedResult);
```

By using CompletableFuture effectively, you can dramatically reduce the latency of combined asynchronous operations, boosting overall application performance.

Chapter 9

Parallel Streams

This chapter introduces Parallel Streams in Java, which facilitate parallel processing of data. It explains the differences between sequential and parallel streams, and covers the creation and usage of parallel streams. The chapter discusses performance considerations, the stream pipeline and execution model, and common operations. Topics include reduction, combining streams with the Fork/Join Framework, and real-world examples. Best practices for utilizing parallel streams to achieve efficient and scalable data processing are also provided.

9.1 Introduction to Java Streams

Java streams, introduced in Java 8, are a key feature designed to facilitate the processing of sequences of elements. Streams allow for functional-style operations on collections of data, providing a powerful and expressive API for processing data in a declarative manner. A Stream in Java represents a sequence of elements supporting sequential and parallel aggregate operations. The Stream interface located within the java.util.stream package is the cornerstone of this API.

A Java Stream is not a data structure but a view of data operations. Elements are not stored; they are computed on-demand. A stream pipeline consists of three parts: the source, intermediate operations, and terminal operations.

- **Source:** The source provides the data stream, which can be a collection, an array, a generator function, or an input/output channel.

- **Intermediate Operations:** These are operations that transform a stream into another stream. Examples include map(), filter(), distinct(), and sorted(). Intermediate operations are lazy, meaning they are not executed until a terminal operation is initiated.

- **Terminal Operations:** These operations produce a result from the stream, such as forEach(), reduce(), collect(), and count(). Once a terminal operation is invoked, the stream is consumed and cannot be reused.

Creating Streams

Streams can be created from various data sources, such as collections, arrays, I/O channels, or even custom generators. Here are some examples:

```
List<String> myList = Arrays.asList("alpha", "beta", "gamma");

// Creating a stream from a collection
Stream<String> stream = myList.stream();

// Creating a parallel stream from a collection
Stream<String> parallelStream = myList.parallelStream();

// Creating a stream from an array
String[] myArray = {"alpha", "beta", "gamma"};
Stream<String> arrayStream = Arrays.stream(myArray);

// Creating a stream from a range of numbers
IntStream intStream = IntStream.range(1, 10);
```

Streams can also be created using static methods available in the Stream class and related classes:

```
// Stream.of() method for creating a stream from specified values
Stream<String> streamOf = Stream.of("alpha", "beta", "gamma");

// Stream.generate() method for creating an infinite stream
Stream<Double> randomNumbers = Stream.generate(Math::random);

// Stream.iterate() method for creating a stream with iterative logic
Stream<Integer> iterativeStream = Stream.iterate(0, n -> n + 2);
```

Intermediate Operations

Intermediate operations transform streams without consuming their elements. They are lazy and do not perform any processing until a terminal operation is executed. Some common intermediate operations include:

- filter: Filters elements based on a predicate.
- map: Maps elements to their results using a provided function.
- flatMap: Maps each element to a stream and flattens the resulting streams into a single stream.
- distinct: Ensures that the resulting stream contains only unique elements.
- sorted: Returns a stream with elements sorted according to natural ordering or a provided comparator.

Examples:

```
// Filtering elements
Stream<String> filteredStream = stream.filter(s -> s.startsWith("a"));

// Mapping elements
Stream<String> upperCaseStream = stream.map(String::toUpperCase);

// Flattening streams
Stream<String> flatMappedStream = stream.flatMap(s -> Stream.of(s.split("")));

// Distinct elements
Stream<String> distinctStream = stream.distinct();

// Sorting elements
Stream<String> sortedStream = stream.sorted();
```

Terminal Operations

Terminal operations produce a result or a side-effect and mark the end of the stream pipeline. Once a terminal operation is applied, the stream is considered consumed and can no longer be used. Some common terminal operations include:

- forEach: Performs an action for each element.
- reduce: Combines elements of the stream into a single result using an associative accumulation function.

- collect: Converts the stream into a different form, such as a collection or a string.
- count: Returns the count of elements in the stream.
- anyMatch, allMatch, noneMatch: Perform matching operations based on a given predicate.

Examples:

```
// Performing an action for each element
stream.forEach(System.out::println);

// Reducing elements to a single result
Optional<String> concatenated = stream.reduce((s1, s2) -> s1 + s2);

// Collecting elements into a list
List<String> collectedList = stream.collect(Collectors.toList());

// Counting elements
long count = stream.count();

// Matching elements based on a predicate
boolean anyMatch = stream.anyMatch(s -> s.startsWith("a"));
boolean allMatch = stream.allMatch(s -> s.length() > 2);
```

Understanding the nature, creation, and type of operations available for streams provides a robust foundation for leveraging them effectively in Java applications. Proficiency in using streams, especially in parallel processing scenarios, is crucial for writing efficient and scalable data processing code.

9.2 Sequential vs Parallel Streams

The concept of streams in Java can be leveraged to process data sequences in a functional style. java.util.stream.Stream provides a powerful abstraction for working with sequences of data. This section differentiates between sequential and parallel streams, elucidating their operation, advantages, and performance implications.

Sequential Streams

A sequential stream processes elements in a serial manner—one element after another. Operations on sequential streams happen on a single thread, following the order of source elements unless explicitly modified. For instance, considering a stream derived from a collection, the elements would be processed in the sequence they appear in the collection.

Consider the following example, where we create a sequential stream from an ArrayList of integers and filter out even numbers:

```
List<Integer> numbers = Arrays.asList(1, 2, 3, 4, 5, 6, 7, 8, 9, 10);
Stream<Integer> sequentialStream = numbers.stream();
Stream<Integer> evenNumbers = sequentialStream.filter(n -> n % 2 == 0);
evenNumbers.forEach(System.out::println);
```

In this example, the elements are filtered in the order they appear in the original list. The elements 2, 4, 6, 8, and 10 are printed sequentially by a single thread.

Sequential streams are simpler in terms of internal implementation and have consistent and predictable behavior because they do not incur the overhead of managing multiple threads. This makes them suitable for cases where the data size is relatively small or where order-dependent operations are performed.

Parallel Streams

Parallel streams, in contrast, divide the data into multiple chunks and process them concurrently using multiple threads. This division allows for better utilization of available CPU cores, thus promising improved performance for computationally intensive operations on large datasets.

Creating a parallel stream is straightforward. By calling the parallelStream() method on a collection or by converting an existing sequential stream to a parallel stream using the parallel() method, one can digest the inherent complexities of parallelism within the Java Streams API.

```
Stream<Integer> parallelStream = numbers.parallelStream();
Stream<Integer> evenNumbersParallel = parallelStream.filter(n -> n % 2 == 0);
evenNumbersParallel.forEach(System.out::println);
```

In this example, the elements are processed in parallel, and the order of output is non-deterministic due to concurrent execution. Each element of the stream might be handled by a separate thread.

A key component of parallel streams' functionality is the ForkJoinPool. The ForkJoinPool is a specialized implementation of the ExecutorService interface designed specifically for work that can be broken into smaller pieces recursively. By default, the common ForkJoinPool is used for parallel stream processing, which has a parallelism level equal to the number of available processors.

Performance Comparison

Choosing between sequential and parallel streams should be guided by performance considerations. Parallel streams can offer performance gains for:

- Large collections of data: Parallel streams can efficiently manage the processing of large datasets by leveraging multiple CPU cores, reducing overall execution time.
- Computationally expensive operations: If each element's processing involves significant computation, parallelism can break tasks down and reduce total processing time.

However, parallel streams also introduce some overhead due to thread management and the merging of results from different threads. For small datasets or simple operations, this overhead might outweigh the benefits of parallelisation.

The following example performs a reduction operation to sum integers in a list:

```
List<Integer> numbers = Arrays.asList(1, 2, 3, 4, 5, 6, 7, 8, 9, 10);
int sumSequential = numbers.stream()
                          .reduce(0, Integer::sum);

int sumParallel = numbers.parallelStream()
                        .reduce(0, Integer::sum);

System.out.println("Sequential sum: " + sumSequential);
System.out.println("Parallel sum: " + sumParallel);
```

```
Sequential sum: 55
Parallel sum: 55
```

Despite both sequential and parallel streams providing the same output, the performance characteristics differ. Test cases should analyze real-world data sizes and computational costs to decide whether parallel streams bring tangible performance benefits.

Order and State

When using parallel streams, the order of operations may not be preserved unless explicitly managed. Considerations must be made when order-dependent results are required. For instance, using methods like forEachOrdered() ensures that elements are processed in the encounter order, though at the cost of potential performance degradation.

Parallel streams also necessitate stateless behaviors within their operations to avoid concurrency issues. Maintaining state in operations like filters, mappings, or reductions introduces risks of inconsistent data or race conditions due to concurrent thread access.

The efficient use of parallel streams depends on balancing the benefits of parallelism against the intricacy of managing multithreaded behavior. Proper benchmark tests and profiling are recommended to make informed decisions about their incorporation into projects.

9.3 Working with Streams in Java

Java Streams API, introduced in Java 8, provides a powerful and expressive way to process collections of objects in a functional and parallelizable manner. Streams represent sequences of elements supporting sequential and parallel aggregate operations. Unlike collections, which are primarily used to store and access data, streams are utilized to perform computations on data. This makes streams an essential feature for modern Java applications focused on both readability and efficiency.

A stream pipeline consists of three components: a source (such as a collection or an array), intermediate operations (such as filter, map), and a terminal operation (such as forEach, collect). This structured approach enables developers to build complex data processing queries that are executed lazily, meaning intermediate operations are not invoked until a terminal operation is initiated.

Typical stream operations can be broken down into several categories: creation, intermediate operations, and terminal operations. Understanding these categories is key to mastering the manipulation of streams.

Stream Creation

Streams can be created from various data sources, such as collections, arrays, or I/O channels. Basic methods to initiate streams include:

- Stream.of(T... values): Creates a stream from a sequence of values.
- Collection.stream(): Creates a sequential stream from a collection.
- Collection.parallelStream(): Creates a parallel stream from a collection.
- Arrays.stream(T[] array): Creates a sequential stream from an array.

- Files.lines(Path path): Creates a stream of lines from a file.

```
Stream<String> streamOfValues = Stream.of("A", "B", "C");
List<String> list = Arrays.asList("A", "B", "C");
Stream<String> sequentialStream = list.stream();
Stream<String> parallelStream = list.parallelStream();
String[] array = {"A", "B", "C"};
Stream<String> arrayStream = Arrays.stream(array);
Stream<String> lines = Files.lines(Paths.get("file.txt"));
```

Intermediate Operations

Intermediate operations transform a stream into another stream. These operations are lazy and only performed when a terminal operation is invoked. Common intermediate operations include:

- filter(Predicate<? super T> predicate): Retains elements that match the given predicate.
- map(Function<? super T, ? extends R> mapper): Transforms each element to another value.
- flatMap(Function<? super T, ? extends Stream<? extends R» mapper): Flattens a stream of streams into a single stream.
- sorted(Comparator<? super T> comparator): Sorts elements based on the provided comparator.
- limit(long maxSize): Truncates the stream to be no longer than the given size.
- distinct(): Eliminates duplicate elements.

```
Stream<String> names = Stream.of("John", "Paul", "George", "John");
Stream<String> distinctNames = names.distinct();
Stream<String> filteredNames = distinctNames.filter(name -> !name.startsWith("J"));
Stream<String> sortedNames = filteredNames.sorted();
```

Terminal Operations

Terminal operations trigger the processing of the stream and produce a result or a side-effect. Key terminal operations include:

- forEach(Consumer<? super T> action): Performs an action for each element.
- collect(Collector<? super T, A, R> collector): Converts the stream into a collection or another data structure.

- reduce(BinaryOperator<T> accumulator): Combines elements into a single result.
- count(): Counts the number of elements in the stream.
- anyMatch(Predicate<? super T> predicate): Returns true if any element matches the predicate.
- findFirst(): Returns the first element of the stream.

```
List<String> names = Arrays.asList("John", "Paul", "George");
names.stream().forEach(System.out::println); // Prints each name
List<String> collectedNames = names.stream().distinct().collect(Collectors.toList());
long count = names.stream().filter(name -> name.startsWith("J")).count();
Optional<String> anyPaul = names.stream().filter(name -> name.equals("Paul")).
    findFirst();
boolean containsJohn = names.stream().anyMatch(name -> name.equals("John"));
```

Lazy Evaluation

Intermediate operations are not evaluated immediately; they are incorporated into the stream's pipeline for potential execution. The actual computation is deferred until a terminal operation invokes the pipeline, ensuring efficiency and enabling optimization opportunities.

```
Stream<String> names = Stream.of("John", "Paul", "George");
Stream<String> filteredNames = names.filter(name -> {
    System.out.println("filter: " + name);
    return name.startsWith("J");
});
System.out.println("Filtered names are not processed yet.");
filteredNames.forEach(name -> System.out.println("forEach: " + name));
```

```
Filtered names are not processed yet.
filter: John
forEach: John
filter: Paul
filter: George
```

The stream's lazy evaluation ensures operations are only executed when necessary, contributing to better performance and resource utilization.

Stream and Parallelism

Parallel streams can leverage multi-core architectures for enhanced performance via concurrent data processing. By opting for parallelStream or invoking parallel() on a sequential stream, developers can enable concurrent execution of operations.

```
List<Integer> numbers = Arrays.asList(1, 2, 3, 4, 5);
Stream<Integer> parallelStream = numbers.parallelStream();
int sum = parallelStream.mapToInt(Integer::intValue).sum();
```

When using parallel streams, it is crucial to be mindful of thread-safety and avoid side-effects in intermediate operations to prevent concurrency issues.

Understanding and applying the Streams API in Java allows developers to write efficient, readable, and maintainable code for data processing tasks. By leveraging both sequential and parallel stream capabilities, various workloads can benefit from optimized performance and scalability.

9.4 Creating Parallel Streams

Parallel streams in Java allow processing tasks concurrently, leveraging multiple processors for improved performance. The Java Stream API, introduced in Java 8, provides an abstraction to define data processing pipelines. When working with streams, the transition from sequential to parallel execution can be achieved straightforwardly.

Creating Parallel Streams from Collections

The most common way to create a parallel stream is from Java collections, such as List, Set, or Map. Any collection can invoke the parallelStream() method, which is a default method available in the Collection interface.

```
List<Integer> numbers = Arrays.asList(1, 2, 3, 4, 5, 6, 7, 8, 9, 10);
Stream<Integer> parallelStream = numbers.parallelStream();
```

The numbers.parallelStream() method converts the sequential stream into a parallel stream, enabling concurrent processing of the elements.

Similarly, you can create parallel streams from other collection types:

```
Set<String> names = new HashSet<>(Arrays.asList("Alice", "Bob", "Charlie", "
    Diana"));
Stream<String> parallelStream = names.parallelStream();
```

Creating Parallel Streams from Arrays

The Arrays.stream() method can be utilized to create both sequential and parallel streams from array elements. Using the parallel() method on a sequential stream transforms it into a parallel stream:

```
int[] numbersArray = {1, 2, 3, 4, 5};
IntStream parallelStream = Arrays.stream(numbersArray).parallel();
```

Arrays.stream(numbersArray).parallel() creates a parallel stream of integers from the array numbersArray.

Creating Parallel Streams from Ranges

The java.util.stream.IntStream, LongStream, and DoubleStream classes provide methods to create ranges, which can be made parallel by calling the parallel() method:

```
IntStream parallelStream = IntStream.range(1, 10).parallel();
```

This example generates a parallel stream of integers from 1 to 9.

Creating Parallel Streams using Stream.generate() and Stream.iterate()

Using the Stream.generate() and Stream.iterate() methods, an infinite stream of values can be generated. These streams can also be transformed into parallel streams by invoking the parallel() method:

```
Stream<Double> parallelStream = Stream.generate(Math::random).parallel();
Stream<Integer> parallelStream = Stream.iterate(0, n -> n + 1).parallel();
```

The examples create parallel streams of random numbers and an infinite stream of integers starting from 0, respectively.

Parallel Streams from the Stream.builder()

The Stream.builder() method offers flexibility in constructing streams. Using the build() method, followed by parallel(), the stream becomes parallel:

```
Stream.Builder<Integer> streamBuilder = Stream.builder();
streamBuilder.add(1).add(2).add(3).add(4).add(5);
Stream<Integer> parallelStream = streamBuilder.build().parallel();
```

Explicitly Parallelizing an Existing Sequential Stream

If there is an existing sequential stream, it can be converted into a parallel stream anytime by invoking the parallel() method:

```
Stream<String> sequentialStream = Stream.of("A", "B", "C", "D");
Stream<String> parallelStream = sequentialStream.parallel();
```

This approach is useful when it is preferable to define the stream pipeline sequentially and switch to parallel processing conditionally.

Performance Considerations

Creating parallel streams is designed to be straightforward; however, it is essential to consider performance implications. Parallel processing is beneficial in scenarios with significant computational tasks or vast amounts of data. The overhead of managing threads can outweigh the benefits if the task is too trivial or the data volume is too small.

It is crucial to understand the nature of the task and data, evaluate the computational cost, and utilize performance monitoring tools to make informed decisions about when to employ parallel streams.

This section provides the foundational methods to create parallel streams, emphasizing the simplicity and flexibility the Java Stream API offers for concurrent data processing. Integrating these techniques effectively allows the full potential of modern multi-core processors to be leveraged.

9.5 Performance Considerations for Parallel Streams

When utilizing parallel streams in Java, it is vital to assess performance considerations to fully leverage the potential advantages of parallel processing. Parallel streams can significantly improve performance but come with their own set of nuances and overheads. Key performance aspects should be meticulously evaluated, including hardware characteristics, data partitioning, and the nature of the operations performed.

Firstly, the underlying hardware plays a crucial role in dictating the performance of parallel streams. Modern processors with multiple cores can handle parallel tasks more efficiently due to their inherent architecture. Java's parallel streams rely on the ForkJoinPool.commonPool(), which is a special kind of thread pool designed to make full use of multiple processors. However, care should be taken to not overwhelm the system's resources. Too many concurrent threads can lead to context switching and memory thrashing, negating the benefits of parallelism.

For example, consider the default size of the common pool, which is usually equal to the number of available processors:

$$\text{int processors} = \text{Runtime.getRuntime().availableProcessors();}$$

Proper tuning of thread pool sizes can have a substantial impact on performance. When performing computationally intensive tasks, the number of threads should generally align with the number of processor cores. This can be configured using the java.util.concurrent.ForkJoinPool class:

```
int parallelism = processors; // This often equals the number of cores
```

```
ForkJoinPool customThreadPool = new ForkJoinPool(parallelism);

List<Integer> list = Arrays.asList(1, 2, 3, 4, 5, 6, 7, 8, 9, 10);
customThreadPool.submit(() ->
        list.parallelStream()
            .forEach(e -> System.out.println(Thread.currentThread().getName() + " : "
                + e))
).join();
customThreadPool.shutdown();
```

Understanding data partitioning is another fundamental aspect. The stream needs to be split into substreams that can be processed independently in parallel. Java's Spliterator supports both sequential and parallel iteration and is designed to divide a stream into multiple parts efficiently:

```
Spliterator<Integer> spliterator = list.spliterator();
Spliterator<Integer> part1 = spliterator.trySplit();
Spliterator<Integer> part2 = spliterator.trySplit();

// Further operations with part1 and part2
```

Efficient parallel stream operation necessitates uniform data partitioning; imbalances can cause some threads to finish early while others are still working, leading to suboptimal CPU utilization. Operations that reorganize or redistribute data within streams can add overhead and should be minimized.

The nature of operations performed on the elements of the stream also influences performance. Stateless operations, where each element is processed independently without reliance on the previous element, are generally more efficient as they fully exploit parallelism. Conversely, stateful operations, such as distinct() and sorted(), can limit the benefits because they often require maintaining a global state.

For instance, contrast the following two cases:

1. Stateless Operation:

```
List<Integer> statelessResult = list.parallelStream()
    .filter(e -> e % 2 == 0)
    .collect(Collectors.toList());
```

2. Stateful Operation:

```
List<Integer> statefulResult = list.parallelStream()
    .sorted()
    .collect(Collectors.toList());
```

Another critical area is reducing task overhead. While parallel streams can speed up performance, the overhead of managing parallel tasks should not be overlooked. Task overhead arises from splitting tasks, managing threads, and coordinating results. These overheads can become significant when dealing with small-sized data sets. Consequently, the performance gains from parallelism become negligible or even negative compared to sequential streams.

The operation reduce() exemplifies this. Reduction in parallel streams combines the results of sub-tasks:

```
int sum = list.parallelStream()
    .reduce(0, Integer::sum);
```

The effectiveness of parallel reduction depends on the capability to decompose tasks optimally and combine results efficiently. Complex reduction tasks or those requiring intricate result handling may not benefit from parallelism.

Resource usage and possible contention issues must also be considered. Shared resources such as I/O operations or memory blocks can become bottlenecks. Parallel streams do not mitigate resource contention; rather, ignoring potential conflicts can exacerbate them. Best practices involve ensuring thread-safety and minimizing synchronized sections.

Lastly, the performance of parallel streams should be continually monitored and benchmarked under varying conditions. Using tools such as Java Microbenchmark Harness (JMH) can provide insights into the performance characteristics of parallel streams:

```
@Benchmark
public void testParallelStreamPerformance() {
    list.parallelStream().forEach(e -> doWork(e));
}
```

Accurate profiling helps identify bottlenecks, enabling effective optimization strategies.

9.6 Stream Pipeline and Execution

In Java, a stream is a sequence of elements that supports various methods which can be pipelined to produce desired results. The concept of a stream pipeline is fundamental to understanding both sequential and parallel streams. A stream pipeline consists of three components: a source, intermediate operations, and terminal operations. This section provides an in-depth exploration of how these components work together and how the execution of streams is handled, especially in the context of parallel streams.

The source is where the stream originates. Common sources include collections, arrays, and I/O channels. For example, given a list of integers, a stream can be created as follows:

```
List<Integer> list = Arrays.asList(1, 2, 3, 4, 5);
Stream<Integer> stream = list.stream();
```

Intermediate operations are methods that transform a stream into another stream. They are always lazy, meaning they do not get executed until a terminal operation is invoked. Examples of intermediate operations include filter, map, and sorted. Each intermediate operation returns a new stream, thereby making it possible to chain multiple operations together. Consider the following sequence of intermediate operations:

```
Stream<Integer> evenNumbersStream = stream.filter(x -> x % 2 == 0).map(x -> x *
    2);
```

Here, the filter operation selects even numbers, and the map operation doubles each selected number.

Terminal operations consume the stream and produce a result or a side-effect, such as collect, forEach, and reduce. Once a terminal operation is executed, the stream cannot be reused. Terminal operations trigger the execution of the entire pipeline:

```
List<Integer> evenNumbersList = evenNumbersStream.collect(Collectors.toList());
```

The execution of parallel streams involves a different mechanism than sequential streams. In parallel streams, the stream is divided into multiple chunks, which are processed in parallel. The task execution framework used under the hood is the Fork/Join Framework. This framework efficiently manages the division and merging of tasks, dynamically balancing the workload among available processor cores.

Parallel processing starts with the stream source potentially being split into multiple parts. This is facilitated by a Spliterator, which partitions the data. For instance:

```
Stream<Integer> parallelStream = list.parallelStream();
```

Here, parallelStream creates a stream that will perform its operations in parallel.

Each chunk is processed independently by different threads. Intermediate operations in a parallel pipeline are also performed in parallel. However, not all operations can be efficiently parallelized. Stateful operations such as sorted require caution because they need knowledge of the entire dataset to guarantee correct results. Therefore, such operations might not achieve significant performance gains when executed in parallel.

The final step involves combining the results from parallel processed chunks. This is where the Fork/Join Framework's task management becomes evident. Forked tasks are joined to produce a single result. For instance, using reduce in parallel mode merges intermediate results from different threads:

```
int sum = parallelStream.reduce(0, Integer::sum);
```

It is essential to understand the internal working mechanism to identify when parallel streams offer performance benefits. Utilizing parallel streams introduces thread management overhead, which can negate the advantages of parallel execution for small data sets or for operations that do not benefit much from parallelism.

A common pitfall is assuming that parallel streams always outperform sequential streams. In reality, the overhead of task partitioning, context switching, and result merging can sometimes slow down execution. Profiling and understanding the operation characteristics are crucial before opting for parallel streams.

In multi-core architectures, common in modern computing environments, parallel streams can significantly optimize processing time by exploiting concurrency. Avoiding shared mutable state during parallel operations is necessary to prevent data races and inconsistent outcomes.

Stream pipelines represent a powerful mechanism for data processing in Java, where intermediate and terminal operations interact seamlessly to produce results. This becomes even more efficient with parallel streams when used appropriately, aligning with the processing capabilities of contemporary hardware. The apt application of these principles allows developers to harness the full potential of streams in Java.

9.7 Common Operations with Parallel Streams

The utilization of parallel streams in Java enables a wide array of operations to be performed concurrently on data collections. This section elaborates on the core operations compatible with parallel streams, ensuring that readers understand both their implementation and their impact on performance and thread management.

Filter Operation

The filter operation allows for the conditional selection of elements from a stream. The specified predicate determines whether an element should be included in the resulting stream.

```
List<Integer> numbers = Arrays.asList(1, 2, 3, 4, 5, 6, 7, 8, 9, 10);
List<Integer> evenNumbers = numbers.parallelStream()
    .filter(n -> n % 2 == 0)
    .collect(Collectors.toList());
```

Here, the filter operation is applied to a parallel stream of numbers, retaining only even numbers. This operation evaluates the predicate concurrently across the stream's elements.

Map Operation

The map operation transforms each element of the stream according to the provided function. It applies the function independently to each element in parallel when executed on a parallel stream.

```
List<String> words = Arrays.asList("apple", "banana", "cherry");
List<Integer> wordLengths = words.parallelStream()
    .map(String::length)
    .collect(Collectors.toList());
```

In this instance, the map operation converts each string into its length, acting on the elements of the stream in parallel.

FlatMap Operation

The flatMap operation flattens nested structures by converting each element into a stream and then concatenating the results. It is particularly useful for handling collections of collections in a parallel context.

```
List<List<Integer>> listOfLists = Arrays.asList(
    Arrays.asList(1, 2, 3),
    Arrays.asList(4, 5, 6),
    Arrays.asList(7, 8, 9)
);
List<Integer> flatList = listOfLists.parallelStream()
    .flatMap(Collection::stream)
    .collect(Collectors.toList());
```

Here, flatMap converts each list element into a stream and merges them into a single stream of integers, processed in parallel.

Reduce Operation

The reduce operation combines the elements of the stream into a single result using an associative accumulation function. This operation leverages parallelism to partition and reduce the data concurrently.

```
List<Integer> numbers = Arrays.asList(1, 2, 3, 4, 5);
int sum = numbers.parallelStream()
    .reduce(0, Integer::sum);
```

The reduce operation here sums up the integers in the stream, taking advantage of concurrent computations to enhance performance.

ForEach Operation

The forEach operation performs an action for each element of the stream. When executed on a parallel stream, it applies the given action concurrently to different elements.

```
List<String> words = Arrays.asList("apple", "banana", "cherry");
words.parallelStream()
    .forEach(word -> System.out.println(word));
```

In this code, forEach prints each word from the parallel stream independently, maximizing CPU resource utilization.

Collect Operation

The collect operation transforms the elements of the stream into a different form, typically a collection. This operation handles the results from parallel processing and combines them efficiently.

```
List<String> words = Arrays.asList("apple", "banana", "cherry");
Set<String> wordSet = words.parallelStream()
    .collect(Collectors.toSet());
```

collect here assembles the stream elements into a Set, reliably merging results from parallel execution paths.

Distinct Operation

The distinct operation removes duplicate elements from the stream. In a parallel stream, duplicates can be eliminated concurrently.

```
List<Integer> numbers = Arrays.asList(1, 2, 3, 2, 4, 3, 5);
List<Integer> distinctNumbers = numbers.parallelStream()
    .distinct()
    .collect(Collectors.toList());
```

This distinct operation filters out duplicate numbers from the parallel stream, maintaining unique elements only.

Sorted Operation

The sorted operation sorts the elements of the stream. When executed on a parallel stream, sorting can be performed in parallel segments before final merging.

```
List<Integer> numbers = Arrays.asList(5, 3, 1, 4, 2);
List<Integer> sortedNumbers = numbers.parallelStream()
    .sorted()
    .collect(Collectors.toList());
```

In this example, the sorted operation arranges the integers in ascending order, utilizing parallel sorting techniques.

Limit and Skip Operations

The limit and skip operations are useful for truncating and slicing streams, respectively. These operations, although intrinsically sequential, can be combined with parallel streams for partial engagement.

```
List<Integer> numbers = Arrays.asList(1, 2, 3, 4, 5, 6, 7, 8, 9, 10);
List<Integer> limitedNumbers = numbers.parallelStream()
    .limit(5)
    .collect(Collectors.toList());
List<Integer> skippedNumbers = numbers.parallelStream()
    .skip(5)
```

```
    .collect(Collectors.toList());
```

In the code above, limit retrieves the first 5 elements, and skip bypasses the initial 5 elements, both executing in parallel but complying with their inherent sequential nature.

This coverage comprehensively elucidates the primary operations that parallel streams support. The examples provided clarify the syntax and parallel execution benefits, while also preparing the reader for advanced uses in subsequent sections.

9.8 Reduction and Parallel Streams

Reduction operations in Java Streams aggregate elements of the stream to form a single resultant value. This functionality is intrinsic to the concept of functional-style data processing and is crucial when working with parallel streams, which allow reductions to be performed in parallel, leveraging multi-core architectures for improved performance.

To begin with, let us understand what reduction operations entail. A reduction operation takes a sequence of input elements and combines them using a binary operation, thereby producing a single result. The most common forms of reduction are the reduce() method, collect() method, and the specialized reductions such as min(), max(), count(), and sum().

The reduce() method is instrumental because it allows the developer to specify a custom reduction operation. It can operate in three forms, each specifically suited for different scenarios:

- Optional<T> reduce(BinaryOperator<T> accumulator)
- T reduce(T identity, BinaryOperator<T> accumulator)
- U reduce(U identity, BiFunction<U, ? super T, U> accumulator, BinaryOperator<U> combiner)

The first variant boils down the stream into an Optional value by applying a binary operator successively to the elements of the stream. Code example:

```
Optional<Integer> sum = integers.stream().reduce((a, b) -> a + b);
```

Here, if the stream is empty, the result will be an empty Optional. Otherwise, the binary operator (a, b) -> a + b sums the elements successively.

The second variant of reduce() involves an identity value, which acts as a starting point for the reduction and as the default result if the stream contains no elements:

```
int sum = integers.stream().reduce(0, (a, b) -> a + b);
```

In the variant shown, 0 is the identity, and the same summing operation is applied. If the stream is empty, 0 is returned.

The third variant of reduce() is most relevant for parallel stream operations. Here, you provide both an accumulative action and a combiner. This allows the reduction to be done in parallel more efficiently:

```
int sum = integers.parallelStream().reduce(0,
    (partialSum, a) -> partialSum + a,
    Integer::sum);
```

In a parallel stream, the stream is divided into multiple sub-streams which are processed independently. Hence, the intermediate results (partial sums) need to be combined using the combiner function Integer::sum.

While reduce() is quite versatile, the collect() method provides greater flexibility and is used when mutable reductions are required.

```
List<String> result = someStream.parallelStream()
    .collect(Collectors.toList());
```

In this case, collect() is leveraging the Collectors.toList() collector to aggregate the elements into a List. The reduction process benefits significantly from parallel execution, as the list construction can occur in different threads.

When working with parallel streams, one must consider certain performance characteristics and potential pitfalls. Ensuring that reduction functions are stateless, associative and thread-safe is key for correctness and efficiency. Non-associative operations can lead to unpredictable results when executed in parallel due to the non-deterministic order of execution. Statelessness ensures that each execution of the function does not depend on external states or past interactions, which can introduce race conditions. Thread safety further ensures that any mutable shared state is correctly synchronized, preventing concurrent modification issues.

Consider a practical example to illustrate the principles discussed:

```
Stream<String> streamOfStrings = Stream.of("a", "b", "c", "d");

String concatenatedString = streamOfStrings.parallel()
    .reduce("", (s1, s2) -> s1 + s2, (s3, s4) -> s3 + s4);
```

In this example, the identity is an empty string "", and the concatenating function (s1, s2) -> s1 + s2 is associative, allowing for proper parallel reduction. The combining function (s3, s4) -> s3 + s4 also ensures that the intermediate results are correctly merged.

Ultimately, mastering reduction operations and understanding their behavior in parallel streams can lead to more efficient, scalable, and maintainable parallel data processing solutions in Java.

9.9 Combining Streams and Fork/Join Framework

The integration of Java Streams and the Fork/Join framework combines the efficiency of parallel streams with a powerful concurrency mechanism. This combination can significantly enhance the performance of parallel data processing tasks by leveraging multi-core processors. Understanding how to effectively combine these two paradigms is essential for developing scalable and efficient applications.

The ForkJoinPool is the heart of the Fork/Join framework, and it operates on the principle of work-stealing to balance the load among threads. By default, parallel streams in Java use a common ForkJoinPool to manage their tasks. However, advanced users can specify their custom ForkJoinPool to gain more control over the execution context.

```
import java.util.Arrays;
import java.util.concurrent.ForkJoinPool;

public class CustomForkJoinPoolExample {

    public static void main(String[] args) {
        ForkJoinPool customThreadPool = new ForkJoinPool(4);

        try {
            customThreadPool.submit(() ->
                Arrays.asList(1, 2, 3, 4, 5, 6, 7, 8, 9, 10)
                .parallelStream()
                .map(e -> e * e)
                .forEach(System.out::println)
            ).get();
        } catch (Exception e) {
            e.printStackTrace();
```

```
        } finally {
            customThreadPool.shutdown();
        }
    }
}
```

In this example, a custom ForkJoinPool with a parallelism level of 4 is created. The tasks executed by the parallel stream use this custom pool, allowing greater control over resource allocation and task execution.

Next, we delve into the mechanics of combining streams and the Fork/Join framework. This involves examining how tasks are divided and processed concurrently.

Task Division and Processing:

The Fork/Join framework divides tasks into smaller subtasks that can be processed in parallel. Similarly, parallel streams automatically split their data source into multiple chunks that can be processed concurrently. The combination follows these steps:

1. *Splitting*: The initial task (stream) is split into multiple subtasks. Each subtask processes a chunk of data.
2. *Processing*: Subtasks are processed in parallel, leveraging multiple threads.
3. *Joining*: Processed results are combined to produce the final output.

The following algorithm demonstrates this concept using the algorithm2e package:

Algorithm 10: Combining Parallel Streams with Fork/Join Framework

Data: Data stream with elements $e_1, e_2, \ldots, e_n$
Result: Processed data

Divide the stream into n chunks;
foreach *chunk* c_i *in parallel* **do**
    Process chunk c_i;
Combine the results of all processed chunks;

Advantages of Combining Streams and Fork/Join:

- **Enhanced Performance**: By utilizing multiple cores, processing large datasets becomes faster.
- **Load Balancing**: The Fork/Join framework balances workload among threads, reducing idle times.
- **Resource Management**: Custom ForkJoinPools allow fine-grained control over resource allocation.

Examples and Applications:

Consider a real-world example where large datasets need to be analyzed for statistical computations. Combining parallel streams with the Fork/Join framework can significantly reduce computation time.

```
import java.util.Arrays;
import java.util.concurrent.ForkJoinPool;
import java.util.stream.Collectors;

public class StatisticalAnalysisExample {

    public static void main(String[] args) {
        ForkJoinPool customThreadPool = new ForkJoinPool(4);

        try {
            Double average = customThreadPool.submit(() ->
                Arrays.asList(1, 2, 3, 4, 5, 6, 7, 8, 9, 10)
                .parallelStream()
                .collect(Collectors.averagingInt(e -> e))
            ).get();

            System.out.println("Average: " + average);
        } catch (Exception e) {
            e.printStackTrace();
        } finally {
            customThreadPool.shutdown();
        }
    }
}
```

In this example, a custom ForkJoinPool is used to execute a parallel stream that calculates the average value of a list of integers. The integration provides a performance boost by concurrently processing different segments of the list.

To achieve optimal performance when combining streams and the Fork/Join framework, consider the following best practices:

- **Avoid Nested Parallelism**: Nesting parallel streams within ForkJoin tasks can lead to performance degradation and increased complexity.

- **Tune** ForkJoin **Pool Size**: Tailor the size of your custom ForkJoinPool based on the hardware capabilities and the nature of the task.
- **Monitor** ForkJoinPool **Utilization**: Use monitoring tools to track the utilization and performance of the ForkJoinPool.
- **Handle Exceptions Gracefully**: Ensure robust error handling to manage exceptions thrown during parallel execution.

Combining parallel streams with the Fork/Join framework enables efficient parallel data processing, enhancing performance and resource management. The following sections will elaborate on additional techniques and strategies to further optimize parallel processing in Java applications.

9.10 Examples of Parallel Streams in Real-World Applications

Java Parallel Streams are a powerful feature for achieving high-performance data processing. This section demonstrates practical examples to illustrate how Parallel Streams can be utilized effectively in real-world applications. Each example highlights important aspects of Parallel Streams, ensuring a clear understanding of their usage and benefits.

Example 1: Processing Large Data Sets

Consider a scenario where a company needs to process a large list of financial transactions to calculate the total revenue. Using Parallel Streams, this can be done efficiently by leveraging multiple cores of the processor.

```
import java.util.List;
import java.util.ArrayList;
import java.util.concurrent.ThreadLocalRandom;

public class ParallelStreamExample {

    public static void main(String[] args) {
        List<Double> transactions = new ArrayList<>();

        // Generating a large list of random transactions
        for (int i = 0; i < 10_000_000; i++) {
            transactions.add(ThreadLocalRandom.current().nextDouble(1.0, 1000.0));
        }
```

```
        // Calculating total revenue using parallel stream
        double totalRevenue = transactions.parallelStream()
                                          .mapToDouble(Double::doubleValue)
                                          .sum();

        System.out.println("Total Revenue: " + totalRevenue);
    }
}
```

```
Total Revenue: 4997973463.232142
```

This example highlights how a simple conversion to a parallel stream (transactions.parallelStream()) can significantly improve performance when processing large data sets, ensuring efficient utilization of system resources.

Example 2: Text Processing

In the context of natural language processing, consider an application that needs to analyze a large collection of documents to find the frequency of a specific word. This task can be parallelized to reduce execution time.

```
import java.util.List;
import java.util.Arrays;
import java.util.concurrent.ConcurrentMap;
import java.util.Map;
import java.util.stream.Collectors;

public class WordFrequency {
    public static void main(String[] args) {
        List<String> documents = Arrays.asList(
            "Parallel computing improves performance",
            "Java Streams provide a powerful framework",
            "Parallel Streams utilize multiple cores",
            "Concurrency is key for efficient applications",
            "Reduce execution time with parallel processing"
        );

        // Count word frequencies in parallel
        ConcurrentMap<String, Long> wordFrequencies = documents.parallelStream()
            .flatMap(line -> Arrays.stream(line.split("\\s+")))
            .collect(Collectors.groupingByConcurrent(word -> word, Collectors.
                counting()));

        for (Map.Entry<String, Long> entry : wordFrequencies.entrySet()) {
            System.out.println(entry.getKey() + ": " + entry.getValue());
        }
    }
}
```

```
Parallel: 3
computing: 1
improves: 1
performance: 1
Java: 1
...
```

The use of parallelStream() and groupingByConcurrent() ensures that the word count operation is performed in parallel, making it efficient even for larger datasets.

Example 3: Image Processing

Image processing tasks, such as applying filters to large batches of images, can benefit greatly from Parallel Streams. Consider an application that applies a grayscale filter to a collection of images.

```
import java.awt.image.BufferedImage;
import java.io.File;
import javax.imageio.ImageIO;
import java.util.List;
import java.util.Arrays;
import java.util.stream.Collectors;

public class ImageProcessing {

    public static void main(String[] args) throws Exception {
        List<String> imagePaths = Arrays.asList("image1.jpg", "image2.jpg", "image3.
            jpg");

        List<BufferedImage> images = imagePaths.parallelStream()
            .map(ImageProcessing::applyGrayscaleFilter)
            .collect(Collectors.toList());

        for (int i = 0; i < images.size(); i++) {
            ImageIO.write(images.get(i), "jpg", new File("grayscale_image" + (i + 1) +
                ".jpg"));
        }
    }
    private static BufferedImage applyGrayscaleFilter(String imagePath) {
        try {
            BufferedImage img = ImageIO.read(new File(imagePath));
            for (int y = 0; y < img.getHeight(); y++) {
                for (int x = 0; x < img.getWidth(); x++) {
                    int rgb = img.getRGB(x, y);
                    int r = (rgb >> 16) & 0xff;
                    int g = (rgb >> 8) & 0xff;
                    int b = rgb & 0xff;
                    int grayLevel = (r + g + b) / 3;
                    int gray = (grayLevel << 16) + (grayLevel << 8) + grayLevel;
                    img.setRGB(x, y, gray);
                }
            }
            return img;
        } catch (Exception e) {
            e.printStackTrace();
            return null;
        }
    }
}
```

By processing the images in parallel, the overall time taken to apply the grayscale filter to all images is reduced, demonstrating the effectiveness of Parallel Streams in real-world image processing tasks.

Example 4: Financial Computations

In financial applications, it is often necessary to compute aggregate statistics over large datasets, such as calculating average portfolio returns. Parallel Streams can expedite such computations.

```
import java.util.List;
import java.util.ArrayList;
import java.util.concurrent.ThreadLocalRandom;

public class FinancialComputations {

    public static void main(String[] args) {
        List<Double> returns = new ArrayList<>();

        // Generating a large list of random returns
        for (int i = 0; i < 1_000_000; i++) {
            returns.add(ThreadLocalRandom.current().nextDouble(-0.1, 0.1));
        }

        // Calculating average return using parallel stream
        double averageReturn = returns.parallelStream()
                                      .mapToDouble(Double::doubleValue)
                                      .average()
                                      .orElse(0.0);

        System.out.println("Average Return: " + averageReturn);
    }
}
```

```
Average Return: -9.738456734643556E-5
```

This example shows how Parallel Streams can be used to perform financial computations efficiently, offering significant performance improvements for computations over large financial datasets.

These examples clearly illustrate the versatility and effectiveness of Parallel Streams in various real-world applications. Whether processing large datasets, performing text analysis, image processing, or financial computations, Parallel Streams provide a robust mechanism for enhancing performance by leveraging parallel processing capabilities inherent in modern multi-core processors.

9.11 Best Practices for Using Parallel Streams

When leveraging parallel streams in Java, adhering to best practices is crucial to maximize performance and ensure correctness. This section presents key considerations and recommended practices for effectively utilizing parallel streams.

1. Assess Parallel Suitability: Before converting a sequential stream to a parallel stream, evaluate whether parallelism will provide a significant performance benefit. Not all tasks are suitable for parallel execution. Tasks that are CPU-bound and require significant processing time, such as complex computations or large-scale data transformations, are ideal candidates. Conversely, I/O-bound tasks with frequent disk or network operations might not benefit from parallelism due to latency and blocking issues.

2. Estimate Overhead: Parallelization introduces overhead, including thread management and inter-thread communication. Too fine-grained tasks may lead to performance degradation due to overhead surpassing the gains from parallel processing. Use larger chunks of data to maintain a good balance between overhead and performance improvement. Empirical testing and profiling tools can help determine the optimal granularity.

3. Avoid Shared Mutable State: Parallel streams process data concurrently across multiple threads, risking race conditions if shared mutable state is involved. Avoid shared mutable state to prevent data corruption and ensure thread safety. Utilize thread-local storage, immutable objects, or atomic data structures to manage shared state safely.

4. Choose Stateless Operations: Stateless operations, such as map, filter, and flatMap, do not depend on any state besides their input elements. These operations are inherently safe for parallel execution. Stateful operations, like reduce and collect, must be used with caution as they accumulate results and can involve synchronization, potentially reducing parallel efficiency. Ensure collectors used in stateful operations are thread-safe.

5. Monitor Thread Pool Size: The default thread pool used by parallel streams is the ForkJoinPool.commonPool(), which has a default size equal to the number of available processors. In certain scenarios, customizing the thread pool size can lead to better resource utilization and performance. This can be done using the ForkJoinPool class:

```
ForkJoinPool customThreadPool = new ForkJoinPool(4);
customThreadPool.submit(() -> {
    // Parallel stream operations
    stream.parallel().forEach(...);
}).join();
customThreadPool.shutdown();
```

6. Ensure Proper Use of Lambda Expressions: Lambda expressions used within parallel streams should be concise and not perform blocking operations (such as I/O). Blocking operations within lambdas can counteract the benefits of parallelism by causing threads to idle while awaiting resource access, thus reducing overall throughput.

7. Leverage Combine Operations for Parallel Streams: Combine function plays a crucial role in parallel reductions. The combining function is applied when intermediate results need to be merged. Ensuring that the combining function is associative and stateless guarantees correct results and efficient parallel execution.

```
List<Integer> numbers = Arrays.asList(1, 2, 3, 4, 5);
int sum = numbers.parallelStream()
                 .reduce(0, Integer::sum);
```

In the above example, Integer::sum is associative, which ensures the parallel reduce operation is correctly applied.

8. Opt for Bulk Data Operations: Make use of bulk data operations that operate on collections in a batched manner to fully leverage the potential of parallel streams. Operations like forEach, reduce, and collect on collections work efficiently with large datasets to distribute the workload among threads.

9. Profile and Tune Performance: Performance tuning of parallel streams is imperative. Utilize Java profiling tools such as VisualVM, JProfiler, or YourKit to analyze the performance of your parallel stream operations. Look for hotspots, thread contention, and bottlenecks that could hinder parallel performance.

10. Utilize Spliterators for Custom Splitting: When working with custom data structures or non-standard collections, implementing a Spliterator can provide enhanced control over data splitting strategies, ensuring optimal parallel processing.

```
public class CustomSpliterator implements Spliterator<T> {
    // Implementation of trySplit, tryAdvance, and forEachRemaining
}
```

Implementing a custom Spliterator provides greater control over how data is portioned and processed concurrently, which can lead to significant performance gains.

Practicing these guidelines enhances the efficiency and correctness of parallel stream operations in Java. Embracing these best practices ensures the full benefits of parallel streams are realized in terms of performance scaling and robust program execution in concurrent environments.

Chapter 10

Concurrency Best Practices and Patterns

This chapter discusses best practices and patterns for effective concurrent programming in Java. It covers the use of immutable objects, strategies to minimize lock contention, and the benefits of higher-level concurrency utilities. The chapter includes advice on thread pool management, avoiding deadlocks, and leveraging functional programming. Scalability and performance considerations are addressed, along with guidelines for testing concurrent applications. It also explores common concurrency patterns, the Actor Model, and designing efficient concurrent algorithms to ensure robust, maintainable, and performant applications.

10.1 Introduction to Concurrency Best Practices

Developing efficient and reliable concurrent applications in Java requires adherence to a set of best practices designed to mitigate common pitfalls and leverage the language's concurrency features optimally. Concurrency introduces complexity due to the interaction of multiple threads as they manipulate shared data. This section outlines key practices for writing robust concurrent applications.

Understand Thread Lifecycle: Every thread in Java goes through several states such as NEW, RUNNABLE, BLOCKED, WAITING, TIMED_WAITING, and TERMINATED. Recognizing these states and transitioning between them is crucial for managing threads effectively. For instance, a thread in the BLOCKED state is waiting for a monitor lock, whereas a thread in the WAITING state is waiting for another thread to perform a specific action.

Use Immutable Objects: Immutable objects are inherently thread-safe because their state cannot be modified after construction. With no changes occurring post-instantiation, synchronization is unnecessary for immutable objects. In Java, an immutable object can be created as follows:

```
// Immutable object example
public final class Person {
    private final String name;
    private final int age;

    public Person(String name, int age) {
        this.name = name;
        this.age = age;
    }

    public String getName() {
        return name;
    }

    public int getAge() {
        return age;
    }
}
```

Minimize Lock Contention: Lock contention occurs when multiple threads compete for the same lock, leading to performance bottlenecks. To minimize lock contention:

- **Reduce Lock Scope:** Keep the synchronized block as short as possible.
- **Use Fine-grained Locking:** Instead of a single lock, utilize multiple locks to separate critical sections in different threads.
- **Read-Write Locks:** Use ReadWriteLock to allow concurrent reads when writes are not happening.

The ReadWriteLock can be implemented as follows:

```
// Example of ReadWriteLock
import java.util.concurrent.locks.ReentrantReadWriteLock;

public class DataContainer {
```

```
    private final ReentrantReadWriteLock rwLock = new ReentrantReadWriteLock();
    private int data;

    public void readData() {
        rwLock.readLock().lock();
        try {
            // Read data
        } finally {
            rwLock.readLock().unlock();
        }
    }

    public void writeData(int newData) {
        rwLock.writeLock().lock();
        try {
            data = newData;
        } finally {
            rwLock.writeLock().unlock();
        }
    }
}
```

Atomic Operations: Atomic operations are indivisible and can be used for simple state management without explicit locking. Java provides classes such as AtomicInteger, AtomicLong, and AtomicReference in the java.util.concurrent.atomic package. These classes provide methods for performing atomic updates:

```
// Example of AtomicInteger
import java.util.concurrent.atomic.AtomicInteger;

public class Counter {
    private final AtomicInteger counter = new AtomicInteger(0);

    public void increment() {
        counter.incrementAndGet();
    }

    public int get() {
        return counter.get();
    }
}
```

Use Higher Level Concurrency Utilities: The java.util.concurrent package includes advanced utilities like ExecutorService, ConcurrentHashMap, CountDownLatch, and CyclicBarrier that abstract low-level threading tasks and offer enhanced functionality. For example:

- **ExecutorService:** Manages a group of worker threads efficiently.
- **ConcurrentHashMap:** Provides thread-safe access with improved performance compared to HashTable.

```
// Using ExecutorService
import java.util.concurrent.ExecutorService;
import java.util.concurrent.Executors;
import java.util.concurrent.TimeUnit;

public class ExecutorServiceExample {
    public static void main(String[] args) {
        ExecutorService executorService = Executors.newFixedThreadPool(10);
        for (int i = 0; i < 100; i++) {
            executorService.submit(() -> {
                // Task to be executed by the thread
            });
        }
        executorService.shutdown();
        try {
            executorService.awaitTermination(1, TimeUnit.MINUTES);
        } catch (InterruptedException e) {
            Thread.currentThread().interrupt();
        }
    }
}
```

Avoid Synchronized Collections: Instead of using synchronized collections like Vector or Hashtable, prefer those designed for concurrency such as ConcurrentHashMap, CopyOnWriteArrayList, and ConcurrentSkipListSet. These collections offer better performance under concurrent access.

```
// Example of ConcurrentHashMap
import java.util.concurrent.ConcurrentHashMap;

public class ConcurrentHashMapExample {
    private final ConcurrentHashMap<String, Integer> map = new
          ConcurrentHashMap<>();

    public void addValue(String key, Integer value) {
        map.put(key, value);
    }

    public Integer getValue(String key) {
        return map.get(key);
    }
}
```

Adopting these best practices significantly enhances the reliability and performance of concurrent Java applications. As we delve further into immutable objects and other advanced concurrency concepts, understanding these foundational principles will be pivotal.

10.2 Immutable Objects

An immutable object is an instance whose state cannot be altered after it has been created. Utilizing immutable objects in concurrent programming offers significant advantages such as thread safety and ease of maintenance. The immutable design helps avoid synchronization issues as the state remains constant once initialized.

Definition and Characteristics of Immutable Objects

An object is considered immutable if it adheres to the following principles:

- All fields of the object are final.
- The object is constructed in a fully initialized state.
- There are no methods provided to modify the object's state.

Java provides a way to create immutable objects through the use of the final keyword. When defining immutable classes, it is essential to declare all fields as final so they can only be assigned once. The constructor is responsible for the complete initialization of these fields.

Example Here is an example of a simple immutable class in Java:

```
public final class ImmutablePoint {
    private final int x;
    private final int y;

    public ImmutablePoint(int x, int y) {
        this.x = x;
        this.y = y;
    }

    public int getX() {
        return x;
    }

    public int getY() {
        return y;
    }
}
```

In this example, ImmutablePoint is immutable because:

- The class is declared as final, thus it cannot be subclassed.
- All fields (x and y) are final and assigned exactly once.

- No setter methods are provided, so the state of the object cannot be changed after construction.

Thread Safety and Immutability

Immutable objects inherently provide thread safety because their state cannot change after their construction. This characteristic eliminates the need for synchronization, making it easier to share the immutable objects across multiple threads without the risk of concurrency-related issues.

Creating and Sharing Immutable Objects

When sharing immutable objects, it's critical that the constructor does not publish references to mutable objects passed to it. Instead, you should make defensive copies of these objects. Here is an example where an immutable class holds an array:

```
public final class ImmutablePerson {
    private final String name;
    private final int age;
    private final int[] favoriteNumbers;

    public ImmutablePerson(String name, int age, int[] favoriteNumbers) {
        this.name = name;
        this.age = age;
        this.favoriteNumbers = favoriteNumbers.clone(); // Defensive copy
    }

    public String getName() {
        return name;
    }

    public int getAge() {
        return age;
    }

    public int[] getFavoriteNumbers() {
        return favoriteNumbers.clone(); // Return copy
    }
}
```

In this example, the constructor makes a defensive copy of the favoriteNumbers array. Similarly, the getter method also returns a copy of this array, ensuring the immutability of the ImmutablePerson class.

Performance Considerations

Although immutable objects simplify thread safety, there are performance implications to consider. Each change to an immutable object requires creating a new instance, which can lead to increased memory allocation and garbage collection overhead. To mitigate this, careful design and consideration of when to use immutability are required. For instance, using immutable objects for frequent state changes may not be ideal, but they are extremely beneficial for simpler, read-only data types.

Effective Use Cases

Immutable objects are particularly effective in the following scenarios:

- **Shared Constants**: Objects that represent fixed values, such as mathematical constants.
- **Configuration Objects**: Objects that store configuration settings which do not change once the application initializes.
- **Keys in Maps and Sets**: Immutable objects make reliable keys since their hash codes and equality checks remain consistent over time.
- **Return Values from Public APIs**: Immutable objects prevent callers from modifying internal state inadvertently.

Java Standard Library Support

The Java standard library includes several classes designed to be immutable, such as String and java.time.LocalDateTime. Understanding their immutability helps to use these classes effectively in concurrent programming.

String objects are commonly used as immutable objects:

```
String str1 = "Hello";
String str2 = str1.substring(1, 3); // Produces "el"

System.out.println(str1); // Output: Hello
System.out.println(str2); // Output: el
```

Here, substring creates a new String with a portion of the original string, leaving str1 unchanged. This reaffirms the immutability property where existing instances remain unaffected by transformations.

Incorporating immutable objects in concurrent applications ensures concurrent accesses are free from race conditions, thereby enhancing the robustness and maintainability of the code while leveraging the inherent thread-safety properties of immutability.

10.3 Minimizing Lock Contention

Minimizing lock contention is crucial for achieving high performance and scalability in concurrent applications. Contention occurs when multiple threads simultaneously attempt to acquire the same lock, resulting in contention and subsequent delays as threads wait for the lock to become available. To minimize lock contention, several strategies can be employed that increase the efficiency and responsiveness of an application.

The first strategy focuses on dividing the locked resources more finely. Instead of using a single lock to guard access to a significant section of code or a large portion of data, multiple locks can be employed to protect smaller, partitioned segments. This technique is known as lock splitting. For example, consider a scenario where multiple threads need to update distinct sections of a shared map. Rather than locking the entire map, each segment or bucket of the map can be locked individually. This approach reduces contention, as threads are less likely to lock the same segment simultaneously.

Listing 10.1: Lock Splitting Example

```
import java.util.concurrent.locks.Lock;
import java.util.concurrent.locks.ReentrantLock;
import java.util.concurrent.ConcurrentHashMap;

public class LockSplittingExample {

    private final ConcurrentHashMap<Integer, String> map = new
         ConcurrentHashMap<>();
    private final Lock[] locks;

    public LockSplittingExample(int numberOfLocks) {
        locks = new ReentrantLock[numberOfLocks];
        for (int i = 0; i < numberOfLocks; i++) {
            locks[i] = new ReentrantLock();
        }
    }

    public void put(Integer key, String value) {
        int lockIndex = key.hashCode() % locks.length;
        Lock lock = locks[lockIndex];
        lock.lock();
        try {
            map.put(key, value);
        } finally {
            lock.unlock();
        }
    }

    public String get(Integer key) {
        int lockIndex = key.hashCode() % locks.length;
        Lock lock = locks[lockIndex];
        lock.lock();
```

```
        try {
            return map.get(key);
        } finally {
            lock.unlock();
        }
    }
}
```

Another effective strategy is lock striping. Similar to lock splitting, lock striping involves partitioning access to a shared resource using multiple locks, but it applies particularly to data structures with a known number of segments or stripes. This technique allows multiple threads to concurrently operate on different portions of the data structure while maintaining thread safety. An example would be a concurrent set that is divided into several stripes, each protected by a separate lock.

Listing 10.2: Lock Striping Example

```
import java.util.concurrent.locks.ReadWriteLock;
import java.util.concurrent.locks.ReentrantReadWriteLock;

public class LockStripingExample<T> {

    private final T[] elements;
    private final ReadWriteLock[] locks;

    @SuppressWarnings("unchecked")
    public LockStripingExample(int capacity) {
        elements = (T[]) new Object[capacity];
        locks = new ReentrantReadWriteLock[capacity];
        for (int i = 0; i < capacity; i++) {
            locks[i] = new ReentrantReadWriteLock();
        }
    }

    public void set(int index, T element) {
        ReadWriteLock lock = locks[index];
        lock.writeLock().lock();
        try {
            elements[index] = element;
        } finally {
            lock.writeLock().unlock();
        }
    }

    public T get(int index) {
        ReadWriteLock lock = locks[index];
        lock.readLock().lock();
        try {
            return elements[index];
        } finally {
            lock.readLock().unlock();
        }
    }
}
```

Lock striping and lock splitting are powerful techniques, but their effectiveness can be further enhanced by combining them with fine-grained locking. Fine-grained locking involves acquiring locks at the most precise levels necessary rather than at broader scopes. This practice reduces the duration for which locks are held and minimizes the lock contention, thereby improving concurrency. For instance, in a linked list structure, it would be more efficient to lock individual nodes or sections of the list rather than the entire list during an update operation.

Beyond structural changes, algorithmic techniques can be integrated into code to reduce lock contention. One such approach is lock-free programming, where data structures are engineered to avoid locks by using atomic operations. Another similar approach is optimistic concurrency control, implemented by retrying operations that experience contention rather than blocking the contending threads. These techniques often leverage the java.util.concurrent.atomic package in Java, which provides classes like AtomicInteger and AtomicReference.

Listing 10.3: Atomic Variable Example

```
import java.util.concurrent.atomic.AtomicInteger;

public class AtomicVariableExample {

    private final AtomicInteger counter = new AtomicInteger(0);

    public void incrementCounter() {
        counter.incrementAndGet();
    }

    public int getCounter() {
        return counter.get();
    }
}
```

Lastly, utilizing high-level concurrency utilities provided by the Java platform contributes to minimizing lock contention. Classes such as ConcurrentHashMap, CopyOnWriteArrayList, and BlockingQueue integrate sophisticated algorithms designed to balance performance and thread safety. When appropriately used, these utilities offload the low-level management of locks and provide efficient concurrent access patterns suitable for many common tasks.

To achieve robust and performant concurrent programs, developers must judiciously apply these strategies in accordance with the specific requirements and constraints of their applications. Lock contention, while inherently challenging, can be significantly mitigated through careful design and consideration, harnessing both structural and algorithmic enhancements to foster efficient multi-threaded execution.

10.4 Using Higher Level Concurrency Utilities

Concurrency in Java can be significantly simplified and made safer through the use of higher-level concurrency utilities provided in the java.util.concurrent package. Unlike low-level constructs such as synchronized blocks or methods, and explicit use of locks, higher-level utilities help abstract complex synchronization logic, reducing the likelihood of errors and making the code more maintainable.

The primary classes and interfaces in the java.util.concurrent package include Executors, Future, Callable, CompletionService, Semaphore, CountDownLatch, CyclicBarrier, Exchanger, and various others. Each of these is designed to tackle specific types of concurrency problems, which we will discuss in detail.

Executors and Thread Pools

The Executor framework provides a replacement for traditional thread management techniques. Instead of manually creating and managing threads, we use Executor implementations to manage thread execution.

Listing 10.4: Atomic Variable Example

```
ExecutorService executor = Executors.newFixedThreadPool(10);
for (int i = 0; i < 100; i++) {
    executor.submit(new Task());
}
executor.shutdown();
```

In this example, a fixed thread pool with a size of 10 is created. The submit method is used to submit tasks for execution. The shutdown method is called after all tasks are submitted to complete the lifecycle of the executor.

ExecutorService interface extends Executor and provides methods to manage the lifecycle of both the executor service and the tasks that it executes:

- shutdown(): Initiates an orderly shutdown in which previously submitted tasks are executed but no new tasks will be accepted.
- shutdownNow(): Attempts to stop all actively executing tasks, halts the processing of waiting tasks, and returns a list of the tasks that were waiting to be executed.

- awaitTermination(long timeout, TimeUnit unit): Blocks until all tasks have completed execution after a shutdown request, or the timeout occurs, or the current thread is interrupted, whichever happens first.

Futures and Callable Interface

The Callable interface is similar to Runnable, but it can return a result and throw a checked exception. This is useful for tasks that are potentially lengthy and need to return a computation result.

Listing 10.5: Atomic Variable Example

```
Callable<Integer> task = () -> {
    TimeUnit.SECONDS.sleep(1);
    return 123;
};
Future<Integer> future = executor.submit(task);

System.out.println(future.get()); // Output: 123
```

The Future interface provides a way to retrieve the result of a computation performed by a Callable and to manage its lifecycle.

Important methods of Future include:

- get(): Waits if necessary for the computation to complete and then retrieves its result.
- get(long timeout, TimeUnit unit): Waits for the computation to complete, up to the specified time limit.
- cancel(boolean mayInterruptIfRunning): Attempts to cancel the execution of the task.
- isCancelled(): Returns true if the task was cancelled before it completed normally.
- isDone(): Returns true if the task completed.

CompletionService

The CompletionService combines the functionality of an Executor with that of a BlockingQueue to facilitate the processing of asynchronous tasks. This is particularly useful in scenarios where it is important to handle tasks as they complete, rather than in the order of submission.

Listing 10.6: Atomic Variable Example

```
CompletionService<Integer> completionService =
    new ExecutorCompletionService<>(executor);
for (int i = 0; i < 10; i++) {
    completionService.submit(() -> {
        TimeUnit.SECONDS.sleep(1);
        return 123;
    });
}

for (int i = 0; i < 10; i++) {
    Future<Integer> future = completionService.take();
    System.out.println(future.get());
}
```

Semaphores

A Semaphore controls access to a shared resource through the use of permits. It can maintain a set of permits and blocks threads until a permit is available. This is useful for controlling access to a resource that has a limited capacity.

Listing 10.7: Atomic Variable Example

```
Semaphore semaphore = new Semaphore(5);
Runnable task = () -> {
    try {
        semaphore.acquire();
        // critical section
    } catch (InterruptedException e) {
        // handle exception
    } finally {
        semaphore.release();
    }
};
```

CountDownLatch

The CountDownLatch is used to make one or more threads wait until a set of operations being performed in other threads completes.

Listing 10.8: Atomic Variable Example

```
CountDownLatch latch = new CountDownLatch(3);
for (int i = 0; i < 3; i++) {
    new Thread(() -> {
        try {
            TimeUnit.SECONDS.sleep(1);
            latch.countDown();
        } catch (InterruptedException e) {
            Thread.currentThread().interrupt();
        }
    }).start();
}
latch.await(); // main thread waits until countDown is called three times
```

CyclicBarrier

A CyclicBarrier allows a set of threads to all wait for each other to reach a common barrier point. It is useful in parallel programming when multiple threads must wait for each other at various points in execution.

Listing 10.9: Atomic Variable Example

```
CyclicBarrier barrier = new CyclicBarrier(3, () -> {
    System.out.println("All parties have arrived at the barrier!");
});
for (int i = 0; i < 3; i++) {
    new Thread(() -> {
        try {
            TimeUnit.SECONDS.sleep(1);
            barrier.await();
        } catch (InterruptedException | BrokenBarrierException e) {
            Thread.currentThread().interrupt();
        }
    }).start();
}
```

Exchanger

An Exchanger is a synchronization point at which threads can pair and swap elements within pairs. This is useful in scenarios where threads must exchange data, and both threads must arrive at the exchange point before the data is exchanged.

Listing 10.10: Atomic Variable Example

```
Exchanger<String> exchanger = new Exchanger<>();
Runnable task1 = () -> {
    try {
        String message = "from Task1";
        message = exchanger.exchange(message);
        System.out.println("Task1 received: " + message);
    } catch (InterruptedException e) {
        Thread.currentThread().interrupt();
    }
};

Runnable task2 = () -> {
    try {
        String message = "from Task2";
        message = exchanger.exchange(message);
        System.out.println("Task2 received: " + message);
    } catch (InterruptedException e) {
        Thread.currentThread().interrupt();
    }
};

new Thread(task1).start();
new Thread(task2).start();
```

The use of higher-level concurrency utilities provided in java.util.concurrent greatly simplifies the development of concurrent programs by abstracting lower-level mechanism details. These abstractions result in more understandable and maintainable code, and they also reduce the likelihood of concurrency-related bugs, making your concurrent applications more robust and efficient.

10.5 Thread Pool Management

Thread pool management is a critical aspect of developing efficient and resource-friendly concurrent applications in Java. Effective management of thread pools not only maximizes performance but also prevents resource exhaustion. This section delves into thread pool basics, strategies for optimal utilization, and considerations for thread pool sizing.

Thread Pool Basics

A thread pool manages a collection of reusable threads for executing tasks, which improves the efficiency and performance of an application by reusing thread resources and reducing the overhead of thread creation and destruction. In Java, the java.util.concurrent package provides robust support for creating and managing thread pools via the ExecutorService interface and the Executors utility class.

The following code demonstrates a simple example of creating a fixed thread pool:

Listing 10.11: Atomic Variable Example

```
import java.util.concurrent.ExecutorService;
import java.util.concurrent.Executors;

public class ThreadPoolExample {
    public static void main(String[] args) {
        ExecutorService executor = Executors.newFixedThreadPool(10);
        for (int i = 0; i < 100; i++) {
            Runnable worker = new WorkerThread("" + i);
            executor.execute(worker);
        }
        executor.shutdown();
        while (!executor.isTerminated()) {
        }
        System.out.println("Finished all threads");
    }
}

class WorkerThread implements Runnable {
    private String command;

    public WorkerThread(String s) {
        this.command = s;
    }

    @Override
    public void run() {
```

```
        System.out.println(Thread.currentThread().getName() + " Start. Command = "
            + command);
        processCommand();
        System.out.println(Thread.currentThread().getName() + " End.");
    }

    private void processCommand() {
        try {
            Thread.sleep(5000);
        } catch (InterruptedException e) {
            e.printStackTrace();
        }
    }

    @Override
    public String toString() {
        return this.command;
    }
}
```

Strategies for Optimal Utilization

Once a thread pool is created, it is essential to manage and utilize it effectively to gain maximum performance benefits. A few key strategies include:

- **Task Granularity:** Ensure that tasks submitted to the thread pool are neither too fine-grained nor too coarse-grained. Fine-grained tasks lead to excessive thread context switching and management overhead, whereas coarse-grained tasks underutilize the pool.
- **Monitoring and Tuning:** Monitoring thread pool metrics, such as active thread count, queue size, and task completion time, helps in identifying bottlenecks and enables appropriate tuning. Java provides tools such as JConsole and VisualVM for this purpose.
- **Handling Rejected Tasks:** When the thread pool and its task queue are both full, new tasks are rejected. Implement rejection policies, such as AbortPolicy, CallerRunsPolicy, DiscardPolicy, or DiscardOldestPolicy, to handle rejected tasks appropriately.

The following code demonstrates configuring a thread pool with a custom rejection policy:

Listing 10.12: Atomic Variable Example

```
import java.util.concurrent.*;

public class CustomRejectionPolicyExample {
    public static void main(String[] args) {
```

```
        ThreadPoolExecutor executor = new ThreadPoolExecutor(2, 4, 10, TimeUnit.
            SECONDS,
             new ArrayBlockingQueue<>(2), new ThreadPoolExecutor.
                 CallerRunsPolicy());

        for (int i = 0; i < 10; i++) {
            executor.execute(new WorkerThread("" + i));
        }
        executor.shutdown();
    }
}
```

Considerations for Thread Pool Sizing

Sizing the thread pool correctly is crucial for achieving optimal performance. An inappropriate size can lead to suboptimal performance or resource exhaustion. The size should be based on the nature of the tasks (CPU-bound or I/O-bound) and the system's hardware capabilities.

- **CPU-bound tasks:** For tasks that predominantly use the CPU, the optimal thread pool size is generally calculated as number of available processors + 1. This formula ensures that each CPU can be kept busy while some threads may be waiting or context switching.

  $$\text{Optimal pool size (CPU-bound)} = \text{Number of available CPUs} + 1$$

- **I/O-bound tasks:** For tasks that involve waiting for I/O operations (e.g., file reading/writing, network communications), the optimal thread pool size can be significantly larger due to the high I/O wait times. A common heuristic is number of available processors * (1 + (wait time / service time)).

  $$\text{Optimal pool size (I/O-bound)} = \text{Number of available CPUs} * (1 + \text{IoWait/ServiceTime})$$

Effectively managing thread pools requires a comprehensive understanding of the application's requirements and the system's capabilities, combined with continuous monitoring and adaptive tuning.

10.6 Avoiding Deadlocks

Deadlocks in concurrent programming occur when two or more threads are indefinitely blocked, each waiting for the other to release a resource. Deadlocks can undermine the reliability and performance of concurrent applications. Several strategies and best practices can help avoid deadlocks in Java applications.

1. Lock Ordering: One of the most effective ways to avoid deadlocks is to impose a strict order in which locks are acquired. By ensuring that all threads acquire multiple locks in a defined order, circular wait conditions can be eliminated.

Consider the following example where two locks, lockA and lockB, are consistently acquired in the same order:

Listing 10.13: Atomic Variable Example

```
public class LockOrderingExample {
    private final Object lockA = new Object();
    private final Object lockB = new Object();

    public void executeTask1() {
        synchronized (lockA) {
            synchronized (lockB) {
                // Perform Task1 actions
            }
        }
    }

    public void executeTask2() {
        synchronized (lockA) {
            synchronized (lockB) {
                // Perform Task2 actions
            }
        }
    }
}
```

In the above code, both executeTask1 and executeTask2 methods acquire lockA before lockB, preventing deadlock scenarios.

2. Try-Lock with Timeout: Java's java.util.concurrent.locks package provides the ReentrantLock class, which supports a tryLock method with timeout. This method attempts to acquire the lock within a specified period, failing gracefully if it cannot do so, thereby allowing the program to back off and avoid deadlock.

Listing 10.14: Atomic Variable Example

```
import java.util.concurrent.locks.ReentrantLock;
import java.util.concurrent.TimeUnit;

public class TryLockExample {
    private final ReentrantLock lockA = new ReentrantLock();
    private final ReentrantLock lockB = new ReentrantLock();

    public void executeTask() {
        boolean acquiredLockA = false;
        boolean acquiredLockB = false;

        try {
            acquiredLockA = lockA.tryLock(1, TimeUnit.SECONDS);
            acquiredLockB = lockB.tryLock(1, TimeUnit.SECONDS);
```

```
            if (acquiredLockA && acquiredLockB) {
                // Perform task actions
            } else {
                // Handle inability to acquire both locks
            }
        } catch (InterruptedException e) {
            // Handle interruption scenario
        } finally {
            if (acquiredLockA) {
                lockA.unlock();
            }
            if (acquiredLockB) {
                lockB.unlock();
            }
        }
    }
}
```

In this example, if both locks cannot be acquired within the specified timeout, the method handles this situation by releasing any acquired locks and potentially retrying or taking alternative actions.

3. Deadlock Detection: While prevention is preferable, detecting deadlocks at runtime can be useful in diagnosing issues. Java provides tools such as ThreadMXBean, which can help identify deadlocked threads.

Here is an example of how to use ThreadMXBean to detect deadlocks:

Listing 10.15: Atomic Variable Example

```
import java.lang.management.ManagementFactory;
import java.lang.management.ThreadInfo;
import java.lang.management.ThreadMXBean;

public class DeadlockDetector {
    private final ThreadMXBean threadMXBean = ManagementFactory.
        getThreadMXBean();

    public void checkForDeadlocks() {
        long[] deadlockedThreadIds = threadMXBean.findDeadlockedThreads();
        if (deadlockedThreadIds != null) {
            ThreadInfo[] threadInfos = threadMXBean.getThreadInfo(
                deadlockedThreadIds);
            for (ThreadInfo threadInfo : threadInfos) {
                System.out.println("Deadlocked Thread:");
                System.out.println(threadInfo);
            }
        } else {
            System.out.println("No deadlocked threads detected.");
        }
    }
}
```

This code periodically checks for deadlocked threads and outputs information about them to assist in debugging.

4. Immutable Objects: Making shared resources immutable can prevent deadlocks by reducing the need for synchronization. When objects are immutable, multiple threads can read them simultaneously without the need for locks, thereby reducing contention and the possibility of deadlocks.

Here's an example of creating an immutable class:

Listing 10.16: Atomic Variable Example

```
public final class ImmutableClass {
    private final int value;

    public ImmutableClass(int value) {
        this.value = value;
    }

    public int getValue() {
        return value;
    }
}
```

In this example, ImmutableClass is immutable, meaning its state cannot change after instantiation. The absence of modification methods guarantees thread-safety without the need for explicit synchronization.

5. Avoid Nested Locks: To avoid deadlocks, it is advisable to minimize the usage of nested locks. Nested locks increase the likelihood of circular wait conditions, leading to deadlocks.

Listing 10.17: Atomic Variable Example

```
public class NestedLockExample {
    private final Object lockA = new Object();
    private final Object lockB = new Object();

    public void performTask() {
        synchronized (lockA) {
            // Perform some actions with lockA
        }
        synchronized (lockB) {
            // Perform some actions with lockB
        }
    }
}
```

In this example, locks are held independently rather than nested, which reduces the risk of deadlocks.

By adopting these strategies and best practices, developers can effectively minimize the occurrence of deadlocks in their concurrent Java applications. Enhanced tool support and careful design considerations are instrumental in creating robust and deadlock-free systems.

10.7 Leveraging Functional Programming

Functional programming (FP) offers a declarative style of writing programs that enhance readability, maintainability, and testability. In the context of concurrent programming in Java, leveraging FP can lead to more robust and scalable applications. This section explores how to utilize functional programming constructs and paradigms to optimize concurrent code.

Functional programming in Java is primarily facilitated through lambda expressions, streams, and the 'java.util.function' package. These features enable developers to create programs in a functional style, reducing the likelihood of bugs commonly associated with mutable state and explicit synchronization.

Listing 10.18: Atomic Variable Example

```
import java.util.Arrays;
import java.util.List;

public class LambdaExample {
    public static void main(String[] args) {
        List<String> strings = Arrays.asList("one", "two", "three");
        strings.forEach(s -> System.out.println(s));
    }
}
```

In the example above, lambda expressions provide a concise way to iterate over a list of strings and perform an action on each element. This enhances readability and eliminates boilerplate code associated with anonymous inner classes.

Streams API and Concurrency:

The Java Streams API allows for declarative processing of sequences of elements, with capabilities for parallel execution. Utilizing the parallelStream() method can significantly improve performance when processing large datasets.

Listing 10.19: Atomic Variable Example

```
import java.util.Arrays;
import java.util.List;

public class ParallelStreamExample {
    public static void main(String[] args) {
        List<Integer> numbers = Arrays.asList(1, 2, 3, 4, 5);
        numbers.parallelStream()
            .map(n -> n * n)
            .forEach(System.out::println);
    }
}
```

In this example, the parallelStream() method is used to create a parallel stream, allowing the map operation to execute concurrently across multiple threads. This can lead to performance improvements on multi-core processors for computationally intensive tasks.

Functional Interfaces:

The java.util.function package defines several functional interfaces, such as Function, Predicate, Supplier, and Consumer. These interfaces facilitate the passing of behavior as parameters, improving code modularity and reuse.

Listing 10.20: Atomic Variable Example

```
import java.util.function.Function;

public class FunctionExample {
    public static void main(String[] args) {
        Function<Integer, Integer> squareFunction = n -> n * n;
        int result = squareFunction.apply(5);
        System.out.println(result); // prints 25
    }
}
```

By utilizing the Function interface, the code encapsulates the behavior of squaring a number, promoting reuse and reducing the possibility of defects.

Immutable Objects:

FP encourages the use of immutable objects which significantly contributes to making concurrent programming safer. Immutable objects are inherently thread-safe since their state cannot be modified after construction. This eliminates issues related to synchronization and data races.

Listing 10.21: Atomic Variable Example

```
public final class ImmutablePoint {
    private final int x;
    private final int y;

    public ImmutablePoint(int x, int y) {
        this.x = x;
        this.y = y;
    }

    public int getX() {
        return x;
    }

    public int getY() {
        return y;
    }
}
```

Higher-Order Functions and Currying:

Higher-order functions, which take other functions as parameters or return them as results, are another feature of FP that can be leveraged in concurrent programming. Currying, the process of transforming a function with multiple arguments into a sequence of functions, each taking a single argument, helps in creating more modular and reusable code.

Listing 10.22: Atomic Variable Example

```
import java.util.function.Function;

public class CurryingExample {
    public static void main(String[] args) {
        Function<Integer, Function<Integer, Integer>> curriedAdder = x -> y -> x +
            y;
        Function<Integer, Integer> addFive = curriedAdder.apply(5);
        int result = addFive.apply(3);
        System.out.println(result); // prints 8
    }
}
```

The ‘curriedAdder‘ function is an example of currying in Java, creating more flexible and composable functions.

Leveraging functional programming constructs in Java can lead to more effective concurrent programming by reducing mutable state and synchronization complexity, promoting immutability and higher-order functions. This paradigm not only enhances code clarity and maintainability but also takes full advantage of modern multi-core processors for parallel execution.

10.8 Scalability and Performance Considerations

When developing concurrent applications, scalability and performance are critical aspects that must be meticulously addressed to ensure that the system can handle increasing loads with minimal degradation in performance. This section delves into various considerations and techniques for achieving an optimally scalable and performant concurrent system in Java.

At the crux of scalability in concurrent applications is the effective utilization of system resources, particularly CPU and memory, while minimizing bottlenecks that can impede performance. The following key strategies are essential for addressing scalability and performance in Java concurrency:

1. Reducing Context Switching Overheads

Context switching occurs when the CPU switches from executing one thread to another. While necessary, excessive context switching can degrade performance due to the associated overhead. The following practices help mitigate context switching overheads:

- Minimize the use of Thread.yield() as it can lead to unnecessary context switches.
- Prefer higher-level concurrency utilities like ExecutorService which manage thread pools efficiently, reducing the need for frequent thread creation and destruction.
- Use the ForkJoinPool for tasks that can be broken down into smaller parallel subtasks, effectively utilizing available CPU cores.

2. Optimal Thread Pool Sizing

Correctly sizing thread pools is crucial for maximizing throughput and maintaining responsive applications. The number of threads should ideally match the number of available CPU cores to prevent excessive context switching and resource contention:

Listing 10.23: Atomic Variable Example

```
ExecutorService executor = Executors.newFixedThreadPool(Runtime.getRuntime().
    availableProcessors());
```

For tasks that involve I/O operations, the thread pool size can be adjusted higher since such tasks frequently wait for I/O operations to complete, freeing up CPU time for other threads.

3. Minimizing Synchronization Overheads

Excessive synchronization can lead to significant performance bottlenecks. Critical sections protected by synchronization prevent other threads from entering the same section, potentially causing delays:

- Use fine-grained locking by splitting synchronized blocks to minimize the time any single thread spends holding a lock.
- Employ lock-free algorithms and data structures such as java.util.concurrent.atomic package where possible. These use

low-level atomic operations (CAS - Compare-And-Swap) to avoid locking.

- Consider ReadWriteLocks (java.util.concurrent.locks.ReadWriteLock) for scenarios where reads are more frequent than writes. This allows multiple readers to access the resource concurrently without blocking each other.

4. Caching and Locality of Reference

Effective use of caching and improving data locality can have a marked impact on performance:

- Employ thread-local storage using ThreadLocal for variables that are frequently accessed by a single thread, reducing contention and improving access speed.
- Use data structures that have good locality of reference, such as ArrayList over LinkedList when random access performance is paramount.

5. Reducing Contention with Non-blocking Algorithms

Non-blocking algorithms can significantly reduce contention:

- Utilize non-blocking data structures such as ConcurrentLinkedQueue and ConcurrentHashMap which are designed to handle high levels of concurrency without locking.
- Apply algorithms that leverage optimistic concurrency control, such as those implemented in the StampedLock class, where operations first execute without locking and only retry under contention.

6. Analyzing and Profiling Performance

Continuous performance monitoring and profiling are essential for identifying and alleviating bottlenecks:

- Use profiling tools such as JProfiler, VisualVM, or YourKit to observe thread activity and identify hot spots or locks causing contention.
- Analyze garbage collection logs and adjust JVM parameters (-Xms, -Xmx, -XX:+UseG1GC) to optimize memory usage and reduce pause times caused by garbage collection.

7. Load Testing and Stress Testing

Conducting thorough load and stress testing is critical for evaluating the scalability and performance of the application under various conditions:

- Use load testing tools like Apache JMeter or Gatling to simulate concurrent user behavior and measure response times, throughput, and resource utilization.
- Perform stress testing to determine the application's breaking point by gradually increasing load until performance degrades or failures occur, helping to identify capacity limits and potential failure points.

By keeping these considerations in mind and applying the aforementioned strategies, developers can build concurrent Java applications that are both scalable and performant, capable of efficiently handling increasing demands while maintaining robust performance characteristics. Integrating these practices into the concurrent application development process is essential for creating systems that not only meet current requirements but are also well-prepared for future scalability.

10.9 Testing Concurrent Applications

Testing concurrent applications poses unique challenges when compared to traditional, sequential software testing. The non-deterministic nature of threads and processes can lead to race conditions, deadlocks, and other synchronization issues that are difficult to reproduce and diagnose. This section covers methodologies, tools, and best practices specifically aimed at testing concurrent Java applications to ensure reliability and robustness.

To systematically test concurrent applications, consider the following approaches:

- **Unit Testing with Concurrent Contexts**
- **Stress and Load Testing**
- **Race Condition Detection**
- **Deadlock Detection**

Unit Testing with Concurrent Contexts: Unit tests in concurrent applications should simulate the concurrent environment to test the correct functioning of individual components under multi-threaded conditions. Tools like JUnit and TestNG facilitate writing unit tests in Java, but additional libraries are needed for handling concurrency.

Listing 10.24: Atomic Variable Example

```
import org.junit.*;
import java.util.concurrent.*;

public class ConcurrentTest {
    @Test
    public void testConcurrentTask() throws InterruptedException {
        ExecutorService executor = Executors.newFixedThreadPool(4);
        CountDownLatch latch = new CountDownLatch(4);

        for (int i = 0; i < 4; i++) {
            executor.execute(() -> {
                // Simulated concurrent task
                doConcurrentWork();
                latch.countDown();
            });
        }
        latch.await(); // Wait for all tasks to complete
        executor.shutdown();
    }

    private void doConcurrentWork() {
        // Simulate task
    }
}
```

The CountDownLatch is essential in synchronizing and ensuring that the unit test waits for all concurrent tasks to complete before moving forward.

Stress and Load Testing: This approach tests the application's behavior under extreme conditions. Stress testing is used to evaluate how the system performs when it is beyond its maximum anticipated load, whereas load testing measures performance under expected usage patterns.

Listing 10.25: Atomic Variable Example

```
import org.junit.*;
import java.util.concurrent.*;

public class LoadTest {
    @Test
    public void testLoad() throws InterruptedException {
        ExecutorService executor = Executors.newFixedThreadPool(100);
        for (int i = 0; i < 1000; i++) {
            executor.submit(this::simulateWorkLoad);
        }
        executor.shutdown();
        executor.awaitTermination(1, TimeUnit.HOURS);
```

```
    }

    private void simulateWorkLoad() {
        // Simulate heavy workload
    }
}
```

By creating multiple threads and pushing the system to its limits, developers can uncover issues that might not appear under normal operating conditions.

Race Condition Detection: Detecting race conditions is complex because they occur sporadically and may not trigger during every execution. Tools like FindBugs, CheckThread, and Java PathFinder can help in identifying potential race conditions in code.

Listing 10.26: Atomic Variable Example

```
import edu.umd.cs.findbugs.annotations.SuppressFBWarnings;

public class ConcurrentComponent {

    private int sharedCounter = 0;

    @SuppressFBWarnings("IS")
    public synchronized void increment() {
        sharedCounter++;
    }
}
```

The \SuppressFBWarnings annotation can suppress false positives when using FindBugs for race condition detection.

Deadlock Detection: Deadlocks are another critical issue in concurrent applications. Tools like Java VisualVM, Deadlock Detection Thread Dump Analyzer, and thread dump analysis are valuable for identifying and resolving deadlocks.

Listing 10.27: Atomic Variable Example

```
public class DeadlockExample {

    private final Object lock1 = new Object();
    private final Object lock2 = new Object();

    public void method1() {
        synchronized(lock1) {
            synchronized(lock2) {
                // Critical section
            }
        }
    }

    public void method2() {
        synchronized(lock2) {
            synchronized(lock1) {
```

```
                // Critical section
            }
        }
    }
}
```

In the above example, a potential deadlock scenario is created by acquiring two locks in different orders, which is a classic case in concurrent programming. Static analysis and runtime monitoring help detect such conditions.

To encapsulate these concepts with an automation strategy, consider the following algorithm for automatic concurrent test execution and monitoring.

Algorithm 11: Automatic Concurrent Test Execution and Monitoring

Input: Test suite T with n tests $\{t_1, t_2, \ldots, t_n\}$
Output: Concurrency issues report R

begin
  Thread pool $P \leftarrow$ initialize(*with fixed thread count*);
  Logger $L \leftarrow$ initialize(*for test results*);
  foreach *test* $t \in T$ **do**
    P.submit((*t*)) // Execute test concurrently
  end
  P.awaitTermination() // Wait for all tests to complete
  foreach *test* $t \in T$ **do**
    if t.detectsConcurrencyIssue() **then**
      L.recordIssue((*t*));
    end
  end
  $R \leftarrow L$.generateReport();
  return R;
end

This algorithm underlines the process of concurrently executing tests and systematically logging any issues detected, thus facilitating automatic detection of concurrency-related problems.

Testing concurrent applications requires meticulous planning and the use of specialized tools to handle the unique challenges posed by multithreaded environments. Through unit tests that account for concurrent execution, load and stress testing, race condition detection, and deadlock detection, it becomes possible to ensure that concurrent Java applications are robust and reliable under various conditions.

10.10 Common Concurrency Patterns

In concurrent programming, specific patterns can significantly enhance the design simplicity and robustness of applications. This section examines prevalent patterns that facilitate efficient and maintainable concurrent applications in Java.

Producer-Consumer Pattern

The Producer-Consumer pattern is a classic concurrency pattern, where one or more threads (producers) create work items and place them into a shared resource, while one or more threads (consumers) remove and process these work items. This pattern is particularly beneficial for decoupling the production and consumption of data, thereby enhancing system efficiency and throughput.

The core component of this pattern is a shared-bound buffer, typically realized through a thread-safe queue. Java's BlockingQueue is a prime candidate for implementing this pattern. It provides thread-safe operations for adding and removing tasks and handles concurrency issues such as thread synchronization and wait-notify logic internally.

Listing 10.28: Atomic Variable Example

```
import java.util.concurrent.BlockingQueue;
import java.util.concurrent.LinkedBlockingQueue;

class Producer implements Runnable {
    private final BlockingQueue<Integer> queue;

    Producer(BlockingQueue<Integer> queue) {
        this.queue = queue;
    }

    @Override
    public void run() {
        try {
            for (int i = 0; i < 100; i++) {
                queue.put(produce(i));
            }
        } catch (InterruptedException ex) {
            Thread.currentThread().interrupt();
        }
    }

    private Integer produce(int i) {
        return i; // Simplified example
    }
}
```

```
class Consumer implements Runnable {
    private final BlockingQueue<Integer> queue;

    Consumer(BlockingQueue<Integer> queue) {
        this.queue = queue;
    }

    @Override
    public void run() {
        try {
            while (true) {
                Integer item = queue.take();
                consume(item);
            }
        } catch (InterruptedException ex) {
            Thread.currentThread().interrupt();
        }
    }

    private void consume(Integer item) {
        System.out.println("Consumed: " + item); // Simplified example
    }
}

public class ProducerConsumerExample {
    public static void main(String[] args) {
        BlockingQueue<Integer> queue = new LinkedBlockingQueue<>();
        Producer producer = new Producer(queue);
        Consumer consumer = new Consumer(queue);

        new Thread(producer).start();
        new Thread(consumer).start();
    }
}
```

Future Pattern

The Future pattern is a concurrency abstraction that allows a thread to perform a computation while another thread can retrieve the result of the computation at a later time. Java's java.util.concurrent.Future and java.util.concurrent.CompletableFuture are key classes for implementing this pattern.

Listing 10.29: Atomic Variable Example

```
import java.util.concurrent.CompletableFuture;
import java.util.concurrent.ExecutionException;

public class FutureExample {
    public static void main(String[] args) {
        CompletableFuture<Integer> future = CompletableFuture.supplyAsync(() ->
                compute(10));

        try {
            Integer result = future.get();
            System.out.println("Result: " + result);
        } catch (InterruptedException | ExecutionException ex) {
            Thread.currentThread().interrupt();
        }
```

```
    }

    private static Integer compute(int value) {
        // Simulated long-running computation
        return value * 2;
    }
}
```

Thread Pool Pattern

Thread Pools manage a pool of worker threads, encapsulating them and providing a higher-level API for task execution. This pattern optimizes resource use by reusing existing threads rather than creating new ones for each task, thus eliminating the overhead associated with thread creation and destruction.

Java's ExecutorService, particularly the Executors factory class, simplifies Thread Pool management.

Listing 10.30: Atomic Variable Example

```
import java.util.concurrent.ExecutorService;
import java.util.concurrent.Executors;

public class ThreadPoolExample {
    public static void main(String[] args) {
        ExecutorService executor = Executors.newFixedThreadPool(5);

        for (int i = 0; i < 10; i++) {
            executor.submit(new Task(i));
        }

        executor.shutdown();
    }
}

class Task implements Runnable {
    private final int taskId;

    Task(int id) {
        this.taskId = id;
    }

    @Override
    public void run() {
        System.out.println("Executing Task " + taskId);
    }
}
```

Read-Write Lock Pattern

The Read-Write Lock Pattern is essential when multiple threads examine the state of an object (read operations) while a few modify it (write operations). This pattern distinguishes between read and write locks, permitting multiple concurrent reads or exclusive write access, thus minimizing lock contention and improving performance.

Java provides ReentrantReadWriteLock for implementing this pattern.

Listing 10.31: Atomic Variable Example

```
import java.util.concurrent.locks.ReentrantReadWriteLock;

public class ReadWriteLockExample {
    private final ReentrantReadWriteLock lock = new ReentrantReadWriteLock();
    private int value = 0;

    public int readValue() {
        lock.readLock().lock();
        try {
            return value;
        } finally {
            lock.readLock().unlock();
        }
    }

    public void writeValue(int newValue) {
        lock.writeLock().lock();
        try {
            value = newValue;
        } finally {
            lock.writeLock().unlock();
        }
    }
}
```

Monitor Object Pattern

The Monitor Object Pattern encapsulates the synchronization logic within a particular class, thereby providing thread-safe methods for accessing its state. This pattern often uses the synchronized keyword to allow mutually exclusive access to an object's methods.

Listing 10.32: Atomic Variable Example

```
public class MonitorObjectExample {
    private int counter = 0;

    public synchronized void increment() {
        counter++;
    }

    public synchronized int getCounter() {
        return counter;
    }
}
```

Exploring and implementing these patterns enriches the toolkit of Java concurrent programming, promoting the development of robust, scalable, and maintainable applications. These patterns address common concurrency issues, providing tested and optimized solutions.

10.11 Actor Model

The Actor Model is a conceptual model in the domain of concurrent computation. It encapsulates the state and behavior of an entity acting within a multithreaded environment. Actors provide a higher-level abstraction for concurrency, decoupling the communication between components, and allowing the development of scalable and resilient systems.

An actor is essentially a computational entity that, in response to a message it receives, can concurrently:

- Send a finite number of messages to other actors.
- Create a finite number of new actors.
- Designate the behavior to be used for the next message it receives.

Characteristics of the Actor Model:

- Isolation: Actors encapsulate state and behavior, ensuring that the state is not shared directly with other actors.
- Message-driven: Actors communicate exclusively via asynchronous messages.
- No Shared State: There is no implicit sharing of state; actors use messages for state sharing, thus avoiding the usual concurrency issues such as race conditions.

Implementation Example in Java:

To implement the Actor Model in Java, the akka framework is typically used. The following example demonstrates the implementation of a simple actor that handles messages:

Listing 10.33: Atomic Variable Example

```
import akka.actor.AbstractActor;
import akka.actor.ActorRef;
import akka.actor.ActorSystem;
import akka.actor.Props;

// Define the Greeter Actor
public class Greeter extends AbstractActor {
    static public Props props() {
```

```
        return Props.create(Greeter.class, Greeter::new);
    }

    static public class Greet {
        public final String name;
        public Greet(String name) {
            this.name = name;
        }
    }

    @Override
    public Receive createReceive() {
        return receiveBuilder()
                .match(Greet.class, greet -> {
                    System.out.println("Hello, " + greet.name);
                })
                .build();
    }
}

// Main class to initialize the system
public class AkkaQuickstart {
    public static void main(String[] args) {
        final ActorSystem system = ActorSystem.create("helloakka");

        try {
            final ActorRef greeter = system.actorOf(Greeter.props(), "greeter");
            greeter.tell(new Greeter.Greet("World"), ActorRef.noSender());

            // Add shutdown hook
            Runtime.getRuntime().addShutdownHook(new Thread() {
                @Override
                public void run() {
                    system.terminate();
                }
            });
        } catch (Exception e) {
            system.terminate();
        }
    }
}
```

In the example, the Greeter class represents an actor that receives a Greet message containing a name. Upon receiving the message, it prints a greeting to the console.

Key Points:

- Props: Used to create actor instances.
- ActorSystem: Manages the lifecycle of actors within a system.
- tell() Method: Asynchronously sends a message to an actor.
- match() and receiveBuilder(): These specify how the actor reacts to different message types.

Actors process messages asynchronously in the order they are received, which helps to maintain isolation. Akka ensures that each actor instance processes only one message at a time, simplifying synchronization.

Advanced Concepts:

- Supervision: Actors can be organized hierarchically, where a parent actor (supervisor) can handle and recover from child actor failures.
- Persistence: Actors can be extended to maintain their state persistently, ensuring resiliency in case of system failures.
- Routers: Special actors that distribute messages across multiple child actors.

Utilizing the Actor Model can significantly improve the scalability and reliability of concurrent applications, particularly those requiring high throughput and minimal downtime.

10.12 Designing Concurrent Algorithms

Designing concurrent algorithms involves careful consideration to ensure correctness, scalability, and performance. Concurrent algorithms must accommodate simultaneous interactions among multiple threads, manage shared resources effectively, and avoid common pitfalls such as deadlocks, race conditions, and high contention. This section delves into the principles and approaches for crafting effective concurrent algorithms in Java.

The first principle when designing concurrent algorithms is **decomposition**. Decompose tasks into smaller independent units of work that can be executed concurrently. This not only facilitates parallel execution but also simplifies the management of shared resources. Consider a sorting algorithm, such as MergeSort, which can be divided into smaller subproblems. The sequence of execution can be described using the ForkJoin framework in Java.

Listing 10.34: Atomic Variable Example

```
import java.util.concurrent.RecursiveTask;
import java.util.concurrent.ForkJoinPool;
```

```
public class ConcurrentMergeSort extends RecursiveTask<int[]> {
    private final int[] array;

    public ConcurrentMergeSort(int[] array) {
        this.array = array;
    }

    @Override
    protected int[] compute() {
        if (array.length <= 1) {
            return array;
        }

        int mid = array.length / 2;

        ConcurrentMergeSort leftTask = new ConcurrentMergeSort(
            Arrays.copyOfRange(array, 0, mid));
        ConcurrentMergeSort rightTask = new ConcurrentMergeSort(
            Arrays.copyOfRange(array, mid, array.length));

        invokeAll(leftTask, rightTask);

        int[] leftResult = leftTask.join();
        int[] rightResult = rightTask.join();

        return merge(leftResult, rightResult);
    }

    private int[] merge(int[] left, int[] right) {
        int[] result = new int[left.length + right.length];
        int i = 0, j = 0, k = 0;
        while (i < left.length && j < right.length) {
            if (left[i] <= right[j]) {
                result[k++] = left[i++];
            } else {
                result[k++] = right[j++];
            }
        }
        while (i < left.length) {
            result[k++] = left[i++];
        }
        while (j < right.length) {
            result[k++] = right[j++];
        }
        return result;
    }

    public static void main(String[] args) {
        int[] array = {3, 5, 1, 2, 4, 6};
        ForkJoinPool pool = new ForkJoinPool();
        ConcurrentMergeSort task = new ConcurrentMergeSort(array);
        int[] sortedArray = pool.invoke(task);
        System.out.println(Arrays.toString(sortedArray));
    }
}
```

The code above demonstrates the use of ForkJoinPool to decompose the merge sort algorithm into smaller tasks that can be executed concurrently. Each sub-array is sorted independently and then merged.

Another important principle is **minimizing synchronization**. Excessive synchronization can create bottlenecks and negate the benefits of concurrency. Techniques such as granular locking, use of non-blocking algorithms, and reducing the critical section scope are effective. Java's ConcurrentHashMap is an example of a concurrent data structure that minimizes synchronization.

Listing 10.35: Atomic Variable Example

```
import java.util.concurrent.ConcurrentHashMap;

public class ConcurrentMapUsage {
    private final ConcurrentHashMap<String, Integer> map = new
          ConcurrentHashMap<>();

    public void putIfAbsent(String key, Integer value) {
        map.putIfAbsent(key, value);
    }

    public Integer getCount(String key) {
        return map.get(key);
    }

    public static void main(String[] args) {
        ConcurrentMapUsage usage = new ConcurrentMapUsage();
        usage.putIfAbsent("key1", 1);
        System.out.println("Count for key1: " + usage.getCount("key1"));
    }
}
```

In this example, ConcurrentHashMap provides thread-safe operations with minimized contention, leveraging fine-grained locks partitioned over the map's elements.

The design of concurrent algorithms must also account for **latency and throughput**. These are critical performance metrics that measure the responsiveness and capacity of the algorithm respectively. To balance these, consider load balancing techniques and efficient task scheduling.

Algorithm 12: Concurrent Task Processing

```
Data: Task list T
Result: Processed tasks
Create a thread pool with fixed number of threads;
foreach task t ∈ T do
    /* Assign each task to a thread in the pool */
    Assign task t to a thread;
    /* Process task concurrently */
    Thread processes task;
```

This simple algorithm outlines assigning tasks to a fixed set of threads. Proper tuning of the thread pool size relative to the task size and computational resources available can significantly impact performance.

Furthermore, **avoiding deadlocks** is essential. A common strategy is to establish a strict order for acquiring multiple locks. Using a try-lock mechanism or employing timeout strategies can also help in handling lock acquisition failures gracefully.

Listing 10.36: Atomic Variable Example

```
import java.util.concurrent.locks.ReentrantLock;
import java.util.concurrent.locks.Lock;

public class AvoidingDeadlock {
    private final Lock lock1 = new ReentrantLock();
    private final Lock lock2 = new ReentrantLock();

    public void performTask() {
        try {
            if (lock1.tryLock()) {
                try {
                    if (lock2.tryLock()) {
                        try {
                            // Critical section
                        } finally {
                            lock2.unlock();
                        }
                    }
                } finally {
                    lock1.unlock();
                }
            }
        } catch (Exception e) {
            e.printStackTrace();
        }
    }

    public static void main(String[] args) {
        AvoidingDeadlock ad = new AvoidingDeadlock();
        ad.performTask();
    }
}
```

In the above code, tryLock() ensures that if a lock is not available, the thread does not get blocked indefinitely, reducing the risk of deadlocks.

Finally, **testing concurrent algorithms** is vital to ensure they work correctly under different scenarios. Unit tests should include tests for race conditions, deadlocks, and other concurrency issues using tools like JUnit and specialized concurrency testing frameworks such as jcStress.

Designing effective concurrent algorithms requires a keen understanding of the underlying principles, careful planning, and diligent testing. Each algorithm must balance the trade-offs between synchronization, performance, and correctness to achieve optimal results in a concurrent environment.

Made in the USA
Monee, IL
13 September 2026

62976631R00184